D0251591

CLASSIC
HORROR
WRITERS

Writers of English: Lives and Works

CLASSIC
HORROR
WRITERS

Edited and with an Introduction by

Harold Bloom

CHELSEA HOUSE PUBLISHERS
New York   Philadelphia

PR
830
.T3
C57
1993

Jacket illustration: Francisco José de Goya y Lucientes (1746–1828), *Nocturne with Witches*, Museum Lazzaro Galdiano, Madrid (courtesy of Art Resource).

CHELSEA HOUSE PUBLISHERS

Editorial Director Richard Rennert
Executive Managing Editor Karyn Gullen Browne
Executive Editor Sean Dolan
Picture Editor Adrian G. Allen
Copy Chief Robin James
Art Director Robert Mitchell
Manufacturing Director Gerald Levine
Production Coordinator Marie Claire Cebrián-Ume

Writers of English: Lives and Works

Senior Editor S. T. Joshi
Senior Designer Rae Grant

Staff for CLASSIC HORROR WRITERS

Research Stefan Dziemianowicz
Editorial Assistants Robert Green, Mary B. Sisson
Picture Researcher Wendy Wills

© 1994 by Chelsea House Publishers, a division of Main Line Book Co.

Introduction © 1994 by Harold Bloom

All rights reserved. No part of this publication may be reproduced or transmitted in any form or by any means without the written permission of the publisher.

Printed and bound in the United States of America.

First Printing

1 3 5 7 9 8 6 4 2

Library of Congress Cataloging-in-Publication Data

Classic horror writers / edited and with an introduction by Harold Bloom.
       p.   cm.—(Writers of English)
       ISBN 0-7910-2201-3.—ISBN 0-7910-2226-9 (pbk.)
    1. Horror tales, English—Bio-bibliography. 2. Horror tales, American—Bio-bibliography. 3. Horror tales, American—Dictionaries. I. Bloom, Harold. II. Series.
PR830.T3C57 1993
823'.0873809—dc20
[B]

93-13020
CIP

▨ Contents

CONCORDIA COLLEGE LIBRARY
2811 NE HOLMAN ST.
PORTLAND, OR 97211-6099

⊞ User's Guide

THIS VOLUME PROVIDES biographical, critical, and bibliographical information on the twelve most significant writers of horror fiction from the late eighteenth century to the end of the nineteenth century. Each chapter consists of three parts: a biography of the author; a selection of brief critical extracts about the author; and a bibliography of the author's published books.

The biography supplies a detailed outline of the important events in the author's life, including his or her major writings. The critical extracts are taken from a wide array of books and periodicals, from the author's lifetime to the present, and range in content from biographical to critical to historical. The extracts are arranged in chronological order by date of writing or publication, and a full bibliographical citation is provided at the end of each extract. Editorial additions or deletions are indicated within carets.

The author bibliographies list every separate publication—including books, pamphlets, broadsides, collaborations, and works edited or translated by the author—for works published in the author's lifetime; selected important posthumous publications are also listed. Titles are those of the first edition; if a work has subsequently come to be known under a variant title, this title is supplied within carets. In selected instances dates of revised editions are given where these are significant. Pseudonymous works are listed but not the pseudonyms under which these works were published. Periodicals edited by the author are listed only when the author has written most or all of the contents. For plays we have listed date of publication, not date of production; unpublished plays are not listed. Titles enclosed in square brackets are of doubtful authenticity. All works by the author, whether in English or in other languages, have been listed; English translations of foreign-language works are not listed unless the author has done the translation.

The Life of the Author

Harold Bloom

NIETZSCHE, WITH EXULTANT ANGUISH, famously proclaimed that God was dead. Whatever the consequences of this for the ethical life, its ultimate literary effect certainly would have surprised the author Nietzsche. His French disciples, Foucault most prominent among them, developed the Nietzschean proclamation into the dogma that all authors, God included, were dead. The death of the author, which is no more than a Parisian trope, another metaphor for fashion's setting of skirt-lengths, is now accepted as literal truth by most of our current apostles of what should be called French Nietzsche, to distinguish it from the merely original Nietzsche. We also have French Freud or Lacan, which has little to do with the actual thought of Sigmund Freud, and even French Joyce, which interprets *Finnegans Wake* as the major work of Jacques Derrida. But all this is as nothing compared to the final triumph of the doctrine of the death of the author: French Shakespeare. That delicious absurdity is given us by the New Historicism, which blends Foucault and California fruit juice to give us the Word that Renaissance "social energies," and not William Shakespeare, composed *Hamlet* and *King Lear*. It seems a proper moment to murmur "enough" and to return to a study of the life of the author.

Sometimes it troubles me that there are so few masterpieces in the vast ocean of literary biography that stretches between James Boswell's great *Life* of Dr. Samuel Johnson and the late Richard Ellmann's wonderful *Oscar Wilde*. Literary biography is a crucial genre, and clearly a difficult one in which to excel. The actual nature of the lives of the poets seems to have little effect upon the quality of their biographies. Everything happened to Lord Byron and nothing at all to Wallace Stevens, and yet their biographers seem equally daunted by them. But even inadequate biographies of strong writers, or of weak ones, are of immense use. I have never read a literary biography from which I have not profited, a statement I cannot make about any other genre whatsoever. And when it comes to figures who are central to us—Dante, Shakespeare, Cervantes, Montaigne, Goethe, Whitman, Tolstoi, Freud, Joyce, Kafka among them—we reach out eagerly for every scrap that the biographers have gleaned. Concerning Dante and Shakespeare we know much too little, yet when we come to Goethe and Freud, where we seem to know more than everything, we still want to know more. The death of the author, despite our current resentniks, clearly was only a momentary fad. Something vital in every authentic lover of literature responds to Emerson's battle-cry sentence: "There is no history, only biography." Beyond that there is a deeper truth, difficult to come at and requiring a lifetime to understand, which is that there is no literature, only autobiography, however mediated, however veiled, however transformed. The events of Shakespeare's life included the composition of *Hamlet,* and that act of writing was itself a crucial act of living, though we do not yet know altogether how to read so doubled an act. When an author takes up a more overtly autobiographical stance, as so many do in their youth, again we still do not know precisely how to accommodate the vexed relation between life and work. T. S. Eliot, meditating upon James Joyce, made a classic statement as to such accommodation:

> We want to know who are the originals of his characters, and what
> were the origins of his episodes, so that we may unravel the web of memory
> and invention and discover how far and in what ways the crude material
> has been transformed.

When a writer is not even covertly autobiographical, the web of memory and invention is still there, but so subtly woven that we may never unravel it. And yet we want deeply never to stop trying, and not merely because we are curious, but because each of us is caught in her own network of memory and invention. We do not always recall our inventions, and long before we age we cease to be certain of the extent to which we have invented our memories. Perhaps one motive for reading is our need to unravel our own webs. If our masters could make, from their lives, what we read, then we can be moved by them to ask: What have we made or lived in relation to what we have read? The answers may be sad, or confused, but the question is likely, implicitly, to go on being asked as long as we read. In Freudian terms, we are asking: What is it that we have repressed? What have we forgotten, unconsciously but purposively: What is it that we flee? Art, literature necessarily included, is regression in the service of the ego, according to a famous Freudian formula. I doubt the Freudian wisdom here, but indubitably it is profoundly suggestive. When we read, something in us keeps asking the equivalent of the Freudian questions: From what or whom is the author in flight, and to what earlier stages in her life is she returning, and why?

Reading, whether as an art or a pastime, has been damaged by the visual media, television in particular, and might be in some danger of extinction in the age of the computer, except that the psychic need for it continues to endure, presumably because it alone can assuage a central loneliness in elitist society. Despite all sophisticated or resentful denials, the reading of imaginative literature remains a quest to overcome the isolation of the individual consciousness. We can read for information, or entertainment, or for love of the language, but in the end we seek, in the author, the person whom we have not found, whether in ourselves or in others. In that quest, there always are elements at once aggressive and defensive, so that reading, even in childhood, is rarely free of hidden anxieties. And yet it remains one of the few activities not contaminated by an entropy of spirit. We read in hope, because we lack companionship, and the author can become the object of the most idealistic elements in our search for the wit and inventiveness we so desperately require. We read biography, not as a supplement to reading the author, but as a second, fresh attempt to understand what always seems to evade us in the work, our drive towards a kind of identity with the author.

This will-to-identity, though recently much deprecated, is a prime basis for the experience of sublimity in reading. *Hamlet* retains its unique position in the Western canon not because most readers and playgoers identify themselves with the prince, who clearly is beyond them, but rather because they find themselves again in the power of the language that represents him with such immediacy and force. Yet we know that neither language nor social energy created Hamlet. Our curiosity about Shakespeare is endless, and never will be appeased. That curiosity itself is a value, and cannot be separated from the value of *Hamlet* the tragedy, or Hamlet the literary character. It provokes us that Shakespeare the man seems so unknowable, at once everyone and no one as Borges shrewdly observes. Critics keep telling us otherwise, yet something valid in us keeps believing that we would know Hamlet better if Shakespeare's life were as fully known as the lives of Goethe and Freud, Byron and Oscar Wilde, or best of all, Dr. Samuel Johnson. Shakespeare never will have his Boswell, and Dante never will have his Richard Ellmann. How much one would give for a detailed and candid *Life of Dante* by Petrarch, or an outspoken memoir of Shakespeare by Ben Jonson! Or, in the age just past, how superb would be rival studies of one another by Hemingway and Scott Fitzgerald! But the list is endless: think of *Oscar Wilde* by Lord Alfred Douglas, or a joint biography of Shelley by Mary Godwin, Emilia Viviani, and Jane Williams. More than our insatiable desire for scandal would be satisfied. The literary rivals and the lovers of the great writers possessed perspectives we will never enjoy, and without those perspectives we dwell in some poverty in regard to the writers with whom we ourselves never can be done.

There is a sense in which imaginative literature *is* perspectivism, so that the reader is likely to be overwhelmed by the work's difficulty unless its multiple perspectives are mastered. Literary biography matters most because it is a storehouse of perspectives, frequently far surpassing any that are grasped by the particular biographer. There are relations between authors' lives and their works of kinds we have yet to discover, because our analytical instruments are not yet advanced enough to perform the necessary labor. Perhaps a novel, poem, or play is not so much a regression in the service of the ego, as it is an amalgam of *all* the Freudian mechanisms of defense, all working together for the apotheosis of the ego. Freud valued art highly, but thought that the aesthetic enterprise was no rival for psycho-analysis, unlike religion and philosophy. Clearly Freud was mistaken; his own anxieties about his indebtedness to Shakespeare helped produce the weirdness of his joining in the lunacy that argued for the Earl of Oxford as the author of

Shakespeare's plays. It was Shakespeare, and not "the poets," who was there before Freud arrived at his depth psychology, and it is Shakespeare who is there still, well out ahead of psychoanalysis. We see what Freud would not see, that psychoanalysis is Shakespeare prosified and systematized. Freud is part of literature, not of "science," and the biography of Freud has the same relations to psychoanalysis as the biography of Shakespeare has to *Hamlet* and *King Lear,* if only we knew more of the life of Shakespeare.

Western literature, particularly since Shakespeare, is marked by the representation of internalized change in its characters. A literature of the ever-growing inner self is in itself a large form of biography, even though this is the biography of imaginary beings, from Hamlet to the sometimes nameless protagonists of Kafka and Beckett. Skeptics might want to argue that all literary biography concerns imaginary beings, since authors make themselves up, and every biographer gives us a creation curiously different from the same author as seen by the writer of a rival *Life*. Boswell's Johnson is not quite anyone else's Johnson, though it is now very difficult for us to disentangle the great Doctor from his gifted Scottish friend and follower. The life of the author is not merely a metaphor or a fiction, as is "the Death of the Author," but it always does contain metaphorical or fictive elements. Those elements are a part of the value of literary biography, but not the largest or the crucial part, which is the separation of the mask from the man or woman who hid behind it. James Joyce and Samuel Beckett, master and sometime disciple, were both of them enigmatic personalities, and their biographers have not, as yet, fully expounded the mystery of these contrasting natures. Beckett seems very nearly to have been a secular saint: personally disinterested, heroic in the French Resistance, as humane a person ever to have composed major fictions and dramas. Joyce, self-obsessed even as Beckett was preternaturally selfless, was the Milton of the twentieth century. Beckett was perhaps the least egoistic post-Joycean, post-Proustian, post-Kafkan of writers. Does that illuminate the problematical nature of his work, or does it simply constitute another problem? Whatever the cause, the question matters. The only death of the author that is other than literal, and that matters, is the fate only of weak writers. The strong, who become canonical, never die, which is what the canon truly is about. To be read forever is the Life of the Author.

◉ Introduction

I AM INCLINED to divide the classic horror writers into two groups: grand stylists such as Henry James and Robert Louis Stevenson, and the rather larger company of rougher storytellers who have a more problematic relation to canonical literature, including Brockden Brown, "Monk" Lewis, Charles Maturin, Bram Stoker, and even Mrs. Shelley. Poe I place in a class by himself, though my rather low estimate of Poe's various styles has provoked the partisans of Poe, including my colleague S. T. Joshi, who in his *The Weird Tale* calls me a "dinosaur" in regard to Poe. Still, if one changes the focus to the life of Poe, there need be no argument. No classic horror writer suffered a more horrifying life, and considerable illumination of Poe's tales results from juxtaposing them with the author's biography.

Henry James, in contrast, is certainly the best writer in this mode, and yet his life is so subtly connected to his *The Turn of the Screw* that Freudian reductions of the story tend to be dismal failures. There appears to be no pattern in the interrelations of life and work among the classic horror writers. Contrast for instance *Frankenstein* to *Dracula*. Knowing Mary Godwin Shelley's life makes an enormous difference in understanding her most famous book. Her relations to her husband, Percy Bysshe Shelley the great Romantic poet, are crucial to the sense in which Victor Frankenstein is "the Modern Prometheus." And the quest for social justice by her father, the revolutionary philosopher-anarchist William Godwin, movingly clarifies the search for acceptance by the poor daemon we now wrongly call "the monster." But it is very difficult to unravel the peculiar social vision of *Dracula* by juxtaposing it with the personal life of Bram Stoker.

Yet all these writers benefit if we come to them again with some informed sense of the life of the author. Somewhere in the sorrow of Stevenson's tubercular fate there lurks the secret of *Dr. Jekyll and Mr. Hyde*, even if we cannot precisely locate it. And we sense that the unlived passional life of Henry James, his long deferral of his own homosexuality, somehow accounts for his excursions into horror. The reader of the classic horror writers will find in this volume much of the background material that will best contextualize the fascination of these terrors.

—H. B.

⬦ ⬦ ⬦

Ambrose Bierce
1842–1914?

AMBROSE GWINNETT BIERCE was born on June 24, 1842, in Meigs County, Ohio, one of thirteen children of Marcus Aurelius and Laura Bierce. He attended the Kentucky Military Institute and saw distinguished service in the Union army in the Civil War, participating in such important battles as Chickamauga and Shiloh and rising to the rank of lieutenant. He later wrote graphically of his war experiences in stories and articles, the latter collected in *Bits of Autobiography* (in the first volume of his *Collected Works* [1909]).

After the war Bierce served briefly as a Treasury aide in Alabama, then joined General William B. Hazen's expedition through the Indian Territory before settling in San Francisco. At that time Bierce began to contribute articles and sketches to California papers, becoming editor of the *News-Letter and California Advertiser* in 1868. His first short story, "The Haunted Valley," was published in 1871.

On Christmas Day, 1871, Bierce married Mollie Day, by whom he had two sons, Leigh and Day, and a daughter, Helen. The marriage was stormy: the couple separated in 1888 and divorced in 1905. Day was killed in a duel in 1889; Leigh died of pneumonia in 1901.

In 1872 Bierce and his wife went to England, where Bierce produced his first book, a collection of humorous pieces entitled *The Fiend's Delight* (1872). Most of the pieces were contributed to Tom Hood's magazine *Fun* or to *Figaro*, and two other humor collections appeared in 1872 and 1873. Returning to San Francisco in 1875, Bierce took a job at the U.S. Mint and then became associate editor of *The Argonaut*, where he began his famous "Prattle" column. With Thomas A. Harcourt he produced the curious hoax *The Dance of Death* (1877), purporting to condemn the immorality of dancing. In 1880 Bierce entered into a venture to mine gold in the Black Hills, but it failed disastrously and he returned to San Francisco.

In 1881 Bierce became editor of the newly founded *Wasp*. Here he continued "Prattle" and began a new column, "The Devil's Dictionary";

1

the latter was eventually collected as *The Cynic's Word Book* (1906), a title supplied by the publisher. In 1887 Bierce began to write for William Randolph Hearst's *San Francisco Examiner* and later lobbied for Hearst interests in Washington. This was his most prolific period: his vast output included his two principal short story collections, *Tales of Soldiers and Civilians* (1891) and *Can Such Things Be?* (1893); *Fantastic Fables* (1899); two collections of poetry; and voluminous essays and reviews.

From 1900 to 1913 Bierce lived in Washington, D.C., where he wrote for *Cosmopolitan* and other periodicals. In 1908 Walter Neale conceived the idea of publishing Bierce's *Collected Works*, and Bierce settled down to the onerous task of editing: the series came out in twelve volumes from 1909 to 1912, although it is by no means complete—an enormous amount of his journalism remains uncollected. In the process, however, Bierce extensively rearranged the contents of his story collections: *Tales of Soldiers and Civilians* (volume 2; now titled *In the Midst of Life*) now contained his war stories and most of his non-supernatural tales of psychological suspense; *Can Such Things Be?* (volume 3) contained nearly all his expressly supernatural tales; and "Negligible Tales" and "The Parenticide Club" (volume 8) contained his sardonic *contes cruels*. Volume 1 of the *Collected Works* contained two lengthy Swiftian satires, *Ashes of the Beacon* and *The Land Beyond the Blow*, as well as shorter proto-science-fiction tales.

In 1913 Bierce left to travel through the South, visiting Civil War battlefields and heading toward Mexico. One of his last recorded utterances is in a letter to Samuel Loveman on September 10, 1913: "I am going away to South America, and have not the faintest notion when I shall return." He vanished without a trace. It is presumed that he was caught up in the Mexican Civil War.

Critical Extracts

AMBROSE BIERCE   So far as I am able to judge, no good novels are now "made in Germany," nor in France, nor in any European country except Russia. The Russians are writing novels which so far as one may venture to judge (dimly discerning their quality through the opacity of translation, for one does not read Russian) are, in their way, admirable; full of fire and light, like an opal. Tourgenieff, Pushkin, Gogol and the early Tolstoi—these be big names. In their hands the novel grew great (as it did in those of Richardson and Fielding, and as it would have done in those of Thackeray and Pater if greatness in that form of fiction had been longer possible in England) because, first, they were great men, and second, the novel was a new form of expression in a world of new thought and life. In Russia the soil is not exhausted: it produces without fertilizers. There we find simple, primitive conditions, and the novel holds something of the elemental passions of the race, unsophisticated by introspection, analysis of motive, problemism, dissection of character, and the other "odious subtleties" that go before a fall. But the blight is upon it even there, with an encroachment visible in the compass of a single lifetime. Compare Tolstoi's *The Cossacks* with his latest work of fiction, and you will see an individual decadence prefiguring a national; just as one was seen in the interval between *Adam Bede* and *Daniel Deronda*. When the story-teller is ambitious to be a philosopher there is an end to good story-telling. Novelists are now all philosophers—excepting those who have "stumbled to eternal mock" as reformers.

With the romance—which in form so resembles the novel that many otherwise worthy persons are but dimly aware of the essential distinction—matters are somewhat otherwise. The romanticist has not to encounter at a disadvantage the formidable competition of his reader's personal experience. He can represent life, not as it is, but as it might be; character, not as he finds it, but as he wants it. His plot knows no law but that of its own artistic development; his incidents do not require the authenticating hand and seal of any censorship but that of taste. The vitality of his art is eternal; it is perpetually young. He taps the great permanent mother-lode of human interest. His materials are infinite in abundance and cosmic in distribution. Nothing that can be known, or thought, or felt, or dreamed, but is available if he can manage it. He is lord of two worlds and may select his characters from both. In the altitudes where his imagination waves her joyous wing there are no bars for her to beat her breast against; the universe is hers, and unlike the sacred bird Simurgh, which is omnipotent on condition of never exerting its power, she may do as she will. And so it comes about that while the novel is accidental and transient, the romance is essential and permanent. The novelist, whatever his ability, writes in the shifting sand; the only age that understands his work is that which has not forgotten the social conditions environing his characters—namely, their own period; but the romancist has cut his work into the living rock. Richardson and Fielding already seem absurd. We are beginning to quarrel with Thackeray, and Dickens needs a glossary. Thirty years ago I saw a list of scores of words used by Dickens that had become obsolete. They were mostly the names

of homely household objects no longer in use; he had named them in giving
"local color" and the sense of "reality." Contemporary novels are read by
none but the reviewers and the multitude—which will read anything if it
is long, untrue and new enough. Men of sane judgment and taste still
illuminate their minds and warm their hearts in Scott's suffusing glow; the
strange, heatless glimmer of Hawthorne fascinates more and more; the
Thousand-and-One Nights holds its captaincy of tale-telling. Whatever a
great man does he is likely to do greatly, but had Hugo set the powers of
his giant intellect to the making of mere novels his superiority to the greatest
of those who have worked in that barren art might have seemed somewhat
less measureless than it is.

> Ambrose Bierce, "The Novel" (1897), *Collected Works* (New York: Neale Publishing
> Co., 1911), Vol. 10, pp. 20–24

GEORGE STERLING

It is now over eight years since ⟨Bierce's⟩
disappearance, and though the likelihood of his existence in the flesh seems
faint indeed, the storm of detraction and obloquy that he always insisted
would follow his demise has never broken, is not even on the horizon.
Instead, he seems to be remembered with tolerance by even those whom
he visited with a chastening pen. Each year of darkness but makes the star
of his fame increase and brighten, but we have, I think, no full conception
as yet of his greatness, no adequate realization of how wide and permanent
a fame he has won. It is significant that some of the discerning admire him
for one phase of his work, some for another. For instance, the clear-headed
H. L. Mencken acclaims him as the first wit of America, but will have none
of his tales; while others, somewhat disconcerted by the cynicism pervading
much of his wit, place him among the foremost exponents of the art of the
short story. Others again prefer his humor (for he was humorist as well as
wit), and yet others like most the force, clarity and keen insight of his
innumerable essays and briefer comments on mundane affairs. Personally,
I have always regarded Poe's "Fall of the House of Usher" as our greatest
tale; close to that come, in my opinion, at least a dozen of Bierce's stories,
whether of the soldier or civilian. He has himself stated in *Prattle:* "I am
not a poet." And yet he wrote poetry, on occasion, of a high order, his
"Invocation" being one of the noblest poems in the tongue. Some of his
satirical verse seems to me as terrible in its withering invective as any that
has been written by classic satirists, not excepting Juvenal and Swift. Like
the victims of their merciless pens, his, too, will be forgiven and forgotten.
Today no one knows, nor cares, whether or not those long-dead offenders

gave just offense. The grave has closed over accuser and accused, and the only thing that matters is that a great mind was permitted to function. One may smile or sigh over the satire, but one must also realize that even the satirist had his own weaknesses, and could have been as savagely attacked by a mentality as keen as his own. Men as a whole will never greatly care for satire, each recognizing, true enough, glimpses of himself in the invective, but sensing as well its fundamental bias and cruelty. However, Bierce thought best of himself as a satirist.

George Sterling, "A Memoir of Ambrose Bierce," *The Letters of Ambrose Bierce*, ed. Bertha Clark Pope (San Francisco: Book Club of California, 1922), pp. xli–xlii

---

H. L. MENCKEN   Another character that marked him, perhaps flowing out of this same cynicism, was his curious taste for the macabre. All of his stories show it. He delighted in hangings, autopsies, dissecting-rooms. Death to him was not something repulsive, but a sort of low comedy— the last act of a squalid and rib-rocking buffoonery. When, grown old and weary, he departed for Mexico, and there—if legend is to be believed— marched into the revolution then going on, and had himself shot, there was certainly nothing in the transaction to surprise his acquaintances. The whole thing was typically Biercian. He died happy, one may be sure, if his executioners made a botch of dispatching him—if there was a flash of the grotesque at the end. Once I enjoyed the curious experience of going to a funeral with him. His conversation to and from the crematory was superb— a long series of gruesome but highly amusing witticisms. He had tales to tell of crematories that had caught fire and singed the mourners, of dead bibuli whose mortal remains had exploded, of widows guarding the fires all night to make sure that their dead husbands did not escape. The gentleman whose carcass we were burning had been a literary critic. Bierce suggested that his ashes be molded into bullets and shot at publishers, that they be presented to the library of the New York Lodge of Elks, that they be mailed anonymously to Ella Wheeler Wilcox. Later on, when he heard that they had been buried in Iowa, he exploded in colossal mirth. The last time I saw him he predicted that the Christians out there would dig them up and throw them over the State line. On his own writing desk, he once told me, he kept the ashes of his son. I suggested idly that the ceremental urn must be a formidable ornament. "Urn hell!" he answered. "I keep them in a cigar-box!"

H. L. Mencken, "Ambrose Bierce," *Prejudices: Sixth Series* (New York: Alfred A. Knopf, 1927), pp. 262–63

CAREY McWILLIAMS   It was the unique distinction of
Ambrose Bierce to be referred to as dead when he was living, and to be
mentioned as living when he was indubitably dead. His reputation is based
on a series of elaborately interwoven paradoxes. Even to attempt a biographical study of his life requires a preliminary analysis of this critical confusion.
His name is already a legend and his reputation is almost mythical so far
has it been divorced from the central values of his work. Such is the fate
that befalls the "obscure" type in letters. Myth becomes imposed on myth,
legend is interlaced with legend, so that in the course of time it becomes
necessary to remove one layer of misunderstanding after another until at
least the outline of the original may be traced over the pattern of errors
that time has somewhat erased. Perhaps the "myth" is already a tradition
and that a dissociation of ideas is impossible. It is a doubt which has often
troubled me.

Some men are predestined to be the subject of misunderstanding, as
though some quality about their lives invited absurd comment and irrelevant
observation. Such a man was Ambrose Bierce. It is seriously to be doubted
if there exists another figure in American literature about whom as much
irregular and unreliable critical comment has been written. He has been
characterized as great, bitter, idealistic, cynical, morose, frustrated, cheerful,
bad, sadistic, obscure, perverted, famous, brutal, kind, a fiend, a God, a
misanthrope, a poet, a realist who wrote romances, a fine satirist and something of a charlatan. Surely such misunderstanding is not an inevitable
condition of fame. There exists no such wildness about the literature on
Emerson, on Melville, or on Twain. If his admirers had realized that Bierce
was a complex figure and that only by the use of paradox could they make
any progress in definition, much confusion might have been avoided. Had
his critics been able to move in both directions, first into his work and
then back to the facts of his life, they might have succeeded in arriving at
a more intelligent appreciation of his work.

Carey McWilliams, "Introduction: The Bierce Myth," *Ambrose Bierce: A Biography*
(New York: Albert & Charles Boni, 1929), pp. 3–4

EDMUND WILSON   ⟨. . .⟩ it is certainly true, not only that, as
has been said by Clifton Fadiman, Death itself is Bierce's favorite character,
but that, except in *The Monk and the Hangman's Daughter,* a rewriting of a
story by someone else, Death may perhaps be said to be Ambrose Bierce's
only real character. In all Bierce's fiction, there are no men or women who
are interesting as men or women—that is, by reason of their passions, their

aspirations or their personalities. They figure only as the helpless butts of sadistic practical jokes, and their higher faculties are so little involved that they might almost as well be trapped animals. But Bierce does succeed in making Death play an almost personal role. His accounts of battles he took part in are among the most attractive of his writings, because here he is able to combine a ceaseless looking Death in the face with a delight in the wonder of the world, as the young man from Elkhart, Indiana, finds himself in a land where "unfamiliar constellations burned in the southern midnights, and the mocking-bird poured out his heart in the moon-gilded magnolia." As in the case of Thomas Wentworth Higginson, the enchantment that Bierce's war memories had for him was partly created by the charms of the South, so different from anything he had previously known. But eventually, in his horror stories, the obsession with death becomes tiresome. If we try to read these stories in bulk, they get to seem not merely disgusting but dull. The horror stories of Poe, with which they have been compared, have always a psychological interest in the sense that the images they summon are metaphors for hidden emotions. The horror stories of Bierce have only in a very few cases such psychological interest as may come from exploiting dramatically some abnormal phenomenon of consciousness. There is, other-wise, merely the Grand Guignol trick repeated again and again. The execu-tioner Death comes to us from outside our human world and, capriciously, gratuitously, cruelly, slices away our lives. It is an unpleasant limitation of Bierce's treatment of violent death that it should seem to him never a tragedy, but merely a bitter jest. He seems rarely to have felt any pity for his dead comrades of the Civil War, and it is characteristic of him that he should write as if in derision, in the passage ⟨. . .⟩ of the soldiers who fell at Shiloh and who were burned, some while still alive, in a forest-fire lit by the battle. "I obtained leave," he writes, "to go down into the valley of death and gratify a reprehensible curiosity"; and then, after a description of the corpses, inhumanly swollen or shrunken, "Faugh! I cannot catalogue the charms of these gallant gentlemen who had got what they enlisted for."

Bierce's short stories are often distinguished from the hackwork of the shudder magazines only by the fact that the shudder is an emotion that for the author is genuine, and by the sharp-edged and flexible style, like the ribbon of a wound-up steel tape-measure. He has also a certain real knack for catching, in his stories about the West, the loneliness of solitary cabins, with their roofs partly fallen in and with a grave or two among the trees; of worked-out diggings in Nevada hills with a skeleton at the bottom of the shaft; of empty buildings in San Francisco of which nobody knows the owners but into which some unknown person creeps at night—all places where the visit of Death seems peculiarly blighting and final, where, in pinching out a tiny human spirit, it renders the great waste complete.

Edmund Wilson, "Ambrose Bierce on the Owl Creek Bridge" (1951), *Patriotic Gore: Studies in the Literature of the American Civil War* (New York: Oxford University Press, 1962), pp. 622–24

MARCUS KLEIN ⟨. . .⟩ the stories ⟨. . .⟩ are still admirable. But
to Bierce's audience there was something greater: they were, in fact, appalling. They irresistibly asserted themselves because, more than craft, they had boldness, they had the courage even to be offensive. What must seem to us today an obstinate, not to say a deranged concern with war, madness, the menace of the supernatural, literally assaulted the public imagination. To a public for whom beauty was joy and tragedy wistful, the story, "Chickamauga," of a child, a deaf mute, romping among dying soldiers and screaming at the sight of its murdered parents, had the impact of a blow. The story of an instant of desperate fantasy of an already hanging man, "An Occurrence at Owl Creek Bridge," had the force almost of truth! The story, "A Son of the Gods," of the gallant young officer whose very courage, excessive and magnetic, provokes a mass slaughter, undermined a public morality. Courage is foolhardy; the hanging man, despite your sentiment and in the nature of things, hangs. These are bearable themes, but they were unexpected. What Bierce precociously revealed was the reader, a reader who hadn't realized the imprisonment of his own romantic inclination; and therein was concealed the shock. It was not realism he committed, but outrage, immediate engagement with a literature and an audience. So he adapts the cheap nostalgia made popular by Riley and Eugene Field to a lyrical tale of parricide; the narrator of "An Imperfect Conflagration" soliloquizes: "Early one June morning in 1872 I murdered my father—an act which made a deep impression on me at the time. This was before my marriage, while I was living with my parents in Wisconsin." So, in the terrible "Oil of Dog," he perverts the worn and oppressive charm of "Little Orphant Annie" to a story of abortion: "My name is Boffer Bings. I was born of honest parents in one of the humbler walks of life, my father being a manufacturer of dog-oil and my mother having a small studio in the shadow of the village church, where she disposed of unwelcome babies." And so in "The Famous Gilson Bequest"—a story which with curious exactness anticipates "The Man That Corrupted Hadleyburg"—the horse-thief Gilson, while exposing the profounder degeneracy of his townsmen, in and out of life remains unrepentingly a thief. With wit real if sometimes mannered, with the good callousness of his intelligence, with skill, Bierce corrupted his contemporaries: death was

possible and unlovely when it came; courage is ridiculous; murder and thievery and other activities of the human spirit are evil only according to a hypocritical ethic. The stories were often gratuitously revolting, but, unlike the satin horrors of Poe, they did a job. They drew an indictment. They served; they broke barriers to show possibilities beyond sentimentality.

Marcus Klein, "San Francisco and Her Hateful Ambrose Bierce," *Hudson Review* 7, No. 3 (Autumn 1954): 406–7

M. E. GRENANDER   The novel had little appeal for Bierce; he thought the short story was much superior to it as a literary form. And it is easy to understand why. It was the sudden, sharp crisis that interested him. This crisis reveals the man for what he is; his past life is important only for what it contributes to this critical juncture. Obviously a writer of narrative prose fiction will find the short story far better suited to portraying this climactic kind of incident than the novel, with its slow accretion of detail.

Bierce's distaste for the novel and his preference for the short story are, accordingly, perfectly consistent with what he was trying to do. The short story may demonstrate a general principle or portray a limited segment of life. But whichever it does, it works within a narrow compass. It cannot develop a plot on the grand scale as the novel does. But at its best what it can do superlatively well is to distill the core of an idea or the essence of a crisis. It can place the brief span of action it represents under a microscope, as it were, to magnify it and show the reader its significance. And just as the microscopic examination of a single cell can tell us something about all similar cells, so a study of Bierce's best short stories about the crises individual men face can tell us something about all men. Such stories, like much lyric poetry—Emily Dickinson comes to mind—have universal implications for humanity. ⟨. . .⟩

⟨. . .⟩ Bierce, at his best, was a consummate craftsman. The key to his technique is that it compresses much in narrow compass. He was master of a fluid and limpid prose, often intentionally ambivalent, in which exactly the right words are chosen to convey precise shades of meaning. Bierce's style is stark and stripped, without excess verbiage but freighted with vast implications. Since it usually operates at more than one level, it poses a continual challenge and may trap the unwary. By its very nature, it forces the reader to think for himself.

M. E. Grenander, *Ambrose Bierce* (New York: Twayne, 1971), pp. 78–79

LAWRENCE I. BERKOVE   The second of Bierce's satires is a narrative written "after the manner of Swift" entitled *The Land Beyond the Blow*. A compilation and revision of at least nine articles written between 1888 and 1899, this work, like *Gulliver's Travels*, is an inverted picture of the narrator's native land. The narrator, transported to a distant region by a blow on the head, moves from country to country, learning the languages of each new land and reacting to each new set of customs from his own perspective. *Ashes of the Beacon* is more a satire of utopian theory and republican government than *The Land Beyond the Blow*, which is aimed more specifically at the values and customs of the United States. From Bierce's point of view, however, a satire on American customs and republican government has fairly direct implications for utopian theory.

The main theme of *The Land Beyond the Blow* appears to be that despite the different customs, religions, and the political creeds of disparate cultures, they all share an essential similarity in reflecting a common human nature. In every one of his voyages the narrator encounters values and national habits so utterly distinct from his own that they suggest a different kind of human being. But in every one of his voyages the narrator observes the same gaps between theory and practice that he did at home, the only difference being that in America he was habituated to his own contradictions, hypocrisies, and rationalizations. On his visit to the land of Tamtonia, for example, which occasions Bierce's most direct satire on republican ideals, the narrator finds a people who have made their government as inefficient as possible and whose conventions of election favor mediocrity. Their private lives are sane but public office is the preserve of fools and ignoramuses. Bierce's clear point is that the only difference between them and us is that they are frank and open. Their candor, however, does not outweigh the disadvantages of their government—an objection which also applies to utopian experiments. In the land of Tortirra the narrator again touches on a point which cuts equally American and utopian values. The Tortirrans are enamored of the phrase "Principles, not men." The narrator's explication of it is pithy: "In the last analysis this is seen to mean that it is better to be governed by scoundrels professing one set of principles than by good men holding another." The skepticism of theory implicit in this view is repeated also in the contrast of Tortirran values with those of another country, Gokeetle-Guk. In Tortirra competition is favored as a way to keep prices low and quality high. In Gokeetle-Guk it is condemned as causing strife and wastefulness. Bierce's resolution of this apparent contradiction is that both of these economic theories have equal validity. The real issue is not economics so much as human nature. Trusts, justly administered, are more efficient than competitive businesses; poorly administered, they are worse. Utopians, therefore, are self-deluded if they think capitalism *per se* is evil; Americans are self-deluded if they think capitalism *per se* is good. Both systems have strengths and limitations, both are imperfect, and it is sheer self-delusion for man to look to any theory he can create as the salvation from his earthly woes.

Lawrence I. Berkove, "Two Impossible Dreams: Ambrose Bierce on Utopia and America," *Huntington Library Quarterly* 44, No. 4 (Autumn 1981): 291–92

CATHY N. DAVIDSON   The uncertainties that most concern Bierce are, finally, the unresolvable problems of mind. Other questions, of course, arise. But such matters as the possible existence of the ghost beyond the ken of some observer or the present whereabouts of Charles Ashmore strangely vanished still bring us back to the real focus in all of Bierce's fiction—the perceiver, what he (very rarely, she) thinks he perceives, how he puts nebulous thought into nebulous words and then reacts to what he thinks he thinks. All of which, contradictory and confused, can be shown only in words. But can language explore the limitations of language? Can story (defined in the late-nineteenth-century primarily as "plot") transcend the "plottedness" of story? It is Bierce's answers, unprecedented in his time, to these difficult questions (questions for the writer and the reader) that distinguish him as an author.

Anticipating more modern fictions, Bierce's experimental stories confuse and confound such fundamental Western dichotomies as reason and superstition, reality and art, even reader and writer. Mimesis, the foundation for late-nineteenth-century realism, is turned inside out. Bierce's texts hold up a mirror, but it is not a mirror held up to nature. It is a mirror held up to consciousness—with all its conscious, subconscious, and unconscious tricks and turnings. When the stories work, the reader necessarily participates in the creation of the fiction. But as we have also seen in stories such as "An Occurrence at Owl Creek Bridge," the reader's participation (being duly "tricked" by the ending) is intended at least partly to make the reader aware of his or her own limitations and, by extension, the limitations of human understanding. In short, Bierce more than any other nineteenth-century American writer anticipates the revolutions in ideas of art and life that characterize the innovative and experimental fictions of the present era.

Cathy N. Davidson, *The Experimental Fictions of Ambrose Bierce: Structuring the Ineffable* (Lincoln: University of Nebraska Press, 1984), pp. 122–23

S. T. JOSHI   Bierce had no overarching view of the world. He once remarked: "We human insects, as a rule, care for nothing but ourselves, and think that is best which most closely touches such emotions and sentiments as grow out of our relations, the one with another. I don't share the preference, and a few others do not, believing that there are things more interesting than men and women." This is close to Lovecraft's "cosmic indifferentism," as is the phrase that Bierce claimed summed up his entire outlook—"Nothing matters." But this is schoolboy philosophy, and in any case I am not certain that Bierce maintained this sort of aloofness with any consistency. He was an atheist but not an especially vociferous one, and it would be simplistic to suppose that the bleakness of his stories could only have been produced by a man who had lost (or never found) God. In truth, the closest he came to uttering a real philosophy is in a newspaper column of 1872:

> The Town Crier does not seek a wider field for his talents. The
> only talents that he has are a knack of hating hypocrisy, cant, and
> all other shams, and a trick of expressing his hatred. . . . Be as
> decent as you can. Don't believe without evidence. Treat
> things divine with marked respect—don't have anything to do
> with them. Do not trust humanity without collateral security;
> it will play you some scurvy trick. Remember that it hurts no
> one to be treated as an enemy entitled to respect until he
> shall prove himself a friend worthy of affection. Cultivate a taste
> for distasteful truths. And, finally . . . endeavor to see things
> as they are, not as they ought to be.

Although the last phrase significantly anticipates his definition of "Cynic" in *The Devil's Dictionary* ("A blackguard whose faulty vision sees things as they are, not as they ought to be"), the whole passage is nothing more than a series of unsupported assertions. And yet had Bierce been asked point-blank why he was a pessimist, cynic, and misanthrope, perhaps his reply would simply have been this: it works. Maybe the world just is a wretched place to be. Maybe people just are, by and large, fools, scoundrels, and hypocrites.

S. T. Joshi, "Ambrose Bierce: Horror as Satire," *The Weird Tale* (Austin: University of Texas Press, 1990), pp. 145–46

▣ *Bibliography*

The Fiend's Delight. 1872.

Nuggets and Dust Panned Out in California. 1872.

Cobwebs: Being the Fables of Zambri, the Parsee. 1873.

Cobwebs from an Empty Skull. 1874.

The Dance of Death (with Thomas A. Harcourt). 1877.

Tales of Soldiers and Civilians ⟨*In the Midst of Life*⟩. 1891.

The Monk and the Hangman's Daughter by Richard Voss (translator; with G. A. Danziger). 1892.

Black Beetles in Amber. 1892.

Can Such Things Be? 1893.

Fantastic Fables. 1899.

Shapes of Clay. 1903.

The Cynic's Word Book ⟨*The Devil's Dictionary*⟩. 1906.

A Son of the Gods and A Horseman in the Sky. 1907.

The Shadow on the Dial. 1909.

Write It Right: A Little Black-List of Literary Faults. 1909.

Collected Works. 1909–12. 12 vols.

My Favorite Murder. 1916.

A Horseman in the Sky; A Watcher by the Dead; The Man and the Snake. 1920.

Letters. Ed. Bertha Clark Pope. 1922.

Twenty-one Letters. Ed. Samuel Loveman. 1922.

Ten Tales. 1925.

An Invocation. 1928.

Selections from Prattle. Ed. Carroll D. Hall. 1936.

Collected Writings. 1946.

The Sardonic Humor of Ambrose Bierce. Ed. George Barkin. 1963.

Ghost and Horror Stories. Ed. E. F. Bleiler. 1964.

The Enlarged Devil's Dictionary. Ed. Ernest Jerome Hopkins. 1967.

The Ambrose Bierce Satanic Reader. Ed. Ernest Jerome Hopkins. 1968.

Complete Short Stories. Ed. Ernest Jerome Hopkins. 1970.

Stories and Fables. Ed. Edward Wagenknecht. 1977.

Skepticism and Dissent: Selected Journalism 1898–1901. Ed. Lawrence I. Berkove. 1980.

A Vision of Doom: Poems. Ed. Donald Sidney-Fryer. 1980.

Charles Brockden Brown
1771–1810

CHARLES BROCKDEN BROWN, the first professional author in the United States, was born in Philadelphia on January 17, 1771. He attended the Friends' Latin School from 1781 to 1786, and then studied law in the office of Alexander Wilcocks from 1787 until 1792, when he decided for moral reasons not to practice. Brown was by that time a member of the Belles Lettres Club, where he came to know like-minded literary men, and had already published "The Rhapsodist," a series of four essays that had appeared in the *Columbia Magazine* (Philadelphia) in 1789. His friendship with Elihu Hubbard Smith, a medical student interested in the theatre, also increased his resolve to become a writer.

In 1794 Brown visited Smith in New York, and there became acquainted with the members of the Friendly Club, including William Dunlap, who was later to become his biographer. Brown's first book, *Sky-Walk*, was completed by the end of 1797 but never released. In the following year he published *Alcuin*, a dialogue on the rights of women, and *Wieland; or, The Transformation*, a Gothic romance set in America. Brown followed this quickly with three more Gothic novels, all published in the next three years: *Ormond; or, The Secret Witness* (1799); *Arthur Mervyn; or, Memoirs of the Year 1793* (1799–1800); and *Edgar Huntly; or, Memoirs of a Sleep-Walker* (1799). Two lesser works, *Clara Howard* and *Jane Talbot*, appeared in 1801. In writing these Gothic novels Brown was influenced not only by Ann Radcliffe but also by Samuel Richardson and William Godwin; in general the novels are intended in part to be morally instructive and are also conscientiously grounded in scientific or pseudo-scientific fact. Among their admirers were Sir Walter Scott, Keats, and Shelley.

After 1801 Brown published no further novels. He worked in his brother's mercantile business between 1800 and 1806, engaged in political pamphleteering (1803–09), and edited the *Monthly Magazine and Literary Review* (New York; 1799–1802) and the *Literary Magazine and American Register* (Philadelphia; 1803–07), both of which printed scientific as well as literary articles. His *Memoirs of Carwin, the Biloquist*, an unfinished story intended as a sequel to *Wieland*, was published serially in the *Literary Magazine* between 1803 and 1805, but was not published in book form. In 1804 Brown married Elizabeth Linn; they had three sons and one daughter. In 1807 Brown began publishing the *American Register, or General Repository of History, Politics and Science*; seven semi-annual volumes appeared before his death on February 21, 1810. A biography attributed to his friend William Dunlap appeared in 1815, although much of it is derived from a manuscript by Paul Allen. The second volume of this biography included many uncollected works by Brown, including *Memoirs of Carwin*, *Memoirs of Stephen Calvert*, and an unpublished final segment of *Alcuin*.

Critical Extracts

CHARLES BROCKDEN BROWN   America has opened new views to the naturalist and politician, but has seldom furnished themes to the moral painter. That new springs of action, and new motives to curiosity should operate; that the field of investigation, opened to us by our own country, should differ essentially from those which exist in Europe; may be readily conceived. The sources of amusement to the fancy and instruction to the heart, that are peculiar to ourselves, are equally numerous and inexhaustible. It is the purpose of this work to profit by some of these sources; to exhibit a series of adventures, growing out of the condition of our country, and connected with one of the most common and most wonderful diseases or affections of the human frame.

One merit the writer may at least claim; that of calling forth the passions and engaging the sympathy of the reader, by means hitherto unemployed by preceding authors. Puerile superstition and exploded manners; Gothic castles and chimeras, are the materials usually employed for this end. The incidents of Indian hostility, and the perils of the western wilderness, are far more suitable; and, for a native of America to overlook these, would admit of no apology.

> Charles Brockden Brown, "To the Public," *Edgar Huntly; or, Memoirs of a Sleep-Walker* (Philadelphia: H. Maxwell, 1799)

GULIAN CROMMELIN VERPLANCK   Brown's mind is distinguished for strong, intense conception. If his thoughts are vast, he is still always master of them. He works with the greatest ease, as if his mind were fully possessed of his subject, and could not but suggest thoughts with freedom and rapidity. In the most monstrous and shocking narrative, he writes with the utmost sincerity, as if he laboured under a delusion which acted with a mischievous but uncontrollable power. He never, indeed, shews a desire to complete a story, nor draws a character so much for what it is to effect in the end, as for the development of mind. The present incident is perhaps fine in itself, and answers the author's purpose, and gives room for display of great strength; but it has little or no connection with others. With the greatest solicitude to tell us everything that passes in the mind before a purpose is formed, he is very careless as to any continuity or dependence in the events, which lead to or flow from that purpose. He sometimes crowds more into one day than we should have expected in many, and at others leaps over so large an interval as to make the narrative improbable to all who are not in the secret. His characters cannot be relied upon: notwithstanding their strength and apparently stubborn singularities, they accommodate themselves readily to the author, sometimes losing all the importance with which they were at first invested, and at others accomplishing something beyond or opposite what was expected, and almost what we can believe to be within the compass of human power in the agent or weakness in the sufferer. This incompleteness of views and inconsistency of characters is not owing to carelessness or haste in the writer; he had never determined how things should end, nor proposed to himself any prevailing object when he began, nor discovered one as he advanced. We generally close a story with a belief that as much more might be said. He was engrossed by single, separate scenes, such as inventions suggested from time to time; and while we can account from this fact for our feeling little solicitude about the story as a whole, we must at the same time form a high estimate of an author's power, who can carry us through almost disconnected scenes without any considerable failure of interest. He seems fond of exciting and vexing curiosity, but when he fails of satisfying it, it is more, we believe, from forgetfulness than design.

There is very little variety in his writings; at least in those where his genius is most clearly discerned. He loves unusual, lawless characters, and extraordinary and tragic incident. There should not be a moment of calm brightness in the world, unless as it may serve to heighten the effect of approaching gloom and tempest. The innocent are doomed to suffer, as if virtue were best capable of enduring and shown most conspicuously in trial, or at least drew the largest sympathy. The suffering is of the mind; bodily pain and death appear but moderate and vulgar evils, and rather a refuge than punishment for the triumphant criminal, who has rioted in mischief till he is weary, and willing to die for repose since his work is ended. In these sad views of life, which make society worse than the wilderness and men's sympathy and promises little better than a mockery, there is no apparent design to mislead the world, or covertly condemn its opinions and awards, but merely to take a firm hold of the heart, by appeals to its pity, terror, indignation or wonder. He wants the universality and justice of a fair observer of the world. He thinks too much in one way, and that a narrow one. His views are of one kind, and shew that he thought more than he observed.

Gulian Crommelin Verplanck, "Charles Brockden Brown," *North American Review* No. 24 (June 1819): 75–76

RICHARD HENRY DANA   If Brown is remarkable for having appeared amongst a people whose pursuits and tastes had, at the time, little or no sympathy with his own, and in a country in which all was new, and partook of the alacrity of hope, and where no old remembrances made the mind contemplative and sad, nor old superstitions conjured up forms of undefined awe, he is scarcely less striking for standing apart, in the character of his mind, from almost every other man of high genius. He is more like Godwin than like any other; but differs from him in making so many of his characters live, and act, and perish, as if they were slaves of supernatural powers, and the victims of a vague and dreadful fatality. Even here his character for truth is maintained, and his invisible agencies mingle with the commonest characters, in the most ordinary scenes of life.

It is true that these mysterious agencies are all very idly explained away, like Mrs. Radcliffe's; yet such a hold do they take upon our minds, that we cannot shake off the mystical influence they have gained over us; and even those who have praised the deceptions seem to have done it not so much from a love of deception as from a hankering after something resembling the supernatural, and an insane sort of delight in watching its strange and dreadful force over others; both he that is wrought upon and he that works seem, the one to suffer, and the other to act, as under some resistless spell. Brown's fatal power is unsparing, and never stops, and through the bitterest griefs and sufferings never draws tears or softens the heart; it wears out the heart and takes away the strength of our spirits, so that we lie helpless under it. A power of this kind holds no associations with nature; for in the gloomiest, and the wildest, and barrenest scenes of nature, there is something enlarging and elevating—something that tells us there is an end to our unmixed sorrow,—something that lifts us above life, and breathes into us immortality. No! it is surrounded by man and the works of man,—man in his ills, and sins, and feebleness; it is there alone that we can feel what is the bitterness and weariness of unmixed helplessness and woe.

So much was gloominess the character of Brown's genius, that he does not, like other authors, begin his story in a state of cheerfulness or quiet, and gradually lead to disappointment and affliction. Some one writes a letter to a friend who has asked him for an account of his suffering life. It hints at mysteries, and sorrows, and remorse,—sorrows and remorse to which there can be no end but in the rest of the grave. He has already passed through years of miseries, and we come in and go on with him to the end of his story. But his sorrows have not ended there; and we leave him, praying that death may at last bring peace to his sick and worn heart. There is woe behind us, and woe before us. The spirit cries, with the Apocalyptic angel, seen flying through the midst of heaven, "Woe, woe, woe, to the inhabitors of earth!"

Richard Henry Dana, "The Novels of Charles Brockden Brown" (1827), *Poems and Prose Writings* (New York: Baker & Scribner, 1850), Vol. 2, pp. 329–31

WILLIAM HAZLITT   Mr Brown, who preceded ⟨Washington Irving⟩, and was the author of several novels which made some noise in this country, was a writer of a different stamp. Instead of hesitating before a scruple, and aspiring to avoid a fault, he braved criticism, and aimed only at effect. He was an inventor, but without materials. His strength and his efforts are convulsive throes—his works are a banquet of horrors. The hint of some of them is taken from *Caleb Williams* and *St Leon*, but infinitely exaggerated, and carried to disgust and outrage. They are full (to disease) of imagination,—but it is forced, violent, and shocking. This is to be expected, we apprehend, in attempts of this kind in a country like America, where there is, generally speaking, no *natural imagination*. The mind must be excited by overstraining, by pulleys and levers. Mr Brown was a man of genius, of strong passion, and active fancy; but his genius was not seconded by early habit, or by surrounding sympathy. His story and his interests are not wrought out, therefore, in the ordinary course of nature; but are, like the monster in *Frankenstein*, a man made by art and determined will. For instance, it may be said of him, as of Gawin Douglas, 'Of Brownies and Bogilis full is his Buik.' But no ghost, we will venture to say, was ever seen in North America. They do not walk in broad day; and the night of ignorance and superstition which favours their appearance, was long past before the

United States lifted up their head beyond the Atlantic wave. The inspired poet's tongue must have an echo in the state of public feeling, or of involuntary belief, or it soon grows harsh or mute. In America, they are 'so well policied,' so exempt from the knowledge of fraud or force, so free from the assaults of *the flesh and the devil*, that in pure hardness of belief they hoot the *Beggar's Opera* from the stage: with them, poverty and crime, pickpockets and highwaymen, the lock-up-house and the gallows, are things incredible to sense! In this orderly and undramatic state of security and freedom from natural foes, Mr Brown has provided one of his heroes with a demon to torment him, and fixed him at his back;—but what is to keep him there? Not any prejudice or lurking superstition on the part of the American reader: for the lack of such, the writer is obliged to make up by incessant rodomontade, and face-making. The want of genuine imagination is always proved by caricature: monsters are the growth, not of passion, but of the attempt forcibly to stimulate it. In our own unrivalled Novelist, and the great exemplar of this kind of writing, we see how ease and strength are united. Tradition and invention meet half way; and nature scarce knows how to distinguish them. The reason is, there is here an old and solid ground in previous manners and opinion for imagination to rest upon. The air of this bleak northern clime is filled with legendary lore: Not a castle without the stain of blood upon its floor or winding steps: not a glen without its ambush or its feat of arms: not a lake without its Lady! But the map of America is not historical; and, therefore, works of fiction do not take root in it; for the fiction, to be good for any thing, must not be in the author's mind, but belong to the age or country in which he lives. The genius of America is essentially mechanical and modern.

William Hazlitt, "American Literature—Dr Channing," *Edinburgh Review* No. 99 (October 1829): 126–28

BARRETT WENDELL   The truth is that, at least in his philosophical speculations and his novels, Brockden Brown, honestly aspiring to prove America civilized, was instinctively true to the American temper of his time in attempting to prove this by conscientious imitations. What he happened to imitate was a temporarily fashionable phase of stagnant English fiction. Nothing better marks the difference between English literature and American in 1798 than that this year produced both the *Lyrical Ballads* and *Wieland*. The former first expressed a new literary spirit in England; the latter, the first serious work of American letters, was as far from new as Wordsworth's verses and the *Ancient Mariner* were from conventional.

Beyond doubt one's first impression is that the novels of Brown are merely imitative.

After a while, however, one begins to feel, beneath his conscientious imitative effort, a touch of something individual. In that epoch-making *Wieland*, the hero is a gentleman of Philadelphia, who in the midst of ideal happiness is suddenly accosted by a mysterious voice which orders him to put to death his superhumanly perfect wife and children. The mysterious voice, which pursues him through increasing moods of horror, declares itself to be that of God. At last, driven to madness by this appalling command, Wieland obeys it and murders his family. To this point, in spite of confusion and turgidity, the story has power. The end is ludicrously weak; the voice of God turns out to have been merely a trick of a malignant ventriloquist. The triviality of this catastrophe tends to make you feel as if all of the preceding horrors had been equally trivial. Really this is not the case. The chapters in which the mind of Wieland is gradually possessed by delusion could have been written only by one who had genuinely felt a sense of what hideously mysterious things may lie beyond human ken. Some such sense as this, in terribly serious form, haunted the imagination of the Puritans. In a meretricious form it appears in the work of Poe. In a form alive with beauty it reveals itself through the melancholy romances of Hawthorne. In Poe's work and in Hawthorne's, it is handled with something like mastery, and few men of letters have been much farther from the mastery of their art than Charles Brockden Brown; but the sense of horror which Brown expressed in *Wieland* is genuine. To feel its power you need only compare it with the similar feeling expressed in Lewis's *Monk*, in the *Mysteries of Udolpho*, or even in *Caleb Williams* itself.

In two of Brown's later novels, *Ormond* and *Arthur Mervyn*, there are touches more directly from life which show another kind of power. Among his most poignant personal experiences was the terrible fact of epidemic yellow fever. During a visitation of this scourge Brown was in New York, where he was on intimate terms with one Dr. Smith, a young physician of about his own age. An Italian gentleman, arriving in town with an introduction to Dr. Smith, was taken with the plague and refused lodging in any respectable hotel. Smith found him, terribly ill, in a cheap lodging-house, whence he took him home. There the Italian died; and Smith, who contracted the disease, died too. Brockden Brown was with them all the while; he came to know the pestilence appallingly well. In both *Ormond* and *Arthur Mervyn* there are descriptions of epidemic yellow fever almost as powerful as Defoe's descriptions of the London plague.

Barrett Wendell, *A Literary History of America* (New York: Scribner's, 1900), pp. 162–64

LESLIE A. FIEDLER   For the haunted castle and the dungeon, Brown substituted the haunted forest (in which nothing is what it seems) and the cave, the natural pit or abyss from which man struggles against great odds to emerge. These are ancient, almost instinctive symbols, the *selva oscura* going back to Dante and beyond, while the cave as a metaphor for the mysteries of the human heart is perhaps as old as literature itself. Brown tries quite consciously to identify the pit in which Edgar Huntly awakes with the terrible womb-tomb dungeons of Mrs. Radcliffe and Monk Lewis. "Methought I was the victim," Huntly says at the moment he becomes aware of where he is, "of some tyrant who had thrust me into a dungeon."

It should be noted that the shift from the ruined castle of the European prototypes to the forest and cave of Brown involves not just a shift in the manner of what the author is after. *The change of myth involves a profound change of meaning.* In the American gothic, that is to say, the heathen, unredeemed wilderness and not the decaying monuments of a dying class, Nature and not society, become the symbol of evil. Similarly, not the aristocrat but the Indian, not the dandified courtier but the savage colored man is postulated as the embodiment of villainy. Our novel of terror, that is to say (even before its founder has consciously shifted his political allegiances), is well on the way to becoming a Calvinist exposé of natural human corruption rather than enlightened attack on a debased ruling class or entrenched superstition. The European gothic identified blackness with the super-ego and was therefore revolutionary in its implications; the American gothic (at least as it followed the example of Brown) identified evil with the id and was conservative at its deepest level of implication, whatever the intent of its authors.

In so far, then, as our response to these natural symbols is determined by the native gothic tradition we are conditioned to regard them, and the life of the unconscious for which they stand, as destructive. There is, however, a counter-tradition, Rousseauistic perhaps in its origins, for which forest, cave and savage, Nature itself, and the instinctive aspects of the psyche they represent are read as beneficent, taken to symbolize a principle of salvation. The dialogue between these two views has continued, basically unresolved, in American life and art until our own time. But it could not even begin until the attitudes of Rousseau had been translated into an American language of myth and symbol, just as the attitudes of the gothic were so translated by Brown.

Leslie A. Fiedler, "Charles Brockden Brown and the Invention of the American Gothic," *Love and Death in the American Novel* (1960; rev. ed. New York: Stein & Day, 1966), pp. 148–49

DAVID PUNTER   Brown, as is well known, held in low regard
the "puerile superstitions and exploded manners" of original Gothic. He
follows Radcliffe in his attitudes toward the power of nature and in his use
of terror, but "romance" was to him an altogether serious business. His most
important definition of it occurs in an essay of 1800, where he distinguishes
it from history on the grounds that romance is principally an enquiry into
motives and causes, whereas history contents itself with the display of facts.
Brown's major works conduct this enquiry on a supra-historical level: that
is, they do not set out to provide reinterpretations of specific historical
conjunctures, but to enquire into the question of social psychology in general.
But in other work, like *Sketches of the History of Carsol* and the *Sketches of
the History of the Carrils and the Ormes* (both of uncertain date), Brown does
apply his investigative technique to real history, albeit a history transmuted
by the deliberate insertion of fictional characters, events and sub-plots, a
mode which recalls to mind the work of Lee and her school. Early in his
life Brown "confessed" his "attachment to fictitious history," and he was
generally interested in fostering American historical writing.

The he saw in romance a way of laying bare the springs of human action
and thereby of understanding the past, although this concern is less clearly
manifested than in the case of Hawthorne. His attempts at understanding the
interrelations of society and ideology were formative in terms of American
Gothic: they look towards both Hawthorne's obsession with religious dogma-
tism and its social effects, and Poe's minute analyses of situations of terror.
Already with Brown one sees a degree of explicitness of purpose in advance
of his English Gothic contemporaries, although the explicitness perhaps
decreases the symbolic force of his writings. The fact that Carwin *teaches*
us more than Schedoni is bound up with the other fact that Carwin is a
far less potently tragic figure than Schedoni; but then, Schedoni reaches
back into depths of historical and religious terror which were hardly available
to a writer in Brown's position. The rational strength and emotional thinness
of Brown's writing are distinctive to his America, his ability to explore
mental worlds with precision peculiar to a situation in which those worlds
were not submerged beneath the pressure of a fearsome past.

David Punter, *The Literature of Terror: A History of Gothic Fictions from 1765 to the
Present Day* (New York: Longman, 1980), pp. 196–97

PAUL WITHERINGTON   Recent criticism seems to slight or
misunderstand Brown's kinship with gothic tradition. A by-product of gothic
literature's revolutionary tendencies is its wariness of conventional plot

logic, and the resulting "carelessness" may disturb both the unreformed New Critic and the sort of psychological or myth critic who insists on matching the bizarre effect with common cause, however far he must abstract them to make them jibe. In Brown and his predecessors, for example, there is a strong sense of infection by proximity, the sort of uncaused misfortune that seems closer to early social realism than to psychological allegory. Gothic novelists were often less concerned with guilt by dissociation than with guilt by association, evil being transferred through confession with all the randomness of a plague. Thus Edgar (Huntly) is blasted by Clithero's story as is the young man by Falkland's story in Godwin's *Caleb Williams*, the shared secret having become the shared sin. Even those historical critics who categorize Brown as a gothic novelist sometimes deny him the prerogatives of that genre. William L. Hedges calls *Edgar Huntly* "the most baffling of all Brown's novels, a botched gothic thriller." "Botched," presumably, because it lacks the authority of later writers (Poe, specifically) and because matters like Waldegrave's murder are left anti-climactically and unsatisfactorily resolved. But surely the gothic tradition is noted as much for works containing supernatural or psychic loopholes as for the kind of thriller that slides back to solid reason at the end.

In truth, Brown both uses and alters traditional gothic to his narrative purposes. For him it works like a dream related by a key character—obviously relevant but not to be taken definitively. The European tradition of "castles and chimeras" referred to by Brown in his introduction is Americanized, but not necessarily made more rational; and despite Brown's social realism and his objective treatment of scientific curiosities such as ventriloquism and somnambulism, his dramas of tangled inner landscapes tend to resist analysis. Even when his plots are laid bare, mysteries remain that beg for the kind of sequel Brown provided to *Wieland* in *Carwin the Biloquist*. *Edgar Huntly* flaunts these loose ends, or as they would be termed in the language usually reserved for calculating modern novels, "open ends," and in burying them, or binding them with the knots of critical hindsight, we do no favor to Brown's intellect or his art.

Paul Witherington, " 'Not My Tongue Only': Form and Language in Brown's *Edgar Huntly*," *Critical Essays on Charles Brockden Brown*, ed. Bernard Rosenthal (Boston: G. K. Hall, 1981), pp. 164–65

DONALD A. RINGE   Because he lays such stress on the psychological state of his characters, the major Gothic romances of Charles Brockden Brown make a new and significant contribution to the developing Gothic mode. The works that he found on the shelves of the bookstores and lending libraries of New York or Philadelphia had no doubt taught him much about the craft and purposes of fiction, and one can certainly trace the influence of some of these books on his own romances. But Brown was not the slavish imitator of any school of fiction, and although he might derive what he could from a Schiller or a Tshinck or Radcliffe or Parsons, he developed the material in a highly original way. He apparently saw at once the possibility of the Gothic mode as a vehicle for psychological themes, and he quickly found a way to relate the mental states of his characters to the objects of external reality. In both *Wieland* and *Edgar Huntly* he established at once his own version of Gothic, creating thereby an American branch of the mode that was to reach its fullest development a generation later in the works of Edgar Allan Poe and Nathaniel Hawthorne.

Donald A. Ringe, "Charles Brockden Brown," *American Gothic: Imagination and Reason in Nineteenth-Century Fiction* (Lexington: University Press of Kentucky, 1982), pp. 56–57

ALAN AXELROD   *Edgar Huntly* and "The Pit and the Pendulum" share the immediate horrors of their common "pit"; but Brown's novel develops another, subtler horror as well. Frightening as Huntly found the wilderness while he was lost in it, returned from it he found that civilized existence held terrors as well. In spite of his fears and over the protest of his civilized sensibilities, Huntly had become a formidably efficient wilderness man, having encountered a panther and killed it, hostile Indians and killed them. Whereas Poe's protagonist is only momentarily effectual, Brown's realizes in himself powers he had never known before. Returned from the wilderness, however, Huntly finds himself as ineffectual as the victim of Poe's Inquisition. ⟨. . .⟩ Only in the wilderness, where the universe's intangible "Inquisitors" are immediately manifest as panthers and savages, does Huntly enjoy a measure of effectual heroism. It is true that there the savage lurks and the panther crouches; but there, in the moment of the attack and the leap, reason must give way to an act of instinct with an unambiguous and immediate result. Civilized life offers few such direct encounters. Conventions, laws and institutions mediate reality, imposing between it and the individual a Daedalian maze. In *Edgar Huntly*, where abstract wilderness figures are grounded in a literal space, the territory offers not only images of confusion and terror but also the opportunity of fulfillment of innate powers and prodigious action.

Alan Axelrod, *Charles Brockden Brown: An American Tale* (Austin: University of Texas Press, 1983), p. 42

A. ROBERT LEE   ⟨Brown⟩ was from the start possessed of his own substantial and truly singular imagination, one worthy of attention in terms which step outside mere antiquarian or historical interest. To encounter him, at least through his four Gothic—and best novels—in turn *Wieland* (1798), *Ormond* (1799), *Arthur Mervyn* (1799) and *Arthur Mervyn . . . Second Part* (1800), and *Edgar Huntley* (1799), is to be faced with the recognition that, beyond all his 'horror', his shocks and melodrama, there lies a far subtler set of designs upon the reader, the upshot of Brown's nothing if not speculative turn of mind. In this he anticipates his fellow Gothic spirit of a generation later, Edgar Allan Poe. Not that, any more than in the case of Poe, such has protected him from the charge of being a 'bungler', the barest survivor of 'defects that would have wrecked an average writer' ⟨Alexander Cowie⟩. Yet, whatever his excesses, the overdone plot lines, the proliferation of characters, the too-energetic fades and dissolves, even the suspicion that he has in mind to keep us reading no matter what the cost, he also manages to persuade that he is about altogether more consequential purposes. He may never quite have managed any single, decisive masterpiece, but the grounds are there for thinking that one never lay too far outside his imaginative grasp. However unlikely, in Hawthorne's terms, his elevation 'in the realms of the imagination' to a 'ruler' or 'demigod', he compares favourably with more established adepts in the art of Gothic—with Horace Walpole, Monk Lewis, Ann Radcliffe and, of later vintage, Bram Stoker. And he does so, in large degree, because to confuse his Gothicism for the whole account does him a genuine disservice.

For Brown's 'Gothic' embodies an authentic force of ideas, his unremitting will to knowledge. Despite 1776, and its accompanying new-born American rhetoric of hope and belief in the perfectibility of mankind, he saw himself as looking out upon the world everywhere still beset by darkness—and a darkness as much within as without. Time and again, he probes the otherness of much of human experience, the play of the unpredictable and random, the deceptiveness of appearance, the self as stranger or exile which without seeming reason can turn wilfully against itself and others. Brown's Gothic is thereby put to greater purpose than mere thrill or titillation. Indeed, in the preface to *Edgar Huntly*, 'To the Public', he actually takes it upon himself to castigate the traditional Gothic as 'puerile superstition', 'exploded manners' and mere 'chimeras'. He speaks of favouring a 'series of adventures, growing out of the country', and of himself as a 'moral painter', an analyst both of 'the heart' and of 'the most wonderful diseases or affectations of the human frame'. Thus, as applied to Brown, Milton's 'darkness visible' does an additional duty. It directs us to the basic push behind his writing, the elucidation of nothing less than our own endemic mystery.

> A. Robert Lee, "A Darkness Visible: The Case of Charles Brockden Brown," *American Horror Fiction from Brockden Brown to Stephen King*, ed. Brian Docherty (New York: St. Martin's Press, 1990), pp. 14–15

▨ Bibliography

Alcuin: A Dialogue. 1798.

Wieland; or, The Transformation: An American Tale. 1798.

Ormond; or, The Secret Witness. 1799.

Arthur Mervyn; or, Memoirs of the Year 1793. 1799–1800. 2 parts.

Edgar Huntly; or, Memoirs of a Sleep-walker. 1799. 3 vols.

Clara Howard. 1801.

Jane Talbot. 1801.

An Address to the Government of the United States, on the Cession of Louisiana to the French. 1803.

Monroe's Embassy; or, The Conduct of the Government, in Relation to Our Claims to the Navigation of the Mississippi, Considered. 1803.

A View of the Soil and Climate of the United States of America by C. F. Volney (translator). 1804.

[*The British Treaty.* 1807.]

An Address to the Congress of the United States, on the Utility and Justice of Restrictions upon Foreign Commerce. 1809.

Novels. 1827. 7 vols.

Novels. 1857. 6 vols.

Complete Novels. 1887. 6 vols.

The Rhapsodist and Other Uncollected Writings. Ed. Harry R. Warfel. 1943.

Novels and Related Works. Ed. Sidney J. Krause et al. 1977–87. 6 vols.

Memoirs of Stephen Calvert. Ed. Hans Borchers. 1978.

Somnambulism and Other Stories. Ed. Alfred Weber. 1987.

Henry James
1843–1916

HENRY JAMES was born in New York City on April 15, 1843. His father was Henry James, Sr., a philosopher and clergyman who was a follower of Swedenborg, and his elder brother was William James, the psychologist. After being educated in New York, London, Paris, and Geneva, James entered Harvard Law School in 1862. From 1865 he was a regular contributor of critical articles to the *Nation* and of stories to the *Atlantic Monthly* and *Galaxy*. His first novel, *Watch and Ward*, appeared serially in the *Atlantic* in 1871, and was followed in 1875 by *Transatlantic Sketches*, *A Passionate Pilgrim*, and a second novel, *Roderick Hudson* (1876).

James moved to Europe in 1875. In 1876, after a brief period in Paris, he settled in England, where he lived for the rest of his life, first in London, and then, after 1898, in Rye. His subsequent novels were all in one way or another a reflection of his changing reactions to the fact of his emigration. At first he chiefly concerned himself with the problem of the American confronted by a more complex civilization, and to this period belong *The American* (1877), *The Europeans* (1878), *Daisy Miller* (1879), and *The Portrait of a Lady* (1881). He then turned to writing more exclusively about the society and character of the English in such novels as *The Tragic Muse* (1890), *The Spoils of Poynton* (1897), and *The Awkward Age* (1899). In his last three great novels, *The Wings of the Dove* (1902), *The Ambassadors* (1903), and *The Golden Bowl* (1904), he again took up the theme of the contrast of American and European culture.

Homesickness for America led to a tour of the United States in 1904–05, and to a fresh reaction against the materialism of American society. After returning to England James spent much time on revising his earlier works and preparing the so-called New York Edition of his works, published in 1907–17 by Charles Scribner's Sons. James became a British subject in 1915, received the Order of Merit in the following year, and died in London on February 28, 1916. Two novels, *The Ivory Tower* and *The Sense of the Past*, were left unfinished at his death; both were published as fragments in 1917.

James also published several other novels, including *Washington Square* (1881), *The Bostonians* (1886), *The Princess Casamassima* (1886), *The Reverberator* (1888), *The Aspern Papers* (1888), and *What Maisie Knew* (1897), as well as tales and short story collections, including *Madonna of the Future* (1879), *The Siege of London* (1883), *The Real Thing* (1893), *Terminations* (1895), *Embarrassments* (1896), *The Other House* (1896), *In the Cage* (1898), and *The Better Sort* (1903). His travel sketches include *Portraits of Places* (1883), *A Little Tour in France* (1884), and *The American Scene* (1907). James also wrote plays (e. g. *Guy Domville*, 1895), critical works (e.g. *Hawthorne*, 1879, for the English Men of Letters series), and autobiographical pieces (e.g. *A Small Boy and Others*, 1913; *Notes of a Son and Brother*, 1914). R. P. Blackmur collected James's prefaces to his novels as *The Art of the Novel* (1934), and Leon Edel has written an exhaustive biography (5 vols., 1953–72) as well as editing his letters (4 vols., 1974–84) and notebooks (1987).

James's famous novella *The Turn of the Screw* first appeared with another tale as *The Two Magics* (1898). It is his most celebrated contribution to ghostly fiction, but by no means his only one; in 1948 Leon Edel gathered together more than a dozen stories in the volume *The Ghostly Tales of Henry James*, which includes "Sir Edmund Orme," "Owen Wingrave," "The Jolly Corner," "The Altar of the Dead," and a number of other tales. *The Turn of the Screw* has engendered perhaps more criticism than any other work in modern literature, and much of the debate focuses on whether the tale genuinely involves the supernatural or whether the "ghosts" seen by the young governess are merely a product of her imagination. James's own remarks on the tale seem to support a supernatural interpretation, but the psychological theory—first espoused by Edna Kenton in 1924 and elaborated by Edmund Wilson and others—has many supporters. Some scholars believe that the ambiguities in the tale are intentionally irresolvable. James referred to his unfinished novel *The Sense of the Past* (begun in 1900) as a "tale of terror," and it too would have included a considerable number of supernatural manifestations.

▧ *Critical Extracts*

HENRY JAMES   Note here the ghost-story told me at Addington (evening of Thursday 10th), by the Archbishop of Canterbury 〈Edward

White Benson⟩: the mere vague, undetailed, faint sketch of it—being all he had been told (very badly and imperfectly), by a lady who had no art of relation, and no clearness: the story of the young children (indefinite number and age) left to the care of servants in an old country-house, through the death, presumably, of parents. The servants, wicked and depraved, corrupt and deprave the children; the children are bad, full of evil, to a sinister degree. The servants *die* (the story vague about the way of it) and their apparitions, figures, return to haunt the house *and* children, to whom they seem to beckon, whom they invite and solicit, from across dangerous places, the deep ditch of a sunk fence, etc.—so that the children may destroy themselves, lose themselves by responding, by getting into their power. So long as the children are kept from them, they are not lost; but they try and try and try, these evil presences, to get hold of them. It is a question of the children 'coming over to where they are.' It is all obscure and imperfect, the picture, the story, but there is a suggestion of strangely gruesome effect in it. The story to be told—tolerably obviously—by an outside spectator, observer.

> Henry James, Notebook entry (12 January 1895), *The Complete Notebooks of Henry James*, ed. Leon Edel and Lyall H. Powers (New York: Oxford University Press, 1987), p. 109

ELISABETH LUTHER CARY   *The Turn of the Screw* is a tale of which the elusive horror cannot be exaggerated. In all its elements, in the choice of the little child as the victim of inexplicable evil, in the veil shrouding in darkness the manifestations of the evil, in the sense of irresistible forces sweeping against and overturning divine innocence of heart, in the downfall of the physical under the fierce assault of the spirit, sheer ghastly, shattering horror is present. In other stories involving excursions into the region of good and evil spirits, a lighter medium is used. The ghosts of "The Real Right Thing," "The Third Person," "Owen Wingrave," "The Romance of Certain Old Clothes"—these ghosts enlist the imagination without appalling it.

> Elisabeth Luther Cary, "Henry James," *Scribner's Magazine* 36, No. 4 (October 1904): 399

HENRY JAMES   The merit of the tale ⟨*The Turn of the Screw*⟩, as it stands, is accordingly, I judge, that it has struggled successfully with its dangers. It is an excursion into chaos while remaining, like Blue-Beard and Cinderella, but an anecdote—though an anecdote amplified and highly emphasised and returning upon itself; as, for that matter, Cinderella and Blue-Beard return. I need scarcely add after this that it is a piece of ingenuity pure and simple, of cold artistic calculation, an *amusette* to catch those not easily caught (the "fun" of the capture of the merely witless being ever but small), the jaded, the disillusioned, the fastidious. Otherwise expressed, the study is of a conceived "tone," the tone of suspected and felt trouble, of an inordinate and incalculable sort—the tone of tragic, yet of exquisite, mystification. ⟨. . .⟩

⟨. . .⟩ Recorded and attested "ghosts" are ⟨. . .⟩ as little expressive, as little dramatic, above all as little continuous and conscious and responsive, as is consistent with their taking the trouble—and an immense trouble they find it, we gather—to appear at all. Wonderful and interesting therefore at a given moment, they are inconceivable figures in an *action*—and *The Turn of the Screw* was an action, desperately, or it was nothing. I had to decide in fine between having my apparitions correct and having my story "good"— that is producing my impression of the dreadful, my designed horror. Good ghosts, speaking by book, make poor subjects, and it was clear that from the first my hovering prowling blighting presences, my pair of abnormal agents, would have to depart altogether from the rules. They would be agents in fact; there would be laid on them the dire duty of causing the situation to reek with the air of Evil. Their desire and their ability to do so, visibly measuring meanwhile their effect, together with their observed and described success—this was exactly my central idea; so that, briefly, I cast my lot with pure romance, the appearances conforming to the true type being so little romantic.

This is to say, I recognise again, that Peter Quint and Miss Jessel are not "ghosts" at all, as we now know the ghost, but goblins, elves, imps, demons as loosely constructed as those of the old trials for witchcraft; if not, more pleasingly, fairies of the legendary order, wooing their victims forth to see them dance under the moon. Not indeed that I suggest their reducibility to any form of the pleasing pure and simple; they please at the best but through having helped me to express my subject all directly and intensely. Here it was—in the use made of them—that I felt a high degree of art really required; and here it is that, on reading the tale over, I find my precautions justified.

Henry James, "Preface" to *The Aspern Papers; The Turn of the Screw; The Liar; The Two Faces* (*The Novels and Tales of Henry James,* New York Edition, Volume 12) (New York: Scribner's, 1908), pp. xvii–xx

---

VIRGINIA WOOLF   Henry James's ghosts have nothing in common with the violent old ghosts—the blood-stained sea captains, the white

horses, the headless ladies of dark lanes and windy commons. They have
their origin within us. They are present whenever the significant overflows
our powers of expressing it; whenever the ordinary appears ringed by the
strange. The baffling things that are left over, the frightening ones that
persist—these are the emotions that he takes, embodies, makes consoling
and companionable. But how can we be afraid? As the gentleman says when
he has seen the ghost of Sir Edmund Orme for the first time: 'I was ready
to answer for it to all and sundry that ghosts are much less alarming and
more amusing than was commonly supposed'. The beautiful urbane spirits
are only not of this world because they are too fine for it. They have taken
with them across the border their clothes, their manners, their breeding,
their band-boxes, and valets and ladies' maids. They remain always a little
worldly. We may feel clumsy in their presence, but we cannot feel afraid.
What does it matter, then, if we do pick up *The Turn of the Screw* an hour
or so before bedtime? After an exquisite entertainment we shall, if the other
stories are to be trusted, end with this fine music in our ears, and sleep the
sounder.

Virginia Woolf, "Henry James's Ghosts" (1921), *Collected Essays* (New York: Harcourt, Brace & World, 1967), Vol. 1, pp. 291–92

EDMUND WILSON   A discussion of Henry James's ambiguity
may appropriately begin with *The Turn of the Screw*. This story, which seems
to have proved more fascinating to the general reading public than anything
else of James's except *Daisy Miller*, apparently conceals another horror behind
the ostensible one. I do not know who first propounded the theory; but
Miss Edna Kenton, whose insight into James is profound, has been one of
its principal exponents, and the late Charles Demuth did a set of illustrations
for the story based on this interpretation.

According to this theory, the young governess who tells the story is a
neurotic case of sex repression, and the ghosts are not real ghosts at all but
merely the hallucinations of the governess. ⟨. . .⟩

When we look back in the light of these hints, we become convinced
that the whole story has been primarily intended as a characterization of
the governess: her visions and the way she behaves about them, as soon as
we look at them from the obverse side, present a solid and unmistakable
picture of the poor country parson's daughter, with her English middle-class
class-consciousness, her inability to admit to herself her sexual impulses and
the relentless English "authority" which enables her to put over on inferiors
even purposes which are totally deluded and not at all to the other people's

best interests. Add to this the peculiar psychology of governesses, who, by reason of their isolated position between the family and the servants, are likely to become ingrown and morbid. The writer knows of an actual case of a governess who used to frighten the servants by opening doors and smashing mirrors and who tortured the parents by mythical stories of kidnappers. The poltergeist, once a figure of demonology, is now a recognized neurotic type.

Edmund Wilson, "The Ambiguity of Henry James" (1934), *The Triple Thinkers: Ten Essays on Literature* (New York: Harcourt, Brace, 1938), pp. 122, 131

LEON EDEL   Henry James's ghosts possess an unusual degree of reality because we see them invariably through the people who see or "feel" them. It is these people's vision of the supernatural that he almost invariably gives us; which is why his ghost stories have seemed to some readers to be among the most terrifying ever written. If we wish to attach him to tradition it must be to Defoe's *True Relation of the Apparition of One Mrs. Veal* rather than to Mrs. Radcliffe and Horace Walpole; although Defoe's tale would have been rejected by James as too closely resembling a case history out of psychical research. These he held to be unusable to a literary artist such as himself, "washed clean of all queerness as by exposure to a flowing laboratory tap, and equipped with credentials vouching for this." Psychical ghosts were static ghosts, devoid of imagination. They "appeared" and that was virtually all that could be said of them. They might be interesting and wonderful at a given moment, but James could not conceive of them as figuring in an *action*. Ghosts had to be active, they had to be agents of terror and usually carry with them an atmosphere charged with evil. ⟨. . .⟩ For Henry James the ghostly narrative could be neither clinical nor analytic; it had to have all the richness of life and all the terror, wonder, excitement, curiosity, the mind is capable of evoking; in a word the ghostly tale was "the most possible form of the fairy tale."

Leon Edel, "Introduction" to *The Ghostly Tales of Henry James* (New Brunswick, NJ: Rutgers University Press, 1948), p. xxvii

DOROTHEA KROOK   I believe that what James is seeking to portray in and through them ⟨Flora and Miles in *The Turn of the Screw*⟩ is a prime fact about the moral constitution of young children, which many have recognised but few have grasped with James's fullness and intensity of understanding. This, stated baldly, is the co-existence of innocence with corruption in the young child. The corruption takes the form, especially in children of more than average intelligence and imagination, of a knowledge, or 'knowingness', that too evidently—and very strangely—exceeds any they could possibly have derived from their own experience of the world; and because this happens as often as not to be a knowledge of 'forbidden' things, disturbingly (so it seems) intimate and first-hand, it argues the presence of a corrupt element.

This, it appears, is the principal psychological insight (which is also a moral insight) that James is concerned to dramatise through the children in *The Turn of the Screw*. The children's innocence is really innocent and their corruption really corrupt—of this James convinces us by his masterly rendering of both; and it is this real, indisputable co-presence of elements so grossly incompatible that accounts for the peculiar mystery and horror of the phenomenon. James himself clearly felt it as such; and for that reason perhaps, among others, chose the traditional literary form of the 'thriller', reinforced by the supernatural—the 'supernatural thriller', one might call it—as the best form in which to project imaginatively the experience of that particular mystery and horror. The supernatural is there, in other words, in the interests of the children's side of the affair, not (as Mr Wilson's theory asks us to believe) in the interests of the governess's: it is there to evoke, as powerfully as possible, the sense of the sheer mysteriousness and inexplicability, with the accompanying sense of horror, that the element of moral corruption in young children induces in a sensitive adult observer.

Dorothea Krook, *The Ordeal of Consciousness in Henry James* (Cambridge: Cambridge University Press, 1962), pp. 109–10

MARGARET LANE   My view of the Kenton-Wilson theory (of *The Turn of the Screw*) is that it has grown out of that very change in our responses which has neutralised our reaction to the ghost-story. *Because* the apparitions were no longer terrifying a more critically acceptable horror had to be invented. And since we are no longer asked to believe in the apparitions we are offered instead the conclusion that the governess's odd behaviour literally frightened the little boy to death.

I find it impossible to read *The Turn of the Screw* and believe that this prosaic interpretation was really all that Henry James intended. His skill in evasions, his providing every clause as it were with apertures, until the texture of the prose is like a net, is prodigious, but in *The Turn of the Screw* it has done him a disservice. Or rather it is we who have done it, with our fondness for illumination and our lack of reticence. Henry James's contemporaries went to bed with candles and could be trusted not to come out with indelicate questions; whereas we have light-switches everywhere and cannot be trusted. That, in the last analysis, is the difference.

Margaret Lane, "The Disappearing Ghost-Story: Some Reflections on Ghost-Stories, in Particular on Henry James's *The Turn of the Screw*," *Cornhill Magazine* No. 1052 (Summer 1967): 145–46

MARTHA BANTA   Between 1881 and 1898 James was exposed to the excitements and controversies stirred up by the Society for Psychical Research. He found new ways of viewing, and expressing, what he had intuited almost from the first about the special nature of psychic sensitivity. Only now he did not need to limit himself to his literary inheritance; he could turn more directly to metaphors and observances taken from the worlds opened up by the séance and the psychologist's study. ⟨. . .⟩

James's *use* of the supernatural as vocabulary, metaphor, theme, and atmosphere altered greatly ⟨. . .⟩ in the *degree* of its quality and importance of symbolic essence. James's *conception* of the supernatural changed in *kind* as well; it changed to an instinctive sense that there was more often "something there" to fascinate than to be lightly dismissed.

James consistently placed emphasis upon man's relationship with man. Because of this, not in spite of it, he produced an extensive body of writing that examines such matters as veridical hallucinations, pursuit of ghostly presences, mental telepathy, clairvoyance, and hauntedness. The reasoned search for the meaning of reality in a universe seen as increasingly hostile, irrational, and unreal remained a constant throughout James's life. Both before and after that significant decade of the 1880's he looked at life with the same disturbing gaze that marks his photographic portraits. In the later years his protuberant eyes bulged further, able to see more clearly that reality might be interior, imperceptible by "Newton's vision" and unprovable by laboratory methods.

Martha Banta, *Henry James and the Occult* (Bloomington: Indiana University Press, 1972), pp. 6–8

E. A. SHEPPARD   Now ⟨*The Turn of the Screw*⟩ is a ghost story with several exceptional features. The majority of ghosts have a local attachment: they 'go with' the haunted house or the haunted room, and anyone who is there at the appointed time may see them. Ghosts of another type have a personal attachment: they haunt certain persons in whatever place they may happen to be—such ghosts have some of the characteristics of the Old Norse *fylgja* or the Irish banshee. Henry James wrote stories of the first type in 'The Third Person' and 'Owen Wingrave', of the second type in 'Sir Edmund Orme' and 'The Friends of the Friends'. But the ghosts of *The Turn of the Screw* haunt certain persons only, at one particular place—the house and grounds of Bly—although both of them died 'off the premises'. Miss Jessel had gone to her distant home to die; Quint was accidentally killed as he was coming home drunk from the village alehouse. Their recall is to Miles and Flora: the governess accidentally intervenes. This, of course, is the crux of the matter; for it is the governess who sees, not, so far as they can be induced to confess it, the children. This is the testing point of the governess's 'credibility', as James has handled it: which is the more convincing, the governess's assertion, or the children's denial? But to resume: Miles, apparently, is not haunted at school—he is 'bad' and expelled at the end of the summer term, because he has been corrupted already. He *might* have been 'bad' from ghostly instigation at his school, since Quint had died during the previous winter, but if so we are not told of it. Flora, apparently, will be safe from Miss Jessel once Mrs. Grose has taken her to London.

Bly, then, harbours ghosts but is not a haunted house; and you note how carefully James emphasizes its ordinariness, its cheerfulness (the white-panelled hall with its red carpet; the wide windows, with their fresh curtains; the comfortable, spacious bedrooms). 'A big, ugly, antique, but convenient house', we are told. The governess insists on the normality of the setting, much as Douglas, in the introduction, insists on the normality of the narrator. James, in fact, quite discards the trappings of horror (the vaults, the dark passages—all the chilling suggestions of antiquity; the monstrous shapes, the weird noises, all the terrifying suggestions of inhuman depravity) which the Gothic novelists pile up around their mysteries (if indeed they are not the macabre encasement of a vacuum), except in the midnight scene in Miles's bedroom, where no ghost appears. The built-over vestiges of a still older building, of which the dizzyingly high 'machicolated square tower' is a feature, carry no menace—they merely suggest 'a castle of romance' with the golden-haired blue-eyed Flora as 'a rosy sprite' to inhabit it. And if there is irony here, and we are meant to recall a towering castle on the Rhine, with the Lorelei combing her golden hair on the rocks below, there is no more than a breath of such association.

It is on this incongruity, carried through particular after particular, that James relies for his effect of horror: it is the ground on which he builds his suggestion of trouble, free 'from weak specifications'. We are presented with a benevolent guardian—who disowns all but a monetary responsibility for his charges; trusted servants—who corrupt their little master and mistress; a perfectly beautiful and charming little girl—who can look like an old woman and rail like a fishwife; a perfectly beautiful and charming little boy—who has 'covered and concealed', as the governess puts it, otherwise, in Victorian slang, 'played gooseberry in', a sordid intrigue, and is an undesirable influence at his school; a devoted governess—whose care results in the death of one of her pupils. At Bly, nothing is, but all things seem.

E. A. Sheppard, Henry James and The Turn of the Screw (Auckland, NZ: Auckland University Press, 1974), pp. 25–26

SERGIO PEROSA   ⟨James⟩ specified that the basis of the idea of *The Sense of the Past* was not simply that of a young American lost in the European past, but rather the fact that he—and not the ghostly figures from the past—was to become a source of terror for the others. The young American was soon identified as the center of consciousness of the story, whose central idea was to be "the *revealed* effect of 'terror,' . . . the fact of the consciousness of it as given, not *received,* on the part of the central, sentient, person of the story." Ingenuity and *expertise* might save the story, if the author succeeded in telling it from the point of view of the protagonist and in compressing his prologue and his exposition ⟨. . .⟩

⟨. . .⟩ "My tale of terror," he wrote ⟨to William Dean Howells, 14 August 1900⟩, "did . . . give way beneath me. It *has,* in short, broken down for the present. I am laying it away on the shelf for the sake of something that *is* in it." He had written two-and-a-half sections (110 pages, according to his statement to Howells), stopping at a crucial moment in what was to become Book 3, in the very middle of the protagonist's talk with the ambassador. Nothing is heard of the project until 1903 when, as it appears from an unpublished letter of 1 September to Scribner's, James had arranged with Harpers to bring out the book toward the end of the next year. He was then busily working on *The Golden Bowl,* which was finished by the end of 1903. The effort involved must have first delayed and then postponed indefinitely his plan of bringing out *The Sense of the Past* together with the three novels of his major phase.

That he had probably given up his project completely is borne out by the fact that he used some of its elements in quite a few of his tales of this period. Although in a dream, the protagonist of "The Great Good Place" (1900) flees from the harassing world of the present into the cherished cloister of tranquility and youth, while his place is taken by a young admirer who is almost his alter ego. In "The Third Person" (1900), in a house haunted by the past like the one in *The Sense of the Past,* two spinsters are visited by the apparitions of a man from another epoch (the "third person" of the title), whom they succeed in laying to rest by doing "a bold deed" for him—an act of smuggling. "The Tone of Time" (1900) deals with the theme of the mysterious portrait—the portrait of a man unknown to the painter, which causes a strange relationship of tension and rivalry between her and the woman who commissioned it. James seems here to be playing with the supernatural in a worldly manner.

Sergio Perosa, *Henry James and the Experimental Novel* (Charlottesville: University Press of Virginia, 1978), pp. 133–35.

JAY MARTIN   James was slow to treat the unconscious for two reasons. Certainly, he was chiefly preoccupied with the problems of consciousness, and regarded the work of sensibility as a work of reclamation, like the draining of the Zuyder Zee. Second, unlike his father, he scorned Christian piety, and unlike his brother William he dismissed psychical research. In the early satiric tale "Professor Fargo" (1874), after the title character contrasts the "earth life and the summer land" of the spirit, the rationalist Gifford speaks for James: "I speak in the name of science. Science recognizes no such thing as 'spiritual magnetism'; no such thing as mysterious fascination; no such thing as spirit-rappings and ghost-raising."

But by the late eighties, James saw that the consciousness could not be represented apart from the unconscious; he could not do without "ghost-raising" in his own fiction. Influenced then by William's "Census of Hallucinations" and even more by Carpenter's concept of "unconscious cerebration" which he refers to in *The Aspern Papers* (1888), he raised many ghosts. These, to be sure, resided in the unconscious rather than in a Christian heaven, but to represent them—in such tales as "Sir Edmund Orme," "The Private Life," *The Turn of the Screw*, "The Great Good Place," "The Jolly Corner," and *The Sense of the Past*—he borrowed the fictive solution of Elizabeth Phelps. If James had earlier dramatized the consciousness as a circle of light, beginning in the nineties he carried his candle into the jolly corners of the psyche, where the unconscious had all the while been living a separate life. "The Jolly Corner" (1908) is, of course, almost a diagrammatic exhibition of the spatial concept of the unconscious, where the subliminal Spencer Brydon has lived out his mutilated existence (James's spirits have houses and furniture just as Phelps's do). Brilliantly, but precisely in line with the tradition I have been exploring, James turned "The Jolly Corner" inside out in *The Sense of the Past* (1917). Here, Ralph Pendrel exchanges identities with a figure in an eighteenth-century portrait and steps through the picture into the past. Then he is the ghost of the future haunting the past, a real past that is living *pari passu* with the present, like Phelps's heaven. The unconsciousness is the ghost of the consciousness in the world of experience, while the consciousness haunts the spirit world of the unconscious. It is, James wrote in planning the novel, "the double consciousness . . . which makes the thrill and curiosity of the affair, the consciousness of being the other and yet himself also, of being himself and yet the other also." James, it appears, had come around to the side of Professor Fargo, or at least to that of Elizabeth Phelps, by the nineties.

Jay Martin, "Ghostly Rentals, Ghostly Purchases: Haunted Imaginations in James, Twain, and Bellamy," *The Haunted Dusk: American Supernatural Fiction 1820–1920*, ed. Howard Kerr, John W. Crowley, and Charles L. Crow (Athens: University of Georgia Press, 1983), pp. 126–27

ADRIAN POOLE   Ghosts are always a good excuse for a story, but James makes these ones ⟨in *The Turn of the Screw*⟩ serve the needs of a particularly pointed story about the production and communication of stories. Stories are made to be shared, but this is particularly true of ghost stories. It is dangerous to keep them from others, as the governess keeps hers from Flora and Miles until it is too late. Writing can be a way of learning to live with ghosts, and so can reading. But writing is also a way of becoming a ghost. The governess's writing may seem to express the desires and fears inspired in her by others. These are initiated by the absent master whose taboo she is determined, impossibly, at once to keep and to break; the power of this double-bind on her produces the vengeful visions of Quint and Miss Jessel. But there is also a sense in which the act of writing takes possession of these desires and fears. The governess who lives again in her writing has assumed the power of the ghosts whom she revives, has even in a sense become the absent master of Bly. And in turn, now, she haunts her readers.

Adrian Poole, *Henry James* (New York: St. Martin's Press, 1991), p. 157

▣ *Bibliography*

A Passionate Pilgrim and Other Tales. 1875.
Transatlantic Sketches. 1875.
Roderick Hudson. 1876.
The American. 1877.
French Poets and Novelists. 1878.

Watch and Ward. 1878.

The Europeans. 1878. 2 vols.

Daisy Miller: A Study. 1879.

An International Episode. 1879.

The Madonna of the Future and Other Tales. 1879. 2 vols.

Confidence. 1879. 2 vols.

Hawthorne. 1879.

A Bundle of Letters. 1880.

The Diary of a Man of Fifty and A Bundle of Letters. 1880.

Washington Square. 1881.

The Portrait of a Lady. 1881. 3 vols.

Daisy Miller: A Comedy (drama). 1883.

The Siege of London, The Pension Beaurepas, and The Point of View. 1883.

[Works] (Collective Edition). 1883. 14 vols.

Portraits of Places. 1883.

Notes (No. 15 of Series) on a Collection of Drawings by Mr. George du Maurier.
      1884.

A Little Tour in France. 1884.

Tales of Three Cities. 1884.

The Art of Fiction (with Walter Besant). 1885.

The Author of Beltraffio; Pandora; Georgina's Reasons; The Path of Duty; Four
      Meetings. 1885.

Stories Revived. 1885. 3 vols.

The Bostonians. 1886. 3 vols.

The Princess Casamassima. 1886. 3 vols.

Partial Portraits. 1888.

The Reverberator. 1888. 2 vols.

The Aspern Papers; Louisa Pallant; The Modern Warning. 1888. 2 vols.

A London Life; The Patagonia; The Liar; Mrs. Temperly. 1889. 2 vols.

The Tragic Muse. 1890.

The Lesson of the Master; The Marriages; The Pupil; Brooksmith; The Solution;
      Sir Edmund Orme. 1892.

The Real Thing and Other Tales. 1893.

Picture and Text. 1893.

The Private Life; The Wheel of Time; Lord Beaupré; The Visits; Collaboration;
      Owen Wingrave. 1893.

Essays in London and Elsewhere. 1893.

The Wheel of Time; Collaboration; Owen Wingrave. 1893.

Theatricals: Two Comedies (Tenants; Disengaged). 1894.

Theatricals, Second Series: The Album; The Reprobate. 1895.

Terminations. 1895.

Embarrassments. 1896.

The Other House. 1896. 2 vols.

The Spoils of Poynton. 1897.

What Maisie Knew. 1897.

In the Cage. 1898.

The Two Magics: The Turn of the Screw; Covering End. 1898.

The Awkward Age. 1899.

The Soft Side. 1900.

The Sacred Fount. 1901.

The Wings of the Dove. 1902. 2 vols.

The Better Sort. 1903.

The Ambassadors. 1903.

William Wetmore Story and His Friends: From Letters, Diaries, and Recollections. 1903. 2 vols.

The Golden Bowl. 1904. 2 vols.

The Question of Our Speech; The Lesson of Balzac: Two Lectures. 1905.

English Hours. 1905.

The American Scene. 1907.

Novels and Tales (New York Edition). 1907–09. 24 vols.

Views and Reviews. Ed. Le Roy Phillips. 1908.

Julia Bride. 1909.

Italian Hours. 1909.

The Finer Grain. 1910.

The Henry James Yearbook. Ed. Evelyn Garnaut Smalley. 1911.

The Outcry. 1911.

A Small Boy and Others. 1913.

Notes of a Son and Brother. 1914.

Notes on Novelists. 1914.

The American Volunteer Motor-Ambulance Corps in France: A Letter to the Editor of an American Journal. 1914.

Uniform Tales. 1915–20. 14 vols.

England at War: An Essay: The Question of the Mind. 1915.

Letters to an Editor. 1916.

Pictures and Other Passages from Henry James. Ed. Ruth Head. 1916.

The Ivory Tower. 1917.

The Sense of the Past. 1917.

The Middle Years. 1917.

Gabrielle de Bergerac. 1918.

Within the Rim and Other Essays 1914–15. 1919.

Travelling Companions. 1919.

A Landscape Painter. 1920.

Refugees in Chelsea. 1920.

Letters. Ed. Percy Lubbock. 1920. 2 vols.

Master Eustace. 1920.

Novels and Stories. Ed. Percy Lubbock. 1921–23. 35 vols.

Notes and Reviews. 1921.

A Letter to Mrs. Linton. 1921.

"A Most Unholy Trade": Being Letters on the Drama. 1923.

Three Letters to Joseph Conrad. 1926.

Letters to Walter Berry. 1928.

Letters to A. C. Benson and Auguste Monod. Ed. E. F. Benson. 1930.

Theatre and Friendship: Some Letters. Ed. Elizabeth Robins. 1932.

The Art of the Novel: Critical Prefaces. Ed. R. P. Blackmur. 1934.

American Novels and Stories. Ed. F. O. Matthiessen. 1947.

Notebooks. Ed. F. O. Matthiessen and Kenneth B. Murdock. 1947.

The Scenic Art: Notes on Acting and the Drama 1872–1901. Ed. Allan Wade.
    1948.

Ghostly Tales. Ed. Leon Edel. 1948.

Henry James and Robert Louis Stevenson: A Record of Friendship and Criticism.
    Ed. Janet Adam Smith. 1948.

Complete Plays. Ed. Leon Edel. 1949.

Eight Uncollected Tales. Ed. Edna Kenton. 1950.

The Portable Henry James. Ed. Morton Dauwen Zabel. 1951.

Selected Letters. Ed. Leon Edel. 1955.

American Essays. Ed. Leon Edel. 1956.

Autobiography. Ed. Frederick W. Dupee. 1956.

The Future of the Novel: Essays on the Art of Fiction. Ed. Leon Edel. 1956.

The Painter's Eye: Notes and Essays on the Pictorial Arts. Ed. John L. Sweeney.
    1956.

Parisian Sketches: Letters to the New York Tribune *1875–1876.* Ed. Leon Edel
    and Ise Dusoir Lind. 1957.

The House of Fiction: Essays on the Novel. Ed. Leon Edel. 1957.

Literary Reviews and Essays on American, English, and French Literature. Ed.
    Albert Mordell. 1957.

French Writers and American Women. Ed. Peter Buitenhuis. 1960.

Complete Tales. Ed. Leon Edel. 1962–64. 12 vols.

Selected Literary Criticism. Ed. Morris Shapira. 1963.

Theory of Fiction. Ed. James E. Miller, Jr. 1972.

Tales. Ed. Maqbool Aziz. 1973– .

Letters. Ed. Leon Edel. 1974–84. 4 vols.

Literary Criticism. 1984. 2 vols.

The Art of Criticism: Henry James on the Theory and the Practice of the Novel. Ed. William Veeder and Susan M. Griffin. 1986.

Complete Notebooks. Ed. Leon Edel and Lyall H. Powers. 1987.

Selected Letters. Ed. Leon Edel. 1987.

Henry James and Edith Wharton: Letters 1900–1915. Ed. Lyall H. Powers. 1990.

The Correspondence of Henry James and Henry Adams 1877–1914. Ed. George Monteiro. 1991.

Joseph Sheridan LeFanu
1814–1873

JOSEPH SHERIDAN LE FANU was born to a Protestant family in Dublin on August 28, 1814; among his forebears was the playwright Richard Brinsley Sheridan. When he was twelve his family moved to Abington, in County Limerick, where LeFanu gained a close acquaintance with the Irish peasantry. He attended Trinity College, Dublin, graduating in 1837. Although called to the Irish bar in 1839, LeFanu decided instead to turn to literary work. His first story, "The Ghost and the Bone-Setter," had appeared in the *Dublin University Magazine* in 1838, and in 1841 he became editor and proprietor of the magazine *The Warden*; he later purchased shares in the *Protestant Guardian, Dublin Evening Packet,* and *Evening Mail.* LeFanu contributed many poems and stories to these periodicals; some were collected posthumously as *The Purcell Papers* (1880).

In 1844 LeFanu married Susan Bennett and the next year published his first novel, *The Cock and Anchor,* an historical novel set in eighteenth-century Dublin. Another historical novel, *The Fortunes of Colonel Torlogh O'Brien,* appeared in 1847. LeFanu devoted the next decade and a half to magazine work, and his only published book of this period was *Ghost Stories and Tales of Mystery* (1851).

In 1858 LeFanu's wife died; grief-stricken, LeFanu became a virtual recluse for the rest of his life. He turned his attention to novel writing (although several of his novels are actually expansions of earlier short stories), producing such works as *The House by the Church-yard* (1863), *Uncle Silas* (1864), *The Rose and the Key* (1871), and others. These novels—as well as such short stories as "Green Tea" and "Carmilla"—established LeFanu as one of the nineteenth century's greatest writers of mystery and supernatural fiction. In 1872 the celebrated collection *In a Glass Darkly* appeared. LeFanu died in Dublin on February 7, 1873. *The Poems of Joseph Sheridan Le Fanu,* edited by Alfred Perceval Graves, was published in 1896. In this century M. R. James and E. F. Benson helped to revive interest in LeFanu's work, and his tales of horror and the supernatural have attracted a wide following.

▣ Critical Extracts

JOSEPH SHERIDAN LE FANU   The writer of this Tale ventures, in his own person, to address a very few words, chiefly of explanation, to his readers. A leading situation in this "Story of Bartram-Haugh" is repeated, with a slight variation, from a short magazine tale of some fifteen pages written by him, and published long ago in a periodical under an altered title. It is very unlikely that any of his readers should have encountered, and still more so that they should remember, this trifle. The bare possibility, however, he has ventured to anticipate by this brief explanation, lest he should be charged with plagiarism—always a disrespect to a reader.

May he be permitted a few words also of remonstrance against the promiscuous application of the term "sensation" to that large school of fiction which transgresses no one of those canons of construction and morality which, in producing the unapproachable *Waverley Novels*, their great author imposed upon himself? No one, it is assumed, would describe Sir Walter Scott's romances as "sensation novels"; yet in that marvellous series there is not a single tale in which death, crime, and, in some form, mystery, have not a place.

Passing by those grand romances of *Ivanhoe*, *Old Mortality*, and *Kenilworth*, with their terrible intricacies of crime and bloodshed, constructed with so fine a mastery of the art of exciting suspense and horror, let the reader pick out those two exceptional novels in the series which profess to paint contemporary manners and the scenes of common life; and remembering in the *Antiquary* the vision in the tapestried chamber, the duel, the horrible secret, and the death of old Elspeth, the drowned fisherman, and above all the tremendous situation of the tide-bound party under the cliffs; and in *St. Ronan's Well*, the long-drawn mystery, the suspicion of insanity, and the catastrophe of suicide—determine whether an epithet which it would be profanation to apply to the structure of any, even the most exciting of Sir Walter Scott's stories, is fairly applicable to tales which, though illimitably inferior in execution, yet observe the same limitations of incident, and the same moral aims.

The author trusts that the Press, to whose masterly criticism and generous encouragement he and other humble labourers in the art owe so much, will insist upon the limitation of that degrading term to the peculiar type of fiction which it was originally intended to indicate, and prevent, as they may, its being made to include the illegitimate school of tragic English romance, which has been ennobled, and in the great measure founded, by the genius of Sir Walter Scott.

Joseph Sheridan LeFanu, "A Preliminary Word," *Uncle Silas* (1864; rpt. London: Cresset Press, 1947), pp. 27–28

RICHARD DOWLING   I am very bad at dates, but I think Le Fanu wrote "Green Tea" before a whole community of Canadian nuns were thrown into the most horrible state of nervous misery by excessive indulgence in that drug. Of all the horrible tales that are not revolting, "Green Tea" is I think the most horrible. The bare statement that an estimable and pious man is haunted by the ghost of a monkey is at first blush funny. But if you have not read the story read it, and see how little of fun is in it. The horror of the tale lies in the fact that this apparition of a monkey is the only *probable* ghost in fiction. I have not the book by me as I write, and I cannot recall the victim's name, but he is a clergyman, and, as far as we know to the contrary, a saint. There is *no reason* on earth why he should be pursued by this malignant spectre. He has committed no crime, no sin even. He labours with all the sincerity of a holy man to regain his health and exorcise his foe. He is as crimeless as you or I and infinitely more faultless. He has not deserved his fate, yet he is driven in the end to cut his throat, and you excuse *that* crime by saying he is mad.

I do not think any additional force is gained in the course of this unique story by the importation of malignant irreverence to Christianity in the latter manifestations of the ape. I think the apparition is at its best and most terrible when it is simply an indifferent pagan, before it assumes the *rôle* of antichrist. This ape is at his best as a mind-destroyer when the clergyman, going down the avenue in the twilight, raises his eyes and finds the awful presence preceding him along the top of the wall. There the clergyman reaches the acme of piteous, insupportable horror. In the pulpit with the brute, the priest is fighting against the devil. In the avenue he has not the strengthening or consoling reflection that he is defending a cause, struggling against hell. The instant motive enters into the story the situation ceases to be dramatic and becomes merely theatrical. Even the "converted" thinker will tell you stirring stories of his wrestling with Satan, forgetting that it takes two to fight, and what a loathsome creature he himself is. But the conflict between a good man and the unnecessary apparition of this ape is pathetic, horribly pathetic, and full of the dramatic despair of the finest tragedy.

It is desirable at this point to focus some scattered words that have been set down above. The reason this apparition of the ape appears probable is *because* it is unnecessary. Any one can understand why Macbeth should see that awful vision at the banquet. The apparition of the murdered dead is little more than was to be expected, and can be explained in an easy fashion. You or I never committed murder, therefore we are not liable to be troubled by the ghost of Banquo. In your life or mine Nemesis is not likely to take heroic dimensions. The spectres of books, as a rule, only excite our imaginative fears, not our personal terrors. The spectres of books have and can have nothing to do with us any more than the sufferings of the Israelites in the desert. When a person of our acquaintance dies, we inquire into the particulars of his disease, and then discover the predisposing causes, so that we prove to ourselves we are not in the same category with him. We do not deny our liability to contract the disease, we deny our likelihood to supply the predisposing causes. He died of aneurysm of the aorta: Ah, we say, induced by the violent exercise he took—we never take violent exercise. If not of aneurysm of the aorta, but fatty degeneration of the heart: Ah, induced by the sedentary habits of his latter years—we take care to secure plenty of exercise. If a man has been careful of his health and dies, we allege that he took all the robustness out of his constitution by over-heedfulness; if he has been careless, we say he took no precaution at all; and from either of these extremes we are exempt, and therefore we shall live for ever.

Now here in this story of "Green Tea" is a ghost which is possible, probable, almost familiar. It is a ghost without genesis or justification. The gods have nothing to do with it. Something, an accident due partly to excessive tea-drinking, has happened to the clergyman's nerves, and the ghost of this ape glides into his life and sits down and abides with him. There is no reason why the ghost should be an ape. When the victim sees the apparition first he does not know it to be an ape. He is coming home in an omnibus one night and describes two gleaming spots of fire in the dark, and from that moment the life of the poor gentleman becomes a ruin. It is a thing that may happen to you or me any day, any hour. That is why Le Fanu's ghost is so horrible. You and I might drink green tea to the end of our days and suffer from nothing more than ordinary impaired indigestion. But you or I may get a fall, or a sunstroke, and ever afterwards have some hideous familiar. To say there can be no such things as ghosts is a paltry blasphemy. It is a theory of the smug, comfortable kind. A ghost need not wear a white sheet and have intelligible designs on personal property. A

ghost need not be a spirit of a dead person. A ghost need have no moral
dimension whatever.

> Richard Dowling, "The Only Real Ghost in Fiction," *Ignorant Essays* (London:
> Ward & Downey, 1887), pp. 15–20

L. BENJAMIN   Le Fanu, popular enough in his day, is now sinking
fast into obscurity. This is not due to the reaction that follows on the heels
of over-praise, as is the case, notably, of Anthony Trollope, but is the
inevitable result of lack of merit in his works. The wonder is that he was
ever regarded very highly, for at his best he is little more than mediocre.
His books recall the once popular riddle 'Why do married men live longer
than single men?' with its answer, 'They don't, but it seems longer.' 'Why,'
one might ask, 'are the stories of Le Fanu so much longer than those of,
say, Wilkie Collins?' The answer would be, 'They are not, but they seem
so.'

> L. Benjamin, "Joseph Sheridan Le Fanu," *Victorian Novelists* (London: Constable,
> 1906), p. 238

S. M. ELLIS   During his last years the mind of Le Fanu became
almost entirely pre-occupied with the supernatural, and all the short stories
he wrote at this time are of that nature—'Green Tea', 'Carmilla' (the most
impressive vampire tale I am acquainted with, for it is written with an
artistry that is lacking in the crudest horrors of *Varney the Vampire*, by
Thomas Preskett Prest), 'Madam Crowl's Ghost', 'The Haunted House in
Westminster' (later entitled 'Mr. Justice Harbottle'), 'The Haunted Baronet',
'The Dead Sexton', 'Dickon the Devil'. His now peculiar habits of life
contributed to this obsession, and there can be little doubt but that many
of these weird tales came to him in the form of dreams. His son, Brinsley
Le Fanu, gave me a remarkable account of his father's methods of work.
He wrote mostly in bed at night, using copy-books for his manuscript. He
always had two candles by his side on a small table; one of these dimly
gleaming tapers would be left burning while he took a brief sleep. Then,
when he awoke about 2 a.m. amid the darkling shadows of the heavy
furnishings and hangings of his old-fashioned room, he would brew himself
some strong tea—which he drank copiously and frequently throughout the
day—and write for a couple of hours in that eerie period of the night when
human vitality is at its lowest ebb and the Powers of Darkness rampant and
terrifying. What wonder then, that, with his brain ever peopled by day and
by night with mysterious and terrible beings, he became afflicted by horrible

dreams, which, as I have suggested, were the bases of his last stories of the supernatural. Apart from imbibing much strong tea—which apparently was not of the Green variety!—he was a most abstemious man, and a nonsmoker. Le Fanu always breakfasted in bed, and at midday went down to the dining-room at the back of the house, where he would resume work, writing at a little table which had been a favourite possession of his granduncle, Richard Brinsley Sheridan. This room opened out to a small garden, pleasant in spring with lilac and flowering shrubs and fruit blossom, and in this small monastic-like close he took the little exercise he fancied, pacing the paths with pencil and copy-book in hand, his mind still and ever with

> The dark folk who live in souls
> Of passionate men, like bats in the dead trees;
> And with the wayward twilight companies.

During these last years he rarely went out into the city. Only under cover of the darkness of night would he venture out, and then generally to the old book-shops in search of works dealing with demonology and ghost lore. 'Any more ghost stories for me?' he would ask with his pleasant voice and smile, and when the desired volumes were handed over to him he would pore over their contents. Although he was, of course, deeply learned in doctrines of Swedenborg and other exponents of demoniacal possession, he would have nothing to do with Spiritualism, and despised its ineffectual messages and mild manifestations. His mind savoured stronger and more frightful meat.

S. M. Ellis, "Joseph Sheridan Le Fanu," *Wilkie Collins, Le Fanu and Others* (New York: Richard R. Smith, 1931), pp. 175–76

E. F. BENSON   But there is one author, far too little known by those in search of creepy lore, who seldom fails in his high mission: his name is Sheridan Le Fanu. He produces, page for page, a far higher percentage of terror than the more widely read Edgar Allan Poe, and whether he deals in ghosts direct or in more material horrors, his success in making his readers very uneasy is amazing. Though we may already know the story we select to give us some insupportable moments on a lonely evening, there is quality about most of his tales which seldom fails to alarm: familiarity with them does not breed comfort. Many ghost stories are efficacious for a first reading, but few, when we already know the worst that the author has to tell us, preserve untainted the atmosphere of horror as do the tales in *In a Glass Darkly*. The best of these, "Green Tea," "The Familiar," and "Mr. Justice Harbottle," are instinct with an awfulness which custom cannot stale, and this quality is due, as in *The Turn of the Screw*, to Le Fanu's admirably artistic methods in setting and narration. They begin quietly enough, the tentacles of terror are applied so softly that the reader hardly notices them till they are sucking the courage from his blood. A darkness gathers like dusk gently falling, and then something stirs in it. . . . Dickens, in his *Christmas Carol*, which is one of the most famous ghost stories in literature, goes the other way about it, and the wrong way. He leads off with the appearance of Marley's ghost, and then he has done his worst. The darkness brightens and we end on a gracious anti-climax of roast goose, Tiny Tim and a regenerated Scrooge. The moral is excellent, but who wants a moral in a ghost story? We can unbend our minds over morals afterwards.

E. F. Benson, "Sheridan Le Fanu," *Spectator*, 21 February 1931, p. 264

V. S. PRITCHETT   LeFanu brought a limpid tributary to the Teutonic stream which had fed mysterious literature for so long. I do not mean that he married the Celtic banshee to the Teutonic poltergeist or the monster, in some Irish graveyard; what he did was to bring an Irish lucidity and imagination to the turgid German flow. LeFanu's ghosts are the most disquieting of all: the ghosts that can be justified, blobs of the unconscious that have floated up to the surface of the mind, and which are not irresponsible and perambulatory figments of family history, mooning and clanking about in fancy dress. The evil of the justified ghosts is not sportive, willful, involuntary or extravagant. In LeFanu the fright is that effect follows cause. Guilt patters two-legged behind its victims in the street, retribution sits adding up its account night after night, the secret doubt scratches away with malignant patience in the guarded mind. We laugh at the headless coachman or the legendary heiress grizzling her way through the centuries in her nightgown; but we pause when we recognize that those other hands on the wardrobe, those other eyes at the window, those other steps on the landing and those small shadows that slip into the room as we open the door, are our own. It is we who are the ghosts. Those are *our* steps which follow us, it is *our* "heavy body" which we hear falling in the attic above. We haunt ourselves. Let illness or strain weaken the catch which we keep fixed so tightly upon the unconscious, and out spring all the hags and animals of moral or Freudian symbolism, just as the "Elemental" burns sharp as a diamond before our eyes when we lie relaxed on the point of sleep.

Some such idea is behind most of LeFanu's tales. They are presented as the cases of a psychiatrist called Dr. Hesselius, whose precise theory appears to be that these fatal visitations come when the psyche is worn to rags and the interior spirit world can then make contact with the external through the holes. A touch of science, even bogus science, gives an edge to the superstitious tale. The coarse hanging judge is tracked down by the man whom he has unjustly hanged and is hanged in turn. The eupeptic sea captain on the point of marrying an Irish fortune is quietly terrorized into the grave by the sailor whom, years before, he had flogged to death in Malta. The fashionable and handsome clergyman is driven to suicide by the persecutions of a phantom monkey who jumps onto his Bible as he preaches, and waits for him at street corners, in carriages, in his very room. A very Freudian animal this. Dark and hairy with original sin and symbolism, he skips straight out of the unchaste jungle of a pious bachelor's unconscious. The vampire girl who preys on the daughter of an Austrian count appears to be displaying the now languid, now insatiate, sterility of Lesbos. I am not, however, advancing LeFanu as an instance of the lucky moralist who finds a sermon in every spook, but as an artist in the dramatic use of evil, the secret, and the fatal, an artist, indeed, in the domestic insinuation of the supernatural. With him it does not break the law, but extends the mysterious jurisdiction of nature.

V. S. Pritchett, "An Irish Ghost" (1947), The Living Novel and Later Appreciations (New York: Random House, 1964), pp. 121–24

PETER PENZOLDT   In 'Green Tea', Le Fanu's psychological insight is probably at its most evident, and his symbolism at its most striking. Disregarding Dr. Hesselius's fantastic theories, the story is the case history of a schizophrenic, or rather an account of the neurotic symptoms which are often observed in connection with this mental disease. The Reverend Dr. Jennings is haunted by an ape-like demon which at first watches him, annoying him merely by its presence, but later begins to speak, uttering terrible blasphemies. Finally it drives the unfortunate clergyman to suicide. The omniscient Dr. Hesselius explains this affair as the result of hereditary suicidal mania, and the opening of an 'interior sense' caused by the excesses of green tea. He finally states that 'spectral illusion' can be created as easily as a 'cold in the head or a trifling dyspepsia'. One of his remedies is 'iced eau-de-Cologne'. But for all this nonsense, which must have sounded a little naïve even when the story was first published, 'Green Tea' contains a strikingly accurate description of the gradual decline of a man suffering from split personality. Le Fanu went so far as to divide it into stages, one, two and three. The ghost monkey, if one may be allowed to regard it as a product of schizoid neurosis rather than of green tea, is the symbol of suppressed sex desire. Dr. Hesselius is for once really perspicacious, when he immediately observes that Jennings must be unmarried. Unfortunately he draws the wrong conclusions from this statement, and perhaps Le Fanu simply wished to suggest that a solitary man is more easily given to nervous brooding. He must have known this better than anyone. But the fact remains that animal ghosts are often the symbols of suppressed sex desire. It is significant that the monkey frequently disturbs its victim when he is praying. If sex is consciously or unconsciously considered as sinful, this fact would be one more point in favour of the theory.

Peter Penzoldt, "Joseph Sheridan Le Fanu (1814–1873)," *The Supernatural in Fiction* (London: Peter Nevill, 1952), pp. 77–78

JULIA BRIGGS   One obsessive anxiety which Le Fanu dramatizes particularly effectively is the terror of invasion or entrance by some feared or hated object, which may ultimately be connected with sexual fear, or with the neurosis derived from some long-concealed repression. However much you shut the hated thing out, it manages to effect an entrance somehow, through some unexpected ruse or trick. Over and over again in Le Fanu's work an evil spirit tricks its way into getting its victim alone just long enough to destroy him or carry him off in triumph. In the three stories of demonic bargains the victims shut themselves away in vain, hoping to avoid the infernal visitant bent on fulfillment of the bargain. In 'Schalken the Painter' the demon lover enters through a window overlooking the canal to abduct Rosa for the last time, after her father has gone to fetch a candle. A gust blows the door closed behind him, and he turns to find it locked. In 'The Familiar', the bedroom door swings shut behind the servant who has briefly looked out for the owl, leaving Barton alone with the creature for the final reckoning. In 'Mr Justice Harbottle', chapter 8 is quite explicitly entitled 'Somebody has got into the house', while in 'Squire Toby's Will' the dead squire and his thwarted heir enter the house in the guise of mourners, soon after the latter's funeral. The horribly dismembered hand in 'The Haunting of the Tiled House' goes round and round knocking outside for some time, and when Mr Prosser takes pistols and a cane to the door to deal with it, 'his arm was jerked up oddly, as it might be with the hollow of a hand, and something passed under it, with a kind of gentle squeeze'. The vampire Carmilla, like so many evil spirits according to tradition, has to be invited into the house, but once in, like the horrible hand, she is not so easily rejected.

Le Fanu's instinctive recognition of the springs of fear, and the kinds of shape fears take, naturally makes him very interested in dreams and in the way they embody these fears. Many of his stories use dreams centrally, or as part of the build-up of suspense, expressing in illogical but concrete form the nature of a particular haunting. Dreams are a particularly useful device for the ghost story-teller, as Scott realized when writing 'Wandering Willie's Tale', for they do not commit him to an assertion of fact. They are often frightening, as much in stories as in fact, but there is no obligation to believe in them, so the story-teller may leave the tale open-ended. Le Fanu wrote to his publisher, George Bentley, about 'The Haunted Baronet' (on which it does not seem a very apt comment) that he was striving for 'the equilibrium between the natural and the *super*-natural, the super-natural phenomena being explained on natural theories—and people left to choose which solution they please'. The use of dreams in ghost stories certainly achieves such an equilibrium.

One of his best stories, 'Strange Disturbances in Aungier Street', uses both dreams and 'natural theories' to create this sense of balance between the natural and super-natural elements of the story. It is basically an account of a haunted house, troubled by the ghost of an evil old judge who had finally hung himself from the bannisters with the skipping rope of his illegitimate child. The occupants of the house, the narrator and his skeptical friend Tom, are initially troubled by evil dreams in which the old man figures prominently. These are followed by sinister noises in the house, and, later, the appearance of a large man and a peculiarly revolting rat (an idea borrowed by Bram Stoker in a similar story, 'The Judge's House'). The psychological reactions of the narrator, alone in the house, are vividly conveyed. He screws himself up to shout 'Who's there?', adding 'There is, I think, something most disagreeably disenchanting in the sound of one's own voice under such circumstances, exerted in solitude, and in vain. It redoubled my sense of isolation. . . .' On the following night he takes a bottle of whiskey up with him, but it too becomes inextricably linked with the ordeal: 'I sat down and stared at the square label on the solemn and reserved-looking black bottle, until "FLANAGAN AND CO'S BEST OLD MALT WHISKEY" grew into a sort of subdued accompaniment to all the fantastic and horrible speculations which chased one another through my brain'. It is the psychological conviction of such details which establishes the credibility of this story. In the later version of this theme, 'Mr Justice Harbottle', the lively character of personal response has given place to an altogether more serious tone. Here we are presented with a vision of the final Court of Judgement, accompanied by lurid, even surreal glimpses of a huge Bosch-like gibbet, and a hellish smithy. There is a new imaginative power, to which the surface realism of the earlier tale has inevitably been sacrificed.

Julia Briggs, *Night Visitors: The Rise and Fall of the English Ghost Story* (London: Faber & Faber, 1977), pp. 48–50

JACK SULLIVAN   "Green Tea" is every bit as twisted, disturbing and unresolvable as it seems. Nevertheless, by imposing orthodox explanations and theoretical systems on the story, critics have done what they could to dissipate its mystery and menace. The orthodoxies divide into two camps, the Freudian and the Christian, each of which has a predictable explanation for Jennings' persecution. To Peter Penzoldt, Jennings' monkey is simply "the product of a schizoid neurosis"; to V. S. Pritchett, it is "dark and hairy with original sin," and its persecutions symbolize "justified" retribution for specific sins; to Michael Begnal, the monkey is sent to punish a clergyman who has "lost his faith" and whose "intellectual pride" has "cut him off from God" ⟨*Joseph Sheridan Le Fanu*, 1971⟩.

The problem with such theories is that they convert possibilities into solutions. M. R. James, who modelled his stories after Le Fanu's, once stated, "It is not amiss sometimes to leave a loophole for a natural explanation, but I would say, let the loophole be so narrow as not to be quite practicable." This teasing, enigmatic quality, so obvious to any writer in the genre, is missed by theory obsessed critics. In "Green Tea," the Freudian "loophole" is narrow indeed. We are not given enough information about the near-anonymous Jennings to conclude that he is "schizoid" or "sexually repressed." We are told only that he is shy and unassuming.

The Christian interpretation is even flimsier. There is no doubt that Jennings's obsession is somehow connected with an intense, unspeakable feeling of guilt. The text contains many references to this feeling: he collapses from the altar "in the agitation of strange shame and horror"; he looks at Hesselius "guiltily" during their first conversation; he even cries "God forgive me!" during a later conversation. What the text does not tell us is what Jennings needs to be forgiven for, what crime he has committed to merit such a hideous, ultimately lethal punishment. As we shall see, the only character who could conceivably be accused of "intellectual pride" is Dr. Hesselius. Indeed, if we assume with Begnal that Jennings committed a mortal sin by researching the non-Christian religious beliefs of the ancients, we must ask why Hesselius is not also pursued to the grave by the avenging monkey, for he is guilty of the same heterodox research. Nor is there any evidence that Jennings has lost his faith; on the contrary, he is a pious, devout Christian who ceases to pray only when the monkey literally prevents him from doing so by shrieking blasphemies in his ear.

The truth is that Jennings has done nothing but drink green tea. The very title of the tale registers the fundamental irony: the awful disjuncture between cause and effect, crime and punishment. What emerges is an irrational, almost Kafkaesque feeling of guilt and persecution. Like Joseph K., Jennings is ceaselessly pursued and tormented for no discernible reason. A persistent experience in modern fiction is a situation in which the main character wakes up one morning on a tightrope and does not know how he got there. This is precisely the predicament Jennings finds himself in. Although S. M. Ellis calls Le Fanu a "tragic" writer, "Green Tea" is closer to modern tragi-comedy. Jennings never experiences even a flash of tragic recognition; on the contrary, he never knows why this horrible thing is happening. There is no insight, no justice, and therefore no tragedy. There is only absurd cruelty, a grim world view which endures in the reader's mind long after the hairs have settled on the back of the neck.

Jack Sullivan, " 'Green Tea': The Archetypal Ghost Story," *Elegant Nightmares: The English Ghost Story from Le Fanu to Blackwood* (Athens: Ohio University Press, 1978), pp. 17–18

W. J. McCORMACK   The final story of *In a Glass Darkly*, 'Carmilla', is perhaps Le Fanu's best-known work. Though its exotic Transylvanian setting, its vampirism, and its powerfully implicit lesbianism may suggest that it is untypical of his fiction, 'Carmilla' integrates itself into the context of the novels and tales through two characteristically extreme areas—allusion and structure. The manner in which it concludes with a theory of vampirism based on the suicide of some earlier villain relates it to those novels where suicide is explicit. And the over-all structure of 'Carmilla' recalls the symmetrical form of *Uncle Silas*; first there is a straightforward narrative of a young girl introduced into a Great House as a result of her mother's need to travel; then the newcomer becomes an intimate friend of the daughter of the house while the traditional signs of vampirism—marks on the throat, listlessness, and so forth—afflict the latter girl. This narrative is then interrupted by a journey during which the victim and her father meet General Spielsdorf. The old soldier then recounts an identical story about his own daughter and the strange girl they had received as a house guest, identical except that the general's daughter had died. The two fathers proceed, with the one surviving daughter, to a place where Spielsdorf supervises the posthumous execution of the vampire who had, under the name Millarca, destroyed his daughter. She is of course identical to Carmilla who had nearly succeeded in destroying the narrator. The vampire is identified as Mircalla, the Countess Karnstein of long ago, whose portrait, after restoration, mirrored the mysterious guest and companion of the narrator. Vampirism, whatever its origins in suicide, is seen as the survival of the past at the expense of the present; just as the rediscovered portrait of 'Carmilla' recalls a similar device in 'The Haunted Baronet', so the reluctance of the narrator and her father to believe in the supernatural reality of their guest recalls the catastrophes of Schalken's demon rival. In 'Carmilla', however, the ultimate disaster is avoided by formal means, by the development of a symmetrical duality in which the narrator undergoes the ordeal and the victim of an interpolated story provides the sombre conclusion. As in *Uncle Silas*, pattern and metaphor overwhelm narrative and characterization. For it is clear that vampirism, like suicide, is exploited here for its symbolic implications. In a manner crudely parallel to the schizophrenic's attempts to escape from the insufficiently real world, the vampire tale presents a second self on which the first literally feeds; vampirism seen as a projection of this kind is suicidal in structure. 'Carmilla' emphasizes this implosive self-destruction by building up a lesbian attraction between the two girls, homosexuality providing yet another example of energies deflected and cancelled. The seductress-vampire murmurs to the narrator of 'Carmilla':

> Dearest, your little heart is wounded; think me not cruel because
> I obey the irresistible law of my strength and weakness; if your dear
> heart is wounded, my wild heart bleeds with yours. In the raptures
> of my enormous humiliation I live in your warm life, and you
> shall die—die, sweetly die—into mine.

Once again the pattern of *Uncle Silas* is repeated: the end of life is death; indeed death becomes a metaphor for life.

W. J. McCormack, "Uncle Silas: A Habitation of Symbols," *Sheridan Le Fanu and Victorian Ireland* (Oxford: Oxford University Press, 1980), pp. 190–91

IVAN MELADA   As a writer of ghost stories, Le Fanu stands between the old-fashioned and the modern, between the belief in the objective and the subjective reality of ghosts. In such a story as "The Familiar," the ghost of the abused sailor writes letters and shoots a pistol, actions that give it existence in nature. On the other hand, the deservedly famous "Green Tea" is a psychological narrative in which the monkey appears to Jennings alone, as a manifestation of his unconscious desires. In "An Account of Some Strange Disturbances on Aungier Street," Le Fanu writes the equivalent of a tract on the objective/subjective existence of ghosts and comes down on the side of modern psychological theory. The experience of the two medical students reveals that the power of suggestion can make a cupboard look like a monster, a phenomenon that Mrs. Radcliffe would acknowledge. But Le Fanu's insight extends beyond rationalizing the supernatural to analyzing the relation between the physiological and the psychological as a factor influencing the manifestation of ghostly phenomena. Thus, an apparition might owe its existence to the unhealthy condition of its beholder's stomach. The old-fashioned ghost as a part of the natural world still figures prominently in Le Fanu's ghost stories, but that is often the result of his retelling the ghostly traditions of Ireland. For the modern reader, Le Fanu's memorable ghost is the hallucination conjured from the private hell of the tormented.

Ivan Melada, *Sheridan Le Fanu* (Boston: Twayne, 1987), p. 126

JOLANTA NALECZ-WOJTCZAK   All LeFanu's most successful characters are tragic characters. The source of their tragedy springs from their desperate, spasmodic struggle for sanity—from a neurotic's awareness that his mind is suddenly on the borderline between what is conventionally considered to be normal and abnormal. Their behaviour is very characteristic—after the very first moments of their encounter with the supernatural they try to control their anxieties and phobias, to find a satisfactory logical explanation for their 'spectral illusions' and 'hallucinations', to conquer them with the help of medicine, philosophy, religion or the warmth of friendship. Jennings ⟨in "Green Tea"⟩ tries to change his diet and style of life, avoids places where the 'thing' is most likely to appear, plunges into specialist literature that might help him solve the mystery of his illness, keeps an objective record of it, and with whole earnestness of faith, supplicates God for deliverance. Sir James Barton ⟨in "The Watcher"⟩ first undertakes some kind of detection, seeks legal advice against the alleged persecutor, consults a physician and, in spite of his materialistic outlook, a theologian as well, tries change of air, place, pastime. Being too passive to take such energetic steps, Sir Philip Feltram ⟨in "The Haunted Baronet"⟩ only tries to find consolation and help pouring out his anxieties and analyzing his state of mind in front of a friendly housekeeper: "I suppose I am not quite well. . . . I think . . . it is getting into me. I think it's like possession. . . . I think there is something trying to influence me. Perhaps it is the way fellows go mad; but it won't let me alone. I've seen it three times, think of that!"

Showing the painful awareness of being on the verge of otherness, the desperate, futile struggle to conquer the unknown force driving one to insanity, LeFanu touched one of the most tragic and pathetic struggles of man. It is impossible to say precisely how much of his success in doing this is due to his sensitiveness as a great artist and how much to his own bitter experience—himself a neurotic, after the death of his wife LeFanu became a recluse suffering heavily from persecution mania. Whatever the reason, this aspect of his ghost stories opened for this genre new perspectives and prepared techniques for later writers impregnated with Freud's ideas.

Jolanta Nalecz-Wojtczak, "Joseph Sheridan LeFanu and New Dimensions for the English Ghost Story," *Literary Interrelations: Ireland, England and the World*, ed. Wolfgang Zach and Heinz Kosok (Tübingen: Narr, 1987), Vol. 2, pp. 195–96

Bibliography

The Cock and Anchor: Being a Chronicle of Old Dublin City. 1845. 3 vols.

The Fortunes of Colonel Torlogh O'Brien: A Tale of the Wars of King James. 1847. 11 parts.

Ghost Stories and Tales of Mystery. 1851.

The House by the Church-yard. 1863. 3 vols.

Wylder's Hand. 1864. 3 vols.

Uncle Silas: A Tale of Bartram-Haugh. 1864. 3 vols.

The Prelude: Being a Contribution towards a History of the Election for the University. 1865.

Guy Deverell. 1865. 3 vols.

All in the Dark. 1866. 2 vols.

The Tenants of Malory. 1867. 3 vols.

A Lost Name. 1868. 3 vols.

Haunted Lives. 1868. 3 vols.

The Wyvern Mystery. 1869. 3 vols.

Checkmate. 1871. 3 vols.

The Rose and the Key. 1871. 3 vols.

Chronicles of Golden Friars. 1871. 3 vols.

In a Glass Darkly. 1872. 3 vols.

Willing to Die. 1873. 3 vols.

The Purcell Papers. 1880. 3 vols.

The Evil Guest. 1895.

Poems. Ed. Alfred Perceval Graves. 1896.

Madam Crowl's Ghost and Other Tales of Mystery. Ed. M. R. James. 1923.

Green Tea and Other Stories. 1945.
Best Ghost Stories. Ed. E. F. Bleiler. 1964.
Ghost Stories and Mysteries. Ed. E. F. Bleiler. 1975.

Matthew Gregory Lewis
1775–1818

MATTHEW GREGORY ("MONK") LEWIS, novelist, playwright, and poet, was born in London on July 9, 1775, and educated at the Westminster School (1783–90) and Christ Church, Oxford (1790–94). In 1791, while still a student at Oxford, Lewis visited Paris, where he wrote a farce, *The Epistolary Intrigue* (the manuscript of which has been lost), and began a never-completed novel, *Effusions of Sensibility*. Returning to Oxford in 1792, Lewis wrote another drama, *The East Indian* (1800; revised as *Rich and Poor*, 1812), performed years later at the Drury Lane Theatre without much success. Later in 1792 Lewis traveled to Weimar to learn German, and there fell under the lasting influence of German Romantic literature.

Upon receiving his B.A. from Oxford, Lewis served briefly as an attaché to the British Embassy at The Hague (1794), and in 1796 entered the House of Commons as the member from Hindon, Wiltshire. Lewis's career in Parliament was undistinguished, and his attendance at sessions became more and more infrequent until he gave up his seat in 1802; by that time, however, his literary success was such that he felt he could concentrate entirely on writing.

The work that established Lewis's reputation—and still his best-known—was his Gothic romance *The Monk* (1796), influenced by Ann Radcliffe as well as by contemporary German literature. Its violence and eroticism made it an immediate *succès de scandale*, and from then on it was the book most associated with its author, who came to be known as "Monk" Lewis. As a dramatist his fame was achieved almost as suddenly and spectacularly: his Gothic play *The Castle Spectre* was produced with great success at Drury Lane in 1797, and was given an initial run of forty-seven nights.

In 1801 Lewis published *Tales of Wonder,* a volume of original and translated verse that was soundly criticized, and so successfully parodied by other writers that the satiric *Tales of Terror,* which appeared the same year, is still spuriously attributed to him. This volume is also frequently confused with a very rare pamphlet, *An Apology for Tales of Terror* (1799), containing poems by Lewis, Sir Walter Scott, Robert Southey, and others.

Also in 1801 Lewis's "romantic drama" *Adelmorn, the Outlaw*, begun in 1795, was produced at Drury Lane and published shortly afterward. This was followed by many other plays, including *Alfonso, King of Castile* (published 1801; produced 1802), *Adelgitha; or, The Fruits of a Single Error* (published 1806; produced 1807), *Timour the Tartar* (produced and published 1811), and *One O'Clock! or, The Knight and the Wood Daemon* (produced and published 1811).

Lewis was also a prolific translator and adaptor, and he produced translations of plays by Schiller (*The Minister*, 1797), Kotzebue (*Rolla; or, The Peruvian Hero*, 1799), and Heinrich Zschokke (*The Bravo of Venice*, 1805), as well as the prose works *The Feudal Tyrants* (1806) and *Romantic Tales* (1808), all translated from German. He also translated Count Anthony Hamilton's *The Four Facardins* (1799) from the French.

In 1812 Lewis's father died, leaving him the bulk of his considerable estate, including several plantations in Jamaica. These Lewis visited twice, and on the second visit he contracted yellow fever, from which he died on his way back to England on May 14, 1818. The diary that he kept to record his experiences in Jamaica (published in 1834 as *Journal of a West Indian Proprietor*) reveals him to be a humanitarian with a strong opposition to slavery. *The Life and Correspondence of M. G. Lewis*, assembled by Margaret Baron-Wilson and incorporating many unpublished pieces of prose and poetry, appeared in 1839.

Critical Extracts

SAMUEL TAYLOR COLERIDGE   The horrible and the preternatural have usually seized on the popular taste, at the rise and decline of literature. Most powerful stimulants, they can never be required except by the torpor of an unawakened, or the languor of an exhausted, appetite. This same phaenomenon, therefore, which we hail as a favourable omen in the belles lettres of Germany, impresses a degree of gloom in the compositions of our countrymen. We trust, however, that satiety will banish what good sense should have prevented; and that, wearied with fiends, incomprehensible characters, with shrieks, murders, and subterraneous dungeons, the public will learn, by the multitude of manufacturers, with how little expense of thought or imagination this species of composition is manufactured. But, cheaply as we estimate romance in general, we acknowledge, in the work before us ⟨*The Monk*⟩, the offspring of no common genius. The tale is similar to that of Santon Barsista ⟨*sic*⟩ in the *Guardian*. Ambrosio, a monk, surnamed the Man of Holiness, proud of his own undeviating rectitude, and severe to the faults of others, is successfully assailed by the tempter of mankind, and seduced to the perpetration of rape and murder, and finally precipitated into a contract in which he consigns his soul to everlasting perdition. ⟨. . .⟩

All events are levelled into one common mass, and become almost equally probable, where the order of nature may be changed whenever the author's purposes demand it. No address is requisite to the accomplishments of any design; and no pleasures therefore can be received from the perception of *difficulty surmounted*. The writer may make us wonder, but he cannot surprise us. For the same reasons a romance is incapable of exemplifying a moral truth. No proud man, for instance, will be made less proud by being told that Lucifer once seduced a presumptuous young monk. *Incredulus odit*. Or even if, believing the story, he should deem his virtue less secure, he would yet acquire no lessons of prudence, no feelings of humility. Human prudence can oppose no sufficient shield to the power and cunning of supernatural beings; and the privilege of being proud might be fairly conceded to him who could rise superior to all earthly temptations, and whom the strength of the spiritual world alone would be adequate to overwhelm. So falling, he would fall with glory, and might reasonably welcome his defeat with the haughty emotions of a conqueror. As far, therefore, as the story is concerned, the praise which a romance can claim, is simply that of having given pleasure during its perusal; and so many are the calamities of life, that he who has done this has not written uselessly. The children of sickness and solitude shall thank him.—To this praise, however, our author has not entitled himself. The sufferings which he describes are so frightful and intolerable, that we break with abruptness from the delusion, and indignantly suspect the man of a species of brutality, who could find a pleasure in wantonly imagining them; and the abominations which he pourtrays with no hurrying pencil, are such as the observation of character by no means demanded, such as 'no observation of character can justify because no good man would willingly suffer them to pass, however transiently, through his own mind.' The merit of a novellist is in proportion (not simply to the effect but) to the *pleasurable* effect which he produces. Situations of torment, and images of naked horror, are easily conceived; and a writer in whose works they abound, deserves our gratitude almost equally with him who would drag us by way of sport through a military hospital, or force us to sit at the dissecting table of a natural philosopher. To trace the nice boundaries, beyond which terror and sympathy are deserted by the pleasurable emotions,—to reach those limits, yet never to pass them,—*hic labor, hic opus est*. Figures that shock the imagination, and narratives that mangle the feelings, rarely discover *genius*, and always betray a low and vulgar *taste*. Nor has our author indicated less ignorance of the human heart in the management of the principal character. The wisdom and goodness of providence have ordered that the tendency of vicious actions to deprave the heart of the perpetrator, should diminish in proportion to the greatness of his temptations. Now, in addition to constitutional warmth and irresistible opportunity, the monk is impelled to incontinence by friendship, by compassion, by gratitude, by all that is amiable, and all that is estimable; yet in a few weeks after his first frailty, the man who had been described as possessing much general humanity, a keen and vigorous understanding, with habits of the most exalted piety, degenerates into an uglier fiend than the gloomy imagination of Dante would have ventured to picture. Again, the monk is described as feeling and acting under the influence of an appetite which could not co-exist with his other emotions. The romance-writer possesses an unlimited power over situations; but he must scrupulously make his characters act in congruity with them. Let him work *physical* wonders only, and we will be content to *dream* with him for a while; but the first *moral* miracle which he attempts, he disgusts and awakens us. Thus, our judgment remains offended, when, announced by thunders and earthquakes, the spirit appears to Ambrosio involved in blue fires that increase the cold of the cavern; and we acquiesce in the power of the silver myrtle which made gates and doors fly open at its touch, and charmed every eye into sleep. But when a mortal, fresh from the impression of that terrible appearance, and in the act of evincing for the first time the witching force of this myrtle, is represented as being at the same moment agitated by so fleeting an appetite as that of lust, our own feelings convince us that this is not improbable, but impossible; not preternatural, but contrary to nature. The extent of the powers that may exist, we can never ascertain; and therefore we feel no great difficulty in yielding a temporary belief to any, the strangest, situation of *things*. But that situation once conceived, how beings like ourselves would feel and act in it, our own feelings insufficiently instruct us; and we instantly reject the clumsy fiction that does not harmonise with them. These are the two *principal* mistakes in *judgment*, which the author has fallen into; but we cannot wholly pass over the frequent incongruity of his style with his subjects. It is gaudy where it should have been severely simple; and too often the mind is offended by phrases the most trite and colloquial, where it demands and had expected a sternness and solemnity of diction.

Samuel Taylor Coleridge, "*The Monk*, A Romance by M. G. Lewis, Esq., M.P." (1797), *Coleridge's Miscellaneous Criticism*, ed. Thomas Middleton Raysor (London: Constable, 1936), pp. 370–73

MATTHEW GREGORY LEWIS Though certain that the clamours against *The Monk* cannot have give you the smallest doubt of the rectitude of my intentions, or the purity of my principles, yet I am conscious that it must have grieved you to find any doubts on the subject existing in the minds of other people. To express my sorrow for having given you pain, is my motive for now addressing you; and also to assure you that you shall not feel that pain a second time on my account. Having made you feel it at all, would be a sufficient reason, had I not others, to make me regret having published the first edition of *The Monk*; but I have others, weaker indeed than the one mentioned, but still sufficiently strong. I perceive that I have put too much confidence in the accuracy of my own judgment; that, convinced of my object being unexceptionable, I did not sufficiently examine whether the means by which I attained that object were generally so; and that upon many accounts, I have to accuse myself of high imprudence. Let me, however, observe that TWENTY is not the age at which prudence is most to be expected. Inexperience prevented my distinguishing what would give offence; but as soon as I found that offence was given, I made the only reparation in my power: I carefully revised the work, and expunged every syllable on which could be grounded the slightest construction of immorality. This, indeed, was no difficult task; for the objections rested entirely on expressions too strong, and words too carelessly chosen; not on the sentiments, characters, or general tendency of the work.

That the latter is undeserving censure, Addison will vouch for me: the moral and outline of the story are taken from an allegory inserted by him in *The Guardian*, and which he commends highly, for ability of invention and propriety of object. Unluckily, in working it up, I thought that the stronger my colours, the more effect my picture would produce; and it never struck me, that the exhibition of vice, in her temporary triumph, might possibly do as much harm as her final exposure and punishment would do good. To do much good, indeed, was more than I expected of my book; having always believed that our conduct depends on our own hearts and characters, not upon the books we read or the sentiments we hear. But though I did not expect much benefit to arise from the perusal of my trifling romance, written by a youth of twenty, I was in my own mind quite certain that no harm could be produced by a work whose subject was furnished by one of the best moralists, and in the composition of which I did not introduce a single incident, or a single character, without meaning to inculcate some maxim universally allowed. It was, then, with infinite surprise that I heard the outcry raised against the book, and found that a few ill-judged and unguarded passages totally obscured its general tendency.

To support my charge of irreligion, a single one only has been, or can be, produced. I am heartily sorry that this passage was ever published; but I must say, that I have been very unfairly treated respecting it. Those who have made it the subject of public censure, have uniformly omitted such parts as would have palliated those offensive expressions. Those expressions, certainly, are much too strong, and I now see that their style is irreverent; but it was not intended to be such, nor was the passage meant to counsel any more than the bible should not be read before a certain age, when its perusers would be capable of benefitting from its precepts and admiring its beauties. It also suggested the propriety of not putting certain passages before the eyes of very young persons. This advice I was induced to give from experience, for I know that schoolboys do not (neither, if my informers may be credited, do schoolgirls) always read particular chapters of the bible for the purpose of edification. In stating this, I thought, by representing the advice as having been given to the heroine by her mother—a woman pious and sensible—I had guarded against the idea of attacking the bible.

My precaution was ineffectual: I have given offence; I am sorry for having given it. I have omitted the passage; and now can do no more than say, that neither in this, nor in any other part of *The Monk,* had I the slightest idea that what I was then writing could injure the principles, moral or religious, of any human being. Since this work, I have published others; and, taught by experience, I have avoided the insertion of any word that could possibly admit of misrepresentation. As their propriety has not been questioned, I trust that I have succeeded in the attempt; and I do not despair of some time or other convincing my censurers that they have totally mistaken both me and my principles.

Matthew Gregory Lewis, Letter to His Father (23 February 1798), *The Life and Correspondence of* M. G. *Lewis,* ed. Margaret Baron-Wilson (London: Henry Colburn, 1839), Vol. 1, pp. 154–58

DAVID MACBETH MOIR   As a man of truly original powers, M. G. Lewis was far behind either Godwin or Coleridge, and stood much on the level of his successor Maturin; but what his imagination lacked in grandeur was made up by energy: he was a high-priest of the intense school. Monstrous and absurd in many things, as were the writings of Lewis, no one could say that they were deficient in interest. Truth and nature, to be sure, he held utterly at arm's-length; but, instead, he had a life-in-death vigour, a spasmodic energy, which answered well for all purposes of astonishment. He wrote of demons, ghouls, ghosts, vampires, and disembodied spirits of every kind, as if they were the common machinery of society. A skeleton "in complete steel," or the spectre of "a bleeding nun," was ever at hand, on emergencies; and wood-demons, fire-kings, and water-sprites, gave a fillip to external scenery. His *Monk*, that strange and extramundane production, made the reader "sup so full of horrors," that mothers were obliged to lock it up from their sickly and sentimental daughters—more especially as its morale was not of the choicest; and when Lewis took a leap from the closet to the stage, his power was equally felt. I yet remember, when a boy, trembling in the very theatre, at the scene in *The Castle Spectre* which brings the murdered maiden on the stage; and if productions are to be judged by their effect, that drama, like *The Robbers* of Schiller, has left on facile imaginations traces never to be obliterated. The *Tales of Wonder*, and the *Tales of Terror*, succeeded; some of them stories of amazing vigour—wild, extravagant, unnatural—but withal highly readable, nay, occasionally of enchaining interest. In spirit Lewis was a thorough convert to the raw-head-and-bloody-bones and the trap-door German school; and his thoughts were ever away amid the Hartz Mountains, seeing "more spirits than vast hell could hold." His every night was Hallowe'en, or a Walpurgis Night; and he is said to have become, in his latter years, the dupe of his own early over-excited feelings, and as sincere a convert to a frequent infringement of the established laws of physics, as Mrs Crowe in her *Night Side of Nature*, or the Baron von Reichenbach himself, with his Odylic light. He conjured up ghosts to affright others, and came to be haunted by them himself—a most natural retribution.

David Macbeth Moir, *Sketches of the Poetical Literature of the Past Half-Century* (Edinburgh: William Blackwood & Sons, 1851; 3rd ed. 1856), pp. 18–20

EINO RAILO   We have dealt already with the storm awakened by the appearance of *The Monk*. The cause of the outburst was Ambrosio, his unquenchable licentiousness and the events occasioned thereby; and in general, the undismayed realism of the narration and the pitilessness of the author in eliminating every hope and possibility of salvation for his monk; these served to arouse in the reader's mind moral indignation and a sense of opposition, though fundamentally the extremely agitating effect of the book was the cause of this. However hard the reader might try to regard the work as the unripe creation of a mere youth, scarcely deserving of attention, he was compelled to admit that it revealed in a perturbingly merciless manner the hidden lust of pleasure biding its opportunity, which bereft of control, exposed to strong temptations, can sweep human beings to destruction. The argument of the book, that the most pious person can, in suitable circumstances, become the slave of his passions is one of the silent truths we are prone to ignore and which, over-boldly expressed, gives rise to hypocritical wrath.

The best proof that the basic argument of Lewis's novel did accord with one of the truths thus silently acquiesced in, is the fact that, as though sprung from the earth, a series of sombre, tragic phantoms of monks appeared to keep Ambrosio company, introducing into the romantic literature of England and the rest of Europe a ghastly, graveyard atmosphere. The passion of the romanticists for the past found in the monk a suitable character, in whose heart deep human conflicts could be laid, making of it a stage for the struggle between good and evil for the ultimate mastery over the human soul. For the romantic movement this denoted a setting aside of mere outward effects and the transference of psychological phenomena into the foreground. Also from this point of view does the appearance of the monk inaugurate a new phase in romanticism, a concentration of interest on the romanticism inherent in tragedies of the soul, which, as a source of "terror-awakening beauty," provided more effective means than those hitherto used. The line of development thus begun by Ambrosio is one of extreme interest in the history of romanticism, and carried to its utmost limits is responsible for many weird literary monsters.

> Eino Railo, "The Criminal Monk," *The Haunted Castle: A Study of the Elements of English Romanticism* (London: Routledge & Sons; New York: E. P. Dutton, 1927), pp. 176–77

MONTAGUE SUMMERS   Mrs. Radcliffe is the romanticist of the Gothic novel; Lewis the realist. His pictures of voluptuous passion are necessary to the narrative; the violence of the orgasm but serves to balance and throw in high relief the charnel horrors. The comeliest forms of man and maid entwined in quivering embrace that Aretine might have imaged in his shameless sonnets, the long rapture of warm honeyed kisses such as Secundus sung, the full swift pulse of life, beauty, love, desire, all these are suddenly shadowed by the dark pall of mortality; those eyes that sparkled with lust's flame must fade and close in the night, those hands whose touch was as a draught of heady wine must palsy, grow cold, and decay, the worm must pasture on those corrupting limbs where lovers' teeth once bit the white flesh in frenzy of sadistic appetite.

> Montague Summers, "Matthew Gregory Lewis," *The Gothic Quest: A History of the Gothic Novel* (London: Fortune Press, 1938), pp. 222–23

BERTRAND EVANS   Lewis's claim to a place of first importance in the history of the Gothic novel is contested by Walpole, Mrs. Radcliffe, and Maturin. His preëminence in Gothic drama is almost uncontested. The number of Gothic plays from his pen equals that of any other playwright, and his novel was adapted several times. His influence upon his contemporaries and successors, both greater and lesser than himself, perhaps exceeded even that of Mrs. Radcliffe. Furthermore, he stood between the two centuries and was most instrumental in passing the Gothic collection over to the romantics. His plays represent better than any others a composite of the traditional, native materials and the foreign and new ones. He wrote at the time that theatrical and literary plays parted company, and such a piece as *Adelmorn* pointed the direction in which each kind was to go. In addition, *The Monk* was translated into German before the flood of German materials reached England, so that the German deluge which came had already received the contribution of Lewis. *The Monk* was also adapted several times for the French stage, and thus when translations and alterations of Pixérécourt began to appear on the English stage, they brought back materials borrowed from Lewis in the first place. Actually, then, Lewis did more than utilize the two foreign sources that were added to the native tradition. He contributed to the English tradition, lent materials to German and French writers for development in their respective countries, and finally capitalized on the results of international circulation when native and foreign elements were reunited in England.

Bertrand Evans, "Lewis and Gothic Drama," *Gothic Drama from Walpole to Shelley* (Berkeley: University of California Press, 1947), pp. 160–61

ROBERT KIELY   The effective representation of any human feeling may be partial justification for a work of art, but the meticulous and deliberate dissection of mental torment and physical abuse which forms the substance of the tale of terror raises aesthetic and moral problems of a complicated sort. Toward what end does such literature aim, if not merely sensational? And in what way is it linked with the major concerns of the romantic aesthetic?

Like most fiction of the period, the novel of terror nearly always made claims, especially on final pages, of high moral intention. Man's inhumanity to man, the dangers of excess, the fate of pride, were all paraded for inspection in the last chapter so that any reader of bad conscience and little discrimination could close the volume content that he had been given a stern lesson. What makes the didactic protestations in *The Monk* ring slightly hollow is the tone rather than the narrative context of the whole book. There is no reason to assume that Lewis set out to write an immoral novel or that his

didactic intrusions are merely cynical compromises with public taste. The
fact is that his novel does show the dangers of excess and the fate of pride,
but the power and originality with which he treats the physical, emotional,
and psychological elements of the story tend to obscure the moral assertions
even when they do not contradict them. Lewis's vocabulary of violent
emotions was part imitation and part artistic creation, but his moral terminol-
ogy was an inherited rhetoric which lacked the energy of belief or discovery.

The Monk Ambrosio is a Faustian protagonist who sells himself to the
devil for the sake of temporary pleasure, but there is little space given to
rational analysis, theological dispute, or metaphysical speculation. Plot and
the conventional implications of chronology and causal relationship are
relegated to a position of unobtrusive significance. The author concentrates
not on how things come about but on how they look and feel. The main
narrative is repeatedly interrupted by the details of a subplot and, at one
point, by a long digressive tale. Nevertheless, The Monk does have a unique
structure which derives from an accumulation of strikingly realized scenes
rather than from a logical knitting together of events. More than any fiction
which preceded it, the novel of terror is picturesque. It appeals first to the
eye and only secondarily to reason and conscience.

Lewis sought to reproduce an intensely private vision of a character in
extreme circumstances, an institutional man suddenly at war with every
kind of convention. Given the novel's roots in social convention and common speech, it would seem that he was attempting the impossible. (It is
no coincidence that, like Walpole and Maturin, he turned from fiction to
poetry and drama.)

        Robert Kiely, The Romantic Novel in England (Cambridge, MA: Harvard University
        Press, 1972), pp. 101–2

PETER BROOKS   The Monk on the one hand tends to assert that
the world is inhabited by irrational and supernatural forces which act upon
man, are implicated and brought into play by man's actions and gestures,
whether he consciously acknowledges them or not, and on the other hand
suggests that these forces do not derive, or no longer derive, from a traditional
conception of the Sacred. What has in fact been left after the desacralization
of the world is not its rationalization—man's capacity to understand and
to manage everything in terms of a rational epistemology and a humanistic
ethics—but rather a terrifying and essentially uncontrollable network of
violent primitive forces and taboos which are surmounted into play by the
dialectics of man's desire. Without any operable idea of the Sacred to refer

himself to, yet surrounded by supernatural forces with which he must reckon, Ambrosio is at last constrained to see himself, by the process of desiring, as a man trapped in this network of forces which he can neither control or deny, which he cannot worship but must sacrifice to.

The Monk, then, seems to give an especially clear and forceful symbolic representation of passage into a world—the Romantic and post-Romantic world, our world—in which the confident rationalism of the Enlightenment has been called into question, yet recognition of the force of the irrational is not accompanied, cannot be accompanied, by reestablishment of the Sacred as true *mysterium tremendum*. The epistemology of the irrational leads rather into ourselves, into the realm of dreams, spooks, interdicted desires. The "primal numinous awe" puts us in touch, not with Godhead, but with the unconscious. Ethically, this universe is one where the support of morals in the Sacred is gone, and the definition of guilt and innocence has to do rather with a primitive and irreducible opposition of purity and pollution. There is no guarantee that in his struggle with his inner daemons man will succeed in asserting his innocence. On the contrary, Matilda's logic looks forward to that of Ivan Karamazov, to the posing of the damned question of whether in a world where there is no Sacred, everything is not permitted. In the sense that there is no respect due to a "wholly other," everything *is* permitted. But if virtue need not be acknowledged, there is nonetheless Terror, which has been shown to inhabit nature, and nature's creature, man.

> Peter Brooks, "Virtue and Terror: *The Monk*," ELH 40, No. 2 (Summer 1973): 262–63

ELIZABETH MacANDREW   Lewis' novel is a deliberate medley of the Sentimental and the Gothic. It also combines the terror of the sublime evoked by the tormented Ambrosio and the horror of the grotesque in the encounter with the bleeding nun or the scene of Agnes cradling her dead and worm-eaten baby. His structures are neither neatly encapsulated one within the other nor juxtaposed in contrast. They seem chaotic and his Gothic devices seem sensationalist, but their very disorder conveys a mixture of hope and despair. Lewis' vision falls somewhere between the neat, optimistic, and common-sensical conclusion of Ann Radcliffe's *Udolpho* and the pessimism of the grotesque in Beckford's *Vathek*. Ambrosio's perversion into evil is complete and he wreaks terrible destruction, yet he might have been good. Every section of Lewis' novel repeats this idea through its structure as well as its events. For this reason, too, Ambrosio is literally bedevilled.

The recurrent theme of imprisonment—in cloister, castle or dungeon—in each plot, subplot, and interpolation, and the repeated transformation of idyll into nightmare say again and again that goodness is locked up inside evil, that innocence is seduced, perverted, but that somehow it might not have been. Ambrosio in the claws of Lucifer is also a victim, a human being of great potential for good betrayed by social forces into a living hell of evil. Later Gothic fiction devises many forms stranger and more subtle than Lewis' but it is perennially preoccupied with the nightmare of uncertainty about the origins and causes of human evil that Lewis expresses in his confusion of victim and villain.

Elizabeth MacAndrew, The Gothic Tradition in Fiction (New York: Columbia University Press, 1979), pp. 138–39

ELIZABETH R. NAPIER   The extreme trials to which Lewis exposes his characters and his often pitiless attitude towards their miseries are supplemented by a stylistic complexity that functions equally to forestall an open response to his narrative. The authorial tone of *The Monk* remains oddly detached (except, perhaps, in the narration of past events (as in Raymond's story) or in the erotic sequences), whether Lewis adopts the cynical attitude of worldly wisdom of the novel's opening scene or the jubilant sadism of the Monk's downfall at the book's close. The voice that introduces the novel is sarcastic and knowing, and aggressively anti-Catholic in tone: 'Scarcely had the Abbey-Bell tolled for five minutes, and already was the Church of the Capuchins thronged with Auditors. Do not encourage the idea that the crowd was assembled either from motives of piety or thirst of information. But very few were influenced by those reasons; and in a city where superstition reigns with such despotic sways as in Madrid, to seek for true devotion would be a fruitless attempt.' In the closing sequence, Lewis's excitement is felt in his allusions to the Creation myth, and his writing gains a new solidity through the controlled biblical rhythms of his prose:

'. . . six miserable days did the Villain languish. On the Seventh a violent storm arose: The winds in fury rent up rocks and forests: The sky was now black with clouds, now sheeted with fire: The rain fell in torrents; It swelled the stream; The waves overflowed their banks; They reached the spot where Ambrosio lay, and when they abated carried with them into the river the Corse of the despairing Monk.' This proud use of biblical parallels (Ambrosio as Adam, experiencing his fall; Ambrosio as Satan, undergoing his expulsion from Heaven; the Decreation; the Flood) was obviously felt by Lewis to be (at least potentially) offensive, for the allusions were removed in the third edition of *The Monk* before he subjected the book to extensive bowdlerization in the fourth printing.

Further disruptions of a unified tone are created by Lewis's inclusion in (and later addition to) *The Monk* of comic characters and episodes. Such a procedure is a hallmark of the Gothic, and it has a particularly disorienting effect here, for the events of the novel are physically and psychologically more horrific than those in, for example, *The Castle of Otranto* or *The Mysteries of Udolpho*. Thus, Leonella's ridiculous behavior with Don Christoval; the scenes in which Cunegonda is carried off, imprisoned in a closet, and eventually silenced by large draughts of cherry brandy; the long episode in which Jacintha details the arrival of Elvira's ghost spewing clouds of fire and rattling with chains grate oddly against the scenes of murder, injustice, and violation that surround them. The Gothic is by nature a mixed genre, and seems to invite such self-conscious comical retreats from tragedy: Lewis's addition (in the fourth section of *The Monk*) of 'Giles Jollup the Grave and Brown Sally Green,' a parody of his 'Alonzo the Brave, and Fair Imogine' (which he based in part on a newspaper parody of his popular ballad from *The Monk*), suggests not only his notion of the form as a sort of 'mixed grill' of prose, poetry, and miscellaneous incident, but as a receptacle for both comedy and tragedy, a genre that allows an experimental (and self-conscious) mixing of tones and incidents in the tradition of the theatrical variety show.

Elizabeth R. Napier, *The Failure of Gothic: Problems of Disjunction in an Eighteenth-Century Literary Form* (Oxford: Clarendon Press, 1987), pp. 124–26

Bibliography

The Monk: A Romance. 1796. 3 vols.
Village Virtues: A Dramatic Satire. 1796.
The Minister by Friedrich Schiller (translator). 1797.
The Castle Spectre. 1798.
Rolla; or, The Peruvian Hero by August von Kotzebue (translator). 1799.
The Love of Gain: Imitated from the Thirteenth Satire of Juvenal. 1799.
An Apology for Tales of Terror (with Sir Walter Scott, Robert Southey, et al.). 1799.
The Four Facardins by Count Anthony Hamilton (translator). 1799.
The East Indian. 1800, 1812 (as *Rich and Poor*).

Tales of Wonder (editor). 1801. 2 vols.

[*Tales of Terror* (editor). 1801.]

Adelmorn, the Outlaw: A Romantic Drama. 1801.

Alfonso, King of Castile. 1801.

The Bravo of Venice by Heinrich Zschokke (translator). 1805.

Adelgitha; or, The Fruits of a Single Error. 1806.

Feudal Tyrants; or, The Counts of Carlsheim and Sargaus: A Romance Taken from the German. 1806. 4 vols.

Romantic Tales. 1808. 4 vols.

Venoni; or, The Novice of St. Mark's. 1809.

Monody on the Death of Sir John Moore. 1809.

Timour the Tartar. 1811.

One O'Clock! or, The Knight and the Wood Daemon. 1811.

Poems. 1812.

The Isle of Devils: An Historical Tale Founded on an Anecdote in the Annals of Portugal. 1827.

Journal of a West Indian Proprietor Kept During a Residence in the Island of Jamaica. 1834.

Life and Correspondence. Ed. Margaret Baron-Wilson. 1839. 2 vols.

Fairy Tales and Romances by Count Anthony Hamilton (translator; with others). 1849.

◈ ◈ ◈

Charles Robert Maturin
c. 1780–1824

CHARLES ROBERT MATURIN, Gothic novelist and playwright, was born in Dublin on September 24, 1780 or 1782, into a well-to-do family descended from French Huguenots. He graduated from Trinity College, Dublin, in 1800, and in 1803 was ordained in the Anglican Church of Ireland. Maturin first served as a curate at the rural parish of Loughrea; after his marriage to Henrietta Kingsbury in 1803 he became a curate at St. Peter's parish, Dublin. He never advanced beyond this poorly paid position, possibly because his personal eccentricities, including his career as a dramatist and writer of Gothic tales, did not impress his superiors favorably.

Maturin's first novel, *Fatal Revenge; or, The Family of Montorio*, a Gothic romance influenced by Ann Radcliffe and Matthew Gregory Lewis, was published at his own expense in 1807 under the pseudonym of Dennis Jasper Murphy. It was a financial failure, as were his next two novels, *The Wild Irish Boy* (1808) and *The Milesian Chief* (1812), in which Maturin turned to traditional Irish themes for inspiration. In 1809 Maturin's father lost his position with the Irish General Post Office, and Maturin was obliged to support himself; he did so for a time by tutoring pupils to prepare them for university. Nonetheless, he still hoped to succeed as a professional writer. He had by this time obtained the literary friendship of Sir Walter Scott (who in 1810 had favorably reviewed *Fatal Revenge*), and it was on Scott's and also Lord Byron's recommendation that Edmund Kean produced Maturin's Gothic drama *Bertram* in 1816 at the Drury Lane Theatre. This was to be Maturin's greatest financial success, although most of the money went to his brother's creditors. His next two dramatic productions, *Manuel* (1817) and *Fredolfo* (1819), were, however, not well received.

In the meantime Maturin had published his fourth novel, *Women; or, Pour et Contre* (1818), followed in 1820 by what is today his best-known work, *Melmoth the Wanderer*. This Gothic novel, considered by many the oustanding example of its genre, was admired by writers as diverse as Baudelaire, Poe, Thackeray, and Dante Gabriel Rossetti; Balzac wrote a sequel to it (*Melmoth reconcilié*), and after his disgrace Oscar Wilde adopted the name Sebastian Melmoth. Maturin produced one further novel, *The Albigenses*, published shortly before his death on October 30, 1824. His play *Osmyn, the Renegade*, written sometime between 1818 and 1820, received a posthumous production in 1830, but was never published in its entirety.

▣ *Critical Extracts*

CHARLES ROBERT MATURIN   I was honored with the receipt of your letter, and am indeed elated by a testimony of approbation from one, whose praise combines all that is valuable in the dignity of Genius, the discernment of Criticism, and the Condescension of Benevolence. When I hinted at the gloom of my writings being borrowed from the shades of my own Mind and feelings, it was not that I might vent the murmurings of a querulous Egotist, or the vanity of a disappointed Author—No Sir—I really believe my own Romances scarce exhibit vicissitudes more extraordinary than my life has furnished.

I am still a very young Man, my father held a situation under Government that enabled him to pass 60 years of life in affluence and luxury, and he had high Connexions in the Church that induced him to put me into orders with the expectations of an ample provision. I married very young, and though my family increased rapidly, I continued to live with my father, as I had only obtained a Curacy.

In November 1809, my father was dismissed from his situation, and at the age of 64 left with my Mother to the horrors of utter Indigence, aggravated by the infirmities of age, the impossibility of applying any other means of subsistence at such a period of life, and above all by bitter recollection of former affluence and honor—it is but a justice to add that the Charge on which he was dismissed was pronounced by the Board of inquiry to be utterly inadequate to the punishment inflicted, and his Character was still more amply justified by the Report of a Committee of the House of Commons— he has made numberless applications for Redress, but while the Country is struggling for Existence, she has little leisure to attend to private com- plaints—in the Battle for life and death we are now fighting, the Cries of the wounded can neither be heard nor pitied.

My father had lived up to his income, and therefore I who was dependent on him, was of course a Sufferer in his Ruin—his interest too was lost with his situation, and their Graces and Lordships the Archbishops and Bishops who had so often feasted at his table, would not now spare him the offals of theirs—in this my extremity, I Betook myself to a source of subsistence which beneficed Clergymen often Resort to in Dublin. I offered to take as boarders and pupils, the sons of those of fortune, who are students in the College of Dublin, but as all the fellows of that university are in the same line, I found the greatest difficulty in procuring the few I have, and almost equal difficulty keeping them—it is impossible to describe the "Variety of wretchedness" attendant on this line of life—the Caprice of parents, the dullness of Children, the Expectation that I am to make a Genius of him whom his Maker has made a dunce, the injunctions of Constraint from the parents, the demand of indulgence from the young Men, the difficulty of maintaining any authority over those who are too old for punishment and too young for self-direction, the insolence of young Men who feel they are more Masters of this house than I am, and who expect in a tutor's house the luxury and splendor in which they live at home, and above all the tremendous Responsibility attached to the Care of their health and Conduct in a great and corrupted City, whose every street is putrid with Vice and disease and infection,—add all this, if any power of mental arithmetic can compute the amount, and then judge how clear my head, and how light my heart must be when I sit down to write—yet what can I do—my wife's fortune was only sufficient to take the spacious house that was necessary for my Establishment, from the Church I have no expectations, for, exclusive of the loss of my father's former interest, I am a high Calvinist in my Religious opinions, and therefore viewed with jealousy by Unitarian Brethren and Arminian Masters—as to my talents (if I possess any) there is no excitement, no literary appetite or impulse in this Country, my most intimate acquaintances scarcely know that I have written, and they care as little as they know.

Under these circumsatances, I look (though with no confident eye) to you—your interest might perhaps introduce me to the Editors of a Review, or some periodical work, and perhaps I might not disgrace that interest—the painfulness of speaking of my own acquirements must be conquered by Necessity—I am a good classical scholar, my acquaintance with Divinity is not superficial, and I am fond of the belles lettres—with all this, I might do something and my introduction to the literary World would be both dignified and Endeared by owing it to one who can stoop from the Summit of Literature to console the humblest wanderer on its rugged Acclivities.

Charles Robert Maturin, Letter to Sir Walter Scott (11 January 1813), *The Correspondence of Sir Walter Scott and Charles Robert Maturin*, ed. Fannie E. Ratchford and William H. McCarthy, Jr. (Austin: University of Texas Press, 1937), pp. 8–10

SIR WALTER SCOTT   I have been recommending to John Kemble (I daresay without any chance of success) to peruse a MS. Tragedy ⟨Bertram⟩ of Maturin's (author of Montorio:) it is one of those things which will either succeed greatly or be damned gloriously, for its merits are marked, deep, and striking, and its faults of a nature obnoxious to ridicule. He had our old friend Satan (none of your sneaking St. John Street devils, but the archfiend himself) brought on the stage bodily. I believe I have exorcised the foul fiend—for, though in reading he was a most terrible fellow, I feared for his reception in public. The last act is ill contrived. He piddles (so to speak) through a cullender, and divides the whole horrors of the catastrophe (though God wot there are enough of them) into a kind of drippity-droppity of four or five scenes, instead of inundating the audience with them at once in the finale, with a grand *"gardez l'eau."* With all this, which I should say had I written the thing myself, it is grand and powerful; the language most animated and poetical; and the characters sketched with a masterly enthusiasm.

Sir Walter Scott, Letter to Daniel Terry (10 November 1814), Letters of Sir Walter Scott, ed. H. J. C. Grierson (London: Constable, 1932), Vol. 3, p. 515

SAMUEL TAYLOR COLERIDGE   I want words to describe the mingled horror and disgust with which I witnessed the opening of the fourth act ⟨of Bertram⟩, considering it as a melancholy proof of the deprivation of the public mind. The shocking spirit of Jacobinism seemed no longer confined to politics. The familiarity with atrocious events and characters appeared to have poisoned the taste, even where it had not directly disorganized the moral principles, and left the feelings callous to all the mild appeals, and craving alone for the grossest and most outrageous stimulants. The very fact then present to our senses, that a British audience could remain passive under such an insult to common decency, nay, receive with a thunder of applause, a human being supposed to have come reeking from the consummation of this complex foulness and baseness, these and the like reflections so pressed as with the weight of lead upon my heart, the actor, author, and tragedy would have been forgotten, had it not been for a plain elderly man sitting beside me, who, with a very serious face, that at once expressed surprize and aversion, touched my elbow, and, pointing to the actor, said to me, in a half-whisper—"Do you see that little fellow there? he has just been committing adultery!" ⟨. . .⟩

Of the fifth act, the only thing noticeable (for rant and nonsense, though abundant as ever, have long before the last act become things of course,) is the profane representation of the high altar in a chapel, with all the vessels and other preparations for the holy sacrament. A hymn is actually sung on the stage by the chorister boys! For the rest, Imogine, who now and then *talks* deliriously, but who is always light-headed as far as her *gown* and *hair* can make her so, wanders about in dark woods with cavern-rocks and precipices in the back-scene; and a number of mute dramatis personae move in and out continually, for whose presence, there is always at least this reason, that they afford something to be *seen*, by that very large part of a Drury-lane audience who have small chance of *hearing* a word. She had, it appears, taken her child with her, but what becomes of the child, whether she murdered it or not, nobody can tell, nobody can learn; it was a riddle at the *representation*, and after a most attentive *perusal* of the Play, a riddle it remains.

Samuel Taylor Coleridge, *Biographia Literaria* (1817), *The Collected Works of Samuel Taylor Coleridge*, ed. James Engell and Walter Jackson Bate (London: Routledge & Kegan Paul; Princeton: Princeton University Press, 1983), Vol. 7, Part II, pp. 229, 231–32

T. NOON TALFOURD   Mr. Maturin gave decisive indications of a morbid sensibility and a passionate eloquence out-running his imaginative faculties, in the commencement of his literary career. His first romance, the *Family of Montorio*, is one of the wildest and strangest of all "false creations proceeding from the heat-oppressed brain." It is for the most part a tissue of magnificent yet unappalling horrors. Its great faults as a work of amusement, are the long and unrelieved series of its gloomy and marvellous scenes, and the unsatisfactory explanation of them all, as arising from mere human agency. This last error he borrowed from Mrs. Radcliffe, to whom he is far inferior in the economy of terrors, but whom he greatly transcends in the dark majesty of his style. As his events are far more wild and wondrous than hers, so his development is necessarily far more incredible and vexatious. There is, in this story, a being whom we are long led to believe is not of this world—who speaks in the tones of the sepulchre, glides through the thickest walls, haunts two distant brothers in their most secret retirements through their strange wanderings, leads one of his victims to a scene which he believes infernal, and there terrifies him with sights of the wildest magic—and who after all this, and after really vindicating to the fancy his claim to the supernatural by the fearful cast of his language—is discovered to be a low impostor, who has produced all by the aid of poor tricks and secret passages! Where is the policy of this? Unless, by his power, the author had given a credibility to magic through four-fifths of his work, it never could have excited any feeling but that of impatience or of scorn. And when we have surrendered ourselves willingly to his guidance—when we have agreed to believe possibilities at his bidding—why does he reward our credence with derision, and tacitly reproach us for not having detected his idle mockeries? After all, too, the reason is no more satisfied than the fancy; for it would be a thousand times easier to believe in the possibility of spiritual influences, than in a long chain of mean contrivances, no one of which would ever succeed. The first is but one wonder, and the one to which our nature has a strange leaning; the last are numberless, and having nothing to reconcile them to our thoughts. In submitting to the former, we contentedly lay aside our reasoning faculties; in approaching the latter our reason itself is appealed to at the moment when it is insulted. Great talent is, however, unquestionably exhibited in this singular story. A stern justice breathes solemnly through all the scenes in the devoted castle. "Fate sits on its dark battlements, and frowns." There is a spirit of deep philosophy in the tracing of the gradual influence of patricidal thoughts on the hearts of the brothers, which would finally exhibit the danger of dallying with evil fancies, if the subject were not removed so far from all ordinary temptations. Some of the scenes of horror, if they were not accumulated until they wear out their impression, would produce an effect inferior to none in the works of Radcliffe or Lewis. The scene in which Filippo escapes from the assassins, deserves to be ranked with the robber scenes in the Monk and Count Fathom. The diction of the whole is rich and energetic—not, indeed, flowing in a calm beauty which may glide on for ever—but impetuous as a mountain torrent, which, though it speedily passes away, leaves behind it no common spoils—

> Depositing upon the silent shore
> Of memory, images and gentle thoughts
> Which cannot die, and will not be destroyed.

T. Noon Talfourd, "Maturin," *Critical and Miscellaneous Writings* (1842; 2nd American ed. Philadelphia: A. Hart, 1852), pp. 20–21

GEORGE SAINTSBURY   *Melmoth the Wanderer* (1820) ⟨. . .⟩ has faults in plenty—especially a narrative method of such involution that, as it has been said, "a considerable part of the book consists of a story told to a certain person, who is a character in a longer story, found in a manuscript which is delivered to a third person, who narrates the greater part of the novel to a fourth person, who is the namesake and descendant of the title-hero." Stripped of these tiresome lendings (which, as has been frequently pointed out, were a mania with the eighteenth century and naturally grew to such intricacy as this,) the central story, though not exactly new, is impressive: and it is told and worked out in manner more impressive, because practically novel, save for, perhaps, a little suggestion from *Vathek*. Melmoth has bartered his soul with the devil for something like immortality and other privileges, including the usual one of escaping doom if he can get someone to take the bargain off his hands. This leads up to numerous episodes or chapters in which Melmoth endeavors to obtain substitutes: and in one of these the love interest of the book—the, of course, fatal love of Melmoth himself for a Spanish-Indian girl Immalee or Isidora—is related with some real pathos and passion, though with a good deal of mere sentiment and twaddle. Maturin is stronger in his terror scenes, and affected his own generation very powerfully: his influence being so great in France that Balzac attempted a variation and continuation, and that there are constant references to the book in the early French Romantics. In fact for this kind of "sensation" Maturin is, putting *Vathek* aside, quite the chief of the whole school. But it is doubtful whether he had many other gifts as a novelist, and this particular one is one that cannot be exercised very frequently, and is very difficult to exercise at all without errors and extravagances.

George Saintsbury, *The English Novel* (London: J. M. Dent, 1913), pp. 185–86

EDITH BIRKHEAD   There are no quiet scenes or motionless figures in *Melmoth*. Everything is intensified, exaggerated, distorted. The very clouds fly rapidly across the sky, and the moon bursts forth with the "sudden and appalling effulgence of lightning." A shower of rain is perhaps "the most violent that was ever precipitated on the earth." When Melmoth stamps his foot "the reverberation of his steps on the hollow and loosened stones almost contended with the thunder." Maturin's use of words like "callosity," "induration," "defecated," "evanition," and his fondness for italics are other indications of his desire to force an impression by fair means or foul.

The gift of psychological insight that distinguishes *Montorio* reappears in a more highly developed form in *Melmoth the Wanderer*. "Emotions," Maturin declares, "are my events," and he excels in depicting mental as well as physical torture. The monotony of a "timeless day" is suggested with dreary reality in the scene where Moncada and his guilt await the approach of night to effect their escape from the monastery. The gradual surrender of resolution before slight, reiterated assaults is cunningly described in the analysis of Isidora's state of mind, when a hateful marriage is forced upon her. Occasionally Maturin astonishes us by the subtlety of his thought:

"While people think it is worth while to torment us we are never without some dignity, though painful and imaginary."

It is his faculty for describing intense, passionate feeling, his power of painting wild pictures of horror, his gifts for conveying his thoughts in rolling, rhythmical periods of eloquence, that make *Melmoth* a memory-haunting book. With all his faults Maturin was the greatest as well as the last of the Goths.

Edith Birkhead, *The Tale of Terror: A Study of the Gothic Romance* (New York: Dutton, 1921), p. 93

NIILO IDMAN   That *Melmoth the Wanderer* is nowadays considered the work by which its author stands or falls, sufficiently explains why Maturin is only mentioned in connection with the school of terror. The 'terrific' elements in *Melmoth* are, it is true, strong enough to render it the greatest novel of that school in the English language. All the same, it is much too complex to be confined within the limits of one single school, while its general purport connects it with some of the greatest works of European literature in its period. ⟨. . .⟩

Maturin's romance belongs to the stories of the supernatural only in so far as the personality of Melmoth is concerned; otherwise the 'Gothic elements' contained in it consist of the usual external apparatus, calculated to appeal to the reader's sense of 'fear arising from objects of invisible terror,' as stated in the preface to *Montorio*.

Niilo Idman, *Charles Robert Maturin: His Life and Works* (London: Constable, 1923), pp. 196, 200

WILLIAM F. AXTON   *Melmoth the Wanderer*'s structure—a system of interpolated tales nested one within the other like the boxes of a child's toy—is a conscious artistic device which serves several important functions. The tales are analogous in theme and pattern of action: each deals in differing terms with social or religious sadism. More important, the succession of narrative interpolations leads the reader, in the "Tale of the Indians," directly but subtly into the heart of the author's themes. Finally, the deliberate variation in point of view and the multiplicity of narrators protect the author, who had already suffered by a false identification with the blasphemous opinions of his characters, from the pious reader's imputation of heterodoxy.

The nested tales, which serve to organize the novel around implicit analogies of character and action, are partially linked by a fairly consistent string of imagery. Wherever the reader turns in *Melmoth*, he is confronted by some new variety of religious perversity, economic injustice, or political and social despotism. An omniscient third-person narrator's account of young John Melmoth's return to the deathbed of his miserly uncle gives way quickly to Biddy Brannigan's account of the Melmoth family's complicity in Cromwell's pitiless reduction of Ireland during the English civil wars and in the ruthless expropriation of Irish Catholics' lands by ambitious Roundheads. She also tells him the strange tale of an immortally young ancestor, the Wanderer. Thus from the beginning Melmoth is closely linked to the interrelated evils of sect and faction, and their exploitation by greedy and ambitious men. The next phase of the narration, the tale of Stanton, a Restoration Englishman whose story survives in a crumbling manuscript, carries these themes farther—in the character of a corrupt inquisitorial priest who has arrogated to himself the divine power of identifying evil, in the ironic contrast between the statue of a compassionate Virgin and a tapestry which depicts the cruelties practiced upon infidel Moors by a savage Christianity, and in the story of Stanton's unjust confinement in Bedlam by a greedy relative.

In Stanton's tale a paradigm of the action and religious theme is provided by the Bedlam sequence, a "nightmare" symbolization of the insanity of factional and sectarian fanaticism that has turned the Christian world into a madhouse. There Stanton finds a Puritan weaver driven insane by the terrors of Hugh Peters' sermons; a loyalist tailor who went mad with joy at the burning of Cromwell's Rump parliament; and an independent preacher who by day damns the errors of every other sect and by night wallows in unspeakable blasphemies. Indeed, Stanton first begins to suspect the character of the surroundings into which he has been decoyed when he finds a manuscript written by another inmate outlining a project for converting Mohammedans by torture and extortion. The Bedlam sequence, in short, depicts the normal world of sectarian and factional violence as insane, and suggests the sense of horrified entrapment felt by a "mere honest man" in a world gone mad.

William F. Axton, "Introduction," *Melmoth the Wanderer* (Lincoln: University of Nebraska Press, 1961), pp. xv–xvi

---

ROBERT KIELY   In the dedication to *The Milesian Chief*, Maturin characterizes his talent as "that of darkening the gloomy, and deepening the sad; of painting life in extremes, and representing those struggles of passion when the soul trembles on the verge of the unlawful and the unhallowed." Like Lewis, he was fascinated by extremes of freedom and repression and the various kinds of anguish which they caused body and mind. But even more than was the case for Lewis or Beckford, painful subjects seem to have stimulated his imagination into an extraordinary state of productivity. According to one of his own characters, "in situations of peril, the imagination is unhappily fertile." This seems to have been true of Maturin's imagination, which initiates "peril" and then divides and multiplies it like a Shakespearian pun. The structure of *Melmoth the Wanderer*, a series of narrations within narrations—often compared with a nest of Chinese boxes—defies conventional chronological sequence and replaces it with obsessive variations on the single theme of human misery. It is like a gruesome contest among the sufferers to tell the worst tale of woe. Though the speakers are different, their narratives are given unity by a common pattern of torment and by the presence of the wraithlike Melmoth, who usually enters at a critical moment to tempt the sufferer into despair.

Though none of the main characters does yield to despair, almost all seem to enjoy lingering close to the edge and analyzing the various moods, emotions, and thoughts produced by enduring the nearly unendurable. While Maturin has his narrators discuss the effects of pain on the human personality, he implicitly suggests much about its uses as a subject for the artist. One of the points first and most often made is that extreme suffering reduces human nature to its essential character, undisguised by artifice and convention. A particularly vicious monk describes the effects of hunger on young lovers: "One physical want, one severe and abrupt lesson from the shrivelled lip of necessity, is worth all the logic of the empty wretches who have presumed to prate it . . . It silences in a second all the feeble sophistry of *conventional* life." His contention is, of course, that human nature is basically selfish, that comfort is a condition of love, and that the young couple's dying bitterly and apart proves it. Maturin himself is not satisfied with so simple a theory and, in fact, presents other examples of love which strengthens under duress. But that pain provides a release from conventional life he appears to acknowledge. It frees the artist from having to portray his characters in terms of their orientation to external custom, but it challenges him too, because it tests whether or not he has the power to portray anything else.

Robert Kiely, *The Romantic Novel in England* (Cambridge, MA: Harvard University Press), pp. 190–91

CORAL ANN HOWELLS Maturin's fascination with the supernatural and his consistent preoccupation with dread, fear and terror would make him a Gothic writer by any definition, but the imaginative range of his psychological speculations and the minutiae of his emotional analyses give him a superiority over those novelists who used the techniques of sensationalism with no other purpose than to shock or frighten their readers. As a practitioner of the craft, Maturin was perfectly aware that the spell of Gothic fiction lay in its power to arouse certain feelings in its readers and he is quite explicit about the compulsion that terror in art exerts ⟨. . .⟩ He used traditional Gothic techniques in a conscious attempt to stimulate his readers into a state of total empathy with his characters but he also used such techniques as instruments for exploration into hitherto uncharted areas of psychology. As in those other romantic novels, Mary Shelley's *Frankenstein* and James Hogg's *Confessions of a Justified Sinner*, Gothic machinery becomes in Maturin's hands a metaphorical language for describing new insights into human suffering and conflict. ⟨. . .⟩

⟨. . .⟩ the imaginative impact of the book (*Melmoth the Wanderer*) comes not from the idea of salvation and damnation but from the description of human responses to fear, terror and oppression. All Maturin's tales are about human beings struggling for survival in a world where man's rôle is that of a victim, tormented by external agents both human and supernatural, and always in danger of betrayal by his own passions and instincts. 'What is Man?', asks Maturin, fascinated by the duality of man's nature, rather as Hamlet marvels that man so capable of love and goodness is also capable of evil and agony, caught between beauty and horror, suspended between Heaven and Hell. The paradox of the human condition is the real area of Maturin's exploration, which has as its starting-point a desperate faith in God's mercy as the only possible means of man's salvation. Given his tormented awareness, it is no wonder that his most powerful literary effects are those of terror and horror, and that the main character is the agent of moral chaos, himself a prey to monstrous spiritual despair.

Coral Ann Howells, "C. R. Maturin, *Melmoth the Wanderer*," *Love, Mystery, and Misery: Feeling in Gothic Fiction* (London: Athlone Press, 1978), pp. 133, 137

WILLIAM PATRICK DAY   Melmoth, who represents the demonic in the novel, is in fact a symbol of humanity. He wanders the earth, one of the living dead, seeking someone who will join him in his rejection of God and his power. As we see in the Indian's Tale, in which Melmoth falls in love with Immalee, to pursue damnation and human love are essentially the same thing. Melmoth's quest to damn souls is also a quest for a fully human world, independent of God, sustaining existence purely through human love and power. Only God makes the terrible suffering of the various characters Melmoth tempts meaningful; Melmoth asks them to substitute pleasure and satisfaction in the human world, the physical world, for the prospect of salvation after death. Melmoth is a very enlightenment demon and comes to represent, not the devil or the principle of evil as it exists in the world of the numinous, but rather the search for a fully human alternative to a spiritual reality whose essential manifestation for human beings is pain. Melmoth is truly a Gothic being, rather than a supernatural one, existing in limbo between the purely physical and the purely spiritual. This is the meaning of his peculiar state beyond death in the human world, with power over time and space but still existing in terms of time and space. The reality represented by Melmoth is what really fires Maturin's imagination. The irony of Maturin's attempt to make the case for God is that while he can portray the Job-like suffering and excruciating horrors undergone by the various victims in the novel, he is unable to make God's restoration and the prospect of salvation in any way convincing. Both the physical world—the world of Spain, the ex-Jesuits, and the Inquisition— and the spiritual world are, in *Melmoth,* simply the sources of pain and suffering.

> William Patrick Day, *In the Circles of Fear and Desire: A Study of Gothic Fantasy* (Chicago: University of Chicago Press, 1985), pp. 39–40

PATRICIA COUGHLIN   Maturin's Melmoth is a Faust-like figure who has sold his soul for arcane and forbidden knowledge; he ranges freely over time and space, seeking a misfortunate victim on whom he may prevail to swap places with him, so that he may shed his monstrous role and cease his wanderings. The tone of Maturin's work is serious, passionate, devastatingly cynical and sardonic. In its representation of repressive institutions—madhouse, monastery, Inquisition dungeon, Cathlic Church—it contains a strong element of socio-intellectual critique, somewhat in the Enlightenment manner. It concentrates on generalized questioning of the role of religions and, by implication, of laws and government, but without applying itself specifically to any contemporary social system in a realistic manner. This sweeping attack is mounted by Melmoth the Wanderer himself, who is a figure of great power and conviction: the demonic quality of his character and attributes, the agony of his solitary existence, renders him heroic, and gives the book an emotional power and tempestuousness which constitutes archetypal representation of the spirit of Romanticism. Melmoth fails to find a dupe upon whom he can visit his fate, and thus passes at the end to violent and mysterious destruction. It is impossible not to feel the Promethean grandeur of Melmoth, and/or to identify in him, rather than in mild orthodoxy, the real centre of energy in the book.

Patricia Coughlin, "The Recycling of Melmoth: 'A Very German Story,'" *Literary Interrelations: Ireland, England and the World*, ed. Wolfgang Zach and Heinz Kosok (Tübingen: Narr, 1987), Vol. 2, pp. 181–82

Bibliography

Fatal Revenge; or, The Family of Montorio: A Romance. 1807. 3 vols.

The Wild Irish Boy. 1808. 3 vols.

The Milesian Chief: A Romance. 1812. 4 vols.

Bertram; or, The Castle of St. Aldobrand. 1816.

Manuel. 1817.

Women; or, Pour et Contre: A Tale. 1818. 3 vols.

Fredolfo. 1819.

Sermons. 1819.

Melmoth the Wanderer: A Tale. 1820. 4 vols.

The Albigenses: A Romance. 1824. 4 vols.

Five Sermons on the Errors of the Roman Catholic Church. 1824.

The Correspondence of Sir Walter Scott and Charles Robert Maturin. Ed. Fannie E. Ratchford and William H. McCarthy, Jr. 1937.

Edgar Allan Poe
1809–1849

EDGAR ALLAN POE was born Edgar Poe in Boston on January 19, 1809, the son of traveling actors. Shortly after his birth his father disappeared, and in 1811 his mother died. He was taken into the home of John Allan (from whom Poe derived his middle name), a wealthy merchant living in Richmond, Virginia. In 1815 the Allans took Poe to England, where he attended the Manor House School at Stoke Newington, later the setting for his story "William Wilson." Poe returned to Richmond with the Allans in 1820. In 1826 he became engaged to Elmira Royster, whose parents broke off the engagement. That fall he entered the University of Virginia. At first he excelled in his studies, but in December 1826 John Allan took him out of school after Poe accumulated considerable gambling debts that Allan refused to pay. Unable to honor these debts himself, Poe fled to Boston, where he enlisted in the army under the name of Edgar A. Perry.

Poe began his literary career with the anonymous publication, at his own expense, of *Tamerlane and Other Poems* (1827), which because of its small print run and poor distribution has become one of the rarest volumes in American literary history. In 1829 Poe was honorably discharged from the army. Later that year he published a second collection of verse, *Al Aaraaf, Tamerlane, and Minor Poems*, containing revisions of poems from his first collection as well as new material. This volume was well received, leading to a tentative reconciliation with John Allan. In 1830 Poe entered West Point, but after another falling out with John Allan, who withdrew his financial support, Poe deliberately got himself expelled in 1831 through flagrant neglect of his duties. Nonetheless, he managed before leaving to gather enough cadet subscriptions to bring out his third collection of verse, *Poems* (1831). In 1833 Poe's final attempt at reconciliation was rejected by the ailing John Allan, who died in 1834 without mentioning Poe in his will.

In the meantime Poe's literary career was progressing. Having settled in Baltimore after leaving West Point, Poe won a prize in 1833 from the *Baltimore Saturday Visitor* for one of his first short stories, "MS. Found in a

Bottle." In 1835 he moved to Richmond to become editor of the recently established *Southern Literary Messenger*, which thrived under his direction. In 1836 Poe felt financially secure enough to marry Virginia Clemm, his fourteen-year-old cousin, but later that year he was fired from the *Messenger*, partly because of what appeared to be chronic alcoholism. In fact, Poe seems to have suffered from a physical ailment that rendered him so sensitive to alcohol that a single drink could induce a drunken state. Poe was later an editor of *Burton's Gentleman's Magazine* (1839–40), *Graham's Magazine* (1841–42), and the *Broadway Journal* (1845–46). In this capacity he wrote many important reviews—notably of Hawthorne, Dickens, and Macaulay—and occasionally gained notoriety for the severity and acerbity of his judgments. In particular he wrote a series of polemics against Henry Wadsworth Longfellow, whom he accused of plagiarism.

Meanwhile Poe continued to write fiction voluminously. His longest tale, *The Narrative of Arthur Gordon Pym* (apparently unfinished), is dated 1838 but appeared in the summer of 1837; *Tales of the Grotesque and Arabesque*, containing "The Fall of The House of Usher" and other important stories, was published in 1840; and *Tales* appeared in 1845. As a fiction writer Poe wrote not only tales of the macabre and the supernatural ("The Pit and the Pendulum," "The Black Cat," "The Tell-Tale Heart," "Ligeia") but also many humorous or parodic pieces ("King Pest," "Some Words with a Mummy"), prose poems ("Silence—a Fable," "Shadow—a Parable"), and what are generally considered the first true detective stories ("The Murders in the Rue Morgue," "The Mystery of Marie Rogêt," "The Gold-Bug," "The Purloined Letter," and others).

In 1844 Poe moved to New York, and in the following year achieved international fame with his poem "The Raven," published in *The Raven and Other Poems* (1845). In 1847 Poe's wife Virginia, who had been seriously ill since 1842, died, leaving him desolate. For the few remaining years of his life he helped support himself by delivering a series of public lectures, including "The Poetic Principle" (published posthumously in 1850). Among his publications were the philosophical treatise *Eureka: A Prose Poem* (1848) and the lyric "Annabel Lee" (1849). His *Marginalia* was published serially from 1844 to 1849. After his wife's death Poe had several romances, including an affair with the Rhode Island poet Sarah Helen Whitman, and in 1849 he became engaged for a second time to Elmira Royster (then Mrs. Shelton). Before they could be married, however, Poe died in Baltimore on October 7, 1849, under mysterious circumstances.

In spite of the fact that Poe's memory was damned by his posthumous editor Rufus Wilmot Griswold, who propagated many long-standing myths about his alcoholism and misanthropy, Poe was one of the first American authors to be widely appreciated in Europe. He had a great influence on the development of French symbolism, much of his work being translated by Baudelaire and Mallarmé. In England he was greatly admired by such figures as Rossetti, Swinburne, and Wilde. His influence on the horror field is incalculable: because of his keen sense of form (he was the virtual inventor of the short story), his acute understanding of abnormal psychology, and his vivid and atmospheric style, Poe single-handedly laid the groundwork for the modern tale of horror, making possible the work of Arthur Machen, Algernon Blackwood, H. P. Lovecraft, and nearly all other writers of weird fiction.

▨ Critical Extracts

EDGAR ALLAN POE   The epithets "Grotesque" and "Arabesque" will be found to indicate with sufficient precision the prevalent tenor of the tales here published. But from the fact that, during a period of some two or three years, I have written five-and-twenty short stories whose general character may be so briefly defined, it cannot be fairly inferred—at all events it is not truly inferred—that I have, for this species of writing, any inordinate, or indeed any peculiar taste or prepossession. I may have written with an eye to this republication in volume form, and may, therefore, have desired to preserve, as far as a certain point, a certain unity of design. This is, indeed, the fact; and it may even happen that, in this manner, I shall never compose anything again. I speak of these things here, because I am led to think it is this prevalence of the "Arabesque" in my serious tales, which has induced one or two critics to tax me, in all friendliness, with what they have been pleased to term "Germanism" and gloom. The charge is in bad taste, and the grounds of the accusation have not been sufficiently considered. Let us admit, for the moment, that the "phantasy-pieces" now given *are* Germanic, or what not. Then Germanism is "the vein" for the time being. To-morrow I may be anything but German, as yesterday I was everything else. These many pieces are yet one book. My friends would be quite as wise in taxing an astronomer with too much astronomy, or an ethical author with treating too largely of morals. But the truth is that, with a single exception, there is no one of these stories in which the scholar should recognise the distinctive features of that species of pseudo-horror which we are taught to call Germanic, for no better reason than that some of the secondary names of German literature have become identified with its folly. If in many of my productions terror has been the thesis, I maintain that terror is not of Germany, but of the soul,—that I have deduced this terror only from its legitimate sources, and urged it only to its legitimate results.

Edgar Allan Poe, "Preface," *Tales of the Grotesque and Arabesque* (1840), *Collected Works*, ed. Thomas Ollive Mabbott et al. (Cambridge, MA: Harvard University Press, 1978), Vol. 2, p. 473

JAMES RUSSELL LOWELL   In his tales, Mr. Poe has chosen to exhibit his power chiefly in that dim region which stretches from the very utmost limits of the probable into the weird confines of superstition and unreality. He combines in a very remarkable manner two faculties which are seldom found united; a power of influencing the mind of the reader by the impalpable shadows of mystery, and a minuteness of detail which does not leave a pin or a button unnoticed. Both are, in truth, the natural results of the predominating quality of his mind, to which we have before alluded, analysis. It is this which distinguishes the artist. His mind at once reaches forward to the effect to be produced. Having resolved to bring about certain emotions in the reader, he makes all subordinate parts tend strictly to the common centre. Even his mystery is mathematical to his own mind. To him x is a known quantity all along. In any picture that he paints, he understands the chemical properties of all his colors. However vague some of his figures may seem, however formless the shadows, to him the outline is as clear and distinct as that of a geometrical diagram. For this reason Mr. Poe has no sympathy with *Mysticism*. The mystic dwells *in* the mystery, is enveloped with it; it colors all his thoughts; it affects his optic nerve especially, and the commonest things get a rainbow edging from it. Mr. Poe, on the other hand, is a spectator *ab extra*. He analyzes, he dissects, he watches

> —with an eye serene,
> The very pulse of the machine,

for such it practically is to him, with wheels and cogs and piston-rods all working to produce a certain end. It is this that makes him so good a critic. Nothing baulks him, or throws him off the scent, *except now and then a prejudice*.

This analyzing tendency of his mind balances the poetical, and, by giving him the patience to be minute, enables him to throw a wonderful reality into his most unreal fancies. A monomania he paints with great power. He loves to dissect these cancers of the mind, and to trace all the subtle ramifications of its roots. In raising images of horror, also, he has a strange success; conveying to us sometimes by a dusky hint some terrible *doubt* which is the secret of all horror. He leaves to imagination the task of finishing the picture, a task to which only she is competent.

James Russell Lowell, "Edgar Allan Poe" (1845), *Complete Works of Edgar Allan Poe*, ed. James A. Harrison (New York: Thomas Y. Crowell Co., 1902), Vol. 1, pp. 377–79

RUFUS WILMOT GRISWOLD   He had made up his mind upon the numberless complexities of the social world, and the whole system was with him an imposture. This conviction gave a direction to his shrewd and naturally unamiable character. Still though he regarded society as composed of villains, the sharpness of his intellect was not of that kind which enabled him to cope with villainy, while it continually caused him overshots, to fail of the success of honesty. He was in many respects like Francis Vivian in Bulwer's novel of the *Caxtons*. Passion, in him, comprehended many of the worst emotions which militate against human happiness. You could not contradict him, but you raised quick choler; you could not speak of wealth, but his cheek paled with gnawing envy. The astonishing natural advantage of this poor boy—his beauty, his readiness, the daring spirit that breathed around him like a fiery atmosphere—had raised his constitutional self-confidence into an arrogance that turned his very claims to admiration into prejudice against him. Irascible, envious—bad enough, but not the worst, for these salient angles were all varnished over with a cold repellant cynicism while his passions vented themselves in sneers. There seemed to him no moral susceptibility; and what was more remarkable in a proud nature, little or nothing of the true point of honour. He had, to a morbid excess, that desire to rise which is vulgarly called ambition, but no wish for the esteem or the love of his species; only the hard wish to succeed—not shine, not serve—succeed, that he might have the right to despise a world which galled his self-conceit.

Rufus Wilmot Griswold, [Obituary] (1849), *Complete Works of Edgar Allan Poe*, ed. James A. Harrison (New York: Thomas Y. Crowell Co., 1902), Vol. 1, pp. 356–57

CHARLES BAUDELAIRE   In Edgar Poe there is no tiresome snivelling; but everywhere and at all times an indefatigable enthusiasm in seeking the ideal. He has a passion for science like Balzac, who died grieved perhaps at not being a pure scientist. He has written a work called *The Conchologist's First Book* which I have forgotten to mention. He has, like

conquerors and philosophers, a compelling yearning for unity; he combines
the spiritual with the physical. It could be said that he seeks to apply to
literature the processes of philosophy, and to philosophy the methods of
algebra. In this constant ascension toward the infinite, one becomes somewhat breathless. The air in this literature is as rarefied as that of a laboratory.
In it can be observed continually the glorification of the will applying itself
to induction and to analysis. It seems that Poe wants to usurp the role of
the prophets and to claim for himself a monopoly on rational explanation.
Thus the landscapes which sometimes serve as a background for his febrile
compositions are pale as phantoms. Poe, who scarcely seemed to share the
passions of other men, sketches trees and clouds which are like the trees
and clouds of a dream, or rather which resemble his strange characters and
which are agitated like them by a supernatural and convulsive shudder.

Charles Baudelaire, "Edgar Allan Poe: His Life and Works" (1852), *Baudelaire on Poe*, tr. Lois and Francis E. Hyslop, Jr. (State College, PA: Bald Eagle Press, 1952), p. 80

SARAH HELEN WHITMAN   His proud reserve, his profound
melancholy, his unworldliness—may we not say his *unearthliness* of nature—
made his character one very difficult of comprehension to the casual observer.
The complexity of his intellect, its incalculable resources, and his masterly
control of those resources when brought into requisition for the illustration
of some favorite theme, or cherished creation, led to the current belief that
its action was purely arbitrary—that he could write without emotion or
earnestness at the deliberate dictation of the will. A certain class of his
writings undeniably exhibits the faculties of ingenuity and invention in a
prominent and distinctive light. But it must not be forgotten that there
was another phase of his mind—one not less distinctive and characteristic
of his genius—which manifested itself in creations of a totally different
order and expression. It can hardly have escaped the notice of the most
careless reader that certain ideas exercised over him the power of fascination.
They return, again and again, in his stories and poems and seem like the
utterances of a mind possessed with thoughts, emotions, and images of which
the will and the understanding take little cognizance. In the delineation of
these, his language often acquires a power and pregnancy eluding all attempts
at analysis. It is then that by a few miraculous words he evokes emotional
states or commands pictorial effects which live forever in the memory and
form a part of its eternal inheritance. No analysis can dissect—no criticism
can disenchant them.

Sarah Helen Whitman, *Edgar Poe and His Critics* (1860; rpt. New Brunswick, NJ: Rutgers University Press, 1949), pp. 57–58

ROBERT LOUIS STEVENSON   Nor should the reader be
surprised if a criticism upon Poe is mostly negative, and rather suggests new
doubts than resolves those already existing; for it is Poe's merit to carry
people away, and it is his besetting sin that he wants altogether such
scrupulous honesty as guides and restrains the finished artist. He was, let
us say it with all sorrow, not conscientious. Hunger was ever at his door,
and he had too imperious a desire for what we call nowadays the sensational
in literature. And thus the critic (if he be more conscientious than the man
he is criticising) dare not greatly praise lest he should be thought to condone
all that is unscrupulous and tinsel in these wonderful stories. They are to
be praised by him in one way only—by recommending those that are least
objectionable. If anyone wishes to be excited, let him read, under favourable
circumstances, "The Gold Bug," "The Descent into the Maelström," "The
Cask of Amontillado," "The Oval Portrait," and the three stories about C.
Auguste Dupin, the philosophical detective. If he should then desire to read
more, he may go on, but warily; there are trap-doors and spring-guns in
these two volumes, there are gins and pitfalls; and the precipitate reader
may stumble unawares upon some nightmare not easily to be forgotten.

> Robert Louis Stevenson, [Review of *The Works of Edgar Allan Poe*, Vols. I and II,
> ed. John H. Ingram], *Academy*, 2 January 1875, p. 2

JOHN MACKINNON ROBERTSON   As a tale-teller, then,
he is to be summed up as having worked in his special line with the same
extraordinary creative energy and intellectual mastery as distinguish his
verse; giving us narratives "of imagination all compact," yet instinct with
life in every detail and particle, no matter how strange, how aloof from
common things, may be the theme. As Dr. Landa remarks, he has been the
first story-writer to exploit the field of science in the department of the
marvellous; and he has further been the first to exploit the marvellous in
morbid psychology with scientific art. These are achievements as commanding, as significant of genius, as the most distinguished success in any of the
commoner walks of fiction; and a contrary view is reasonably to be described
as a fanatical development of an artistic doctrine perfectly sound and of
vital importance in its right application, but liable, like other cults, to incur
reaction when carried to extremes. After *The Idiot Boy* and *The Prelude*
came *The Lady of Shalott* and the *Idylls of the King;* after Trollope came King
Romance again; and even if Poe were eclipsed for a time, posterity would
still be to reckon with.

> John Mackinnon Robertson, "Poe" (1885), *New Essays towards a Critical Method*
> (London: John Lane/The Bodley Head, 1897), pp. 103–4

LEWIS E. GATES   The world that Poe's genuinely fantastic tales take us into has the burnish, the glow, the visionary radiance of the world of Romantic poetry; it is as luxuriantly unreal, too, as phantasmagoric—though it lacks the palpitating, buoyant loveliness of the nature that such poets as Shelley reveal, and is somewhat enamelled or metallic in its finish. Its glow and burnish come largely from the concreteness of Poe's imagination, from his inveterate fondness for sensations, for colour, for light, for luxuriant vividness of detail. Poe had the tingling senses of the genuine poet, senses that vibrated like delicate silver wire to every impact. He was an amateur of sensations and loved to lose himself in the O *Altitudo* of a perfume or a musical note. He pored over his sensations and refined upon them, and felt to the core of his heart the peculiar thrill that darted from each. He had seventy times seven colours in his emotional rainbow, and was swift to fancy the evanescent hue of feeling that might spring from every sight or sound—from the brazen note, for example, of the clock in "The Masque of the Red Death," from "the slender stems" of the ebony and silver trees in "Eleonora," or from the "large and luminous orbs" of Ligeia's eyes. Out of the vast mass of these vivid sensations—"passion-wingèd ministers of thought"—Poe shaped and fashioned the world in which his romances confine us, a world that is, therefore, scintillating and burnished and vibrant, quite unlike the world in Hawthorne's tales, which is woven out of dusk and moonlight.

Yet, curiously enough, this intense brilliancy of surface does not tend to exorcise mystery, strangeness, terror from Poe's world, or to transfer his stories into the region of everyday fact. Poe is a conjurer who does not need to have the lights turned down. The effects that he is most prone to aim at are, of course, the shivers of awe, crispings of the nerves, shuddering thrills that come from a sudden, overwhelming sense of something uncanny, abnormal, ghastly, lurking in the heart of life. And these nervous perturbations are even more powerfully excited by those of his stories that, like "Eleonora" and "Ligeia," have a lustrous finish, than by sketches that, like "Shadow" and "Silence," deal with twilight lands and half-visualized regions. In "The Masque of the Red Death," in "The Fall of the House of Usher," and in "A Descent into the Maelström," the details of incident and background flash themselves on our imaginations with almost painful distinctness.

The terror in Poe's tales is not the terror of the child that cannot see in the dark, but the terror of diseased nerves and morbid imaginations, that see with dreadful visionary vividness and feel a mortal pang. Poe is a past master of the moods of diseased mental life, and in the interests of some one or other of these semi-hysterical moods many of his most uncannily prevailing romances are written. They are prose-poems that realize for us

such half-frenetic glimpses of the world as madmen have; and *suggest* in us
for the moment the breathless, haggard mood of the victim of hallucinations.

Lewis E. Gates, "Edgar Allan Poe," *Studies and Appreciations* (New York: Macmillan, 1900), pp. 112–14

D. H. LAWRENCE   Moralists have always wondered helplessly
why Poe's "morbid" tales need have been written. They need to be written
because old things need to die and disintegrate, because the old white psyche
has to be gradually broken down before anything else can come to pass.

Man must be stripped even of himself. And it is a painful, sometimes a
ghastly process.

Poe had a pretty bitter doom. Doomed to seethe down his soul in a great
continuous convulsion of disintegration, and doomed to register the process.
And then doomed to be abused for it, when he had performed some of the
bitterest tasks of human experience, that can be asked of a man. Necessary
tasks, too. For the human soul must suffer its own disintegration, *consciously*,
if ever it is to survive.

But Poe is rather a scientist than an artist. He is reducing his own self
as a scientist reduces a salt in a crucible. It is an almost chemical analysis
of the soul and consciousness. Whereas in true art there is always the double
rhythm of creating and destroying.

This is why Poe calls his things "tales." They are a concatenation of
cause and effect.

His best pieces, however, are not tales. They are more. They are ghastly
stories of the human soul in its disruptive throes.

Moreover, they are "love" stories.

"Ligeia" and "The Fall of the House of Usher" are really love stories.

D. H. Lawrence, "Edgar Allan Poe," *Studies in Classic American Literature* (New York: Thomas Seltzer, 1923), pp. 93–94

H. P. LOVECRAFT   Before Poe the bulk of weird writers had
worked largely in the dark; without an understanding of the psychological
basis of the horror appeal, and hampered by more or less of conformity to
certain empty literary conventions such as the happy ending, virtue
rewarded, and in general a hollow moral didacticism, acceptance of popular
standards and values, and striving of the author to obtrude his own emotions
into the story and take sides with the partisans of the majority's artificial
ideas. Poe, on the other hand, perceived the essential impersonality of the
real artist; and knew that the function of creative fiction is merely to express

and interpret events and sensations as they are, regardless of how they tend or what they prove—good or evil, attractive or repulsive, stimulating or depressing—with the author always acting as a vivid and detached chronicler rather than as a teacher, sympathiser, or vendor of opinion. He saw clearly that all phases of life and thought are equally eligible as subject-matter for the artist, and being inclined by temperament to strangeness and gloom, decided to be the interpreter of those powerful feelings and frequent happenings which attend pain rather than pleasure, decay rather than growth, terror rather than tranquillity, and which are fundamentally averse or indifferent to the tastes and traditional outward sentiments of mankind, and to the health, sanity, and normal expansive welfare of the species.

Poe's spectres thus acquired a convincing malignity possessed by none of their predecessors, and established a new standard of realism in the annals of literary horror. The impersonal and artistic intent, moreover, was aided by a scientific attitude not often found before; whereby Poe studied the human mind rather than the usages of Gothic fiction, and worked with an analytical knowledge of terror's true sources which doubled the force of his narratives and emancipated him from all the absurdities inherent in merely conventional shudder-coining. This example having been set, later authors were naturally forced to conform to it in order to compete at all; so that in this way a definite change began to affect the main stream of macabre writing. Poe, too, set a fashion in consummate craftsmanship; and although today some of his own work seems slightly melodramatic and unsophisticated, we can constantly trace his influence in such things as the maintenance of a single mood and achievement of a single impression in a tale, and the rigorous paring down of incidents to such as have a direct bearing on the plot and will figure prominently in the climax. Truly may it be said that Poe invented the short story in its present form. His elevation of disease, perversity, and decay to the level of artistically expressible themes was likewise infinitely far-reaching in effect; for avidly seized, sponsored, and intensified by his eminent French admirer Charles Pierre Baudelaire, it became the nucleus of the principal aesthetic movements in France, thus making Poe in a sense the father of the Decadents and the Symbolists.

Poet and critic by nature and supreme attainment, logician and philosopher by taste and mannerism, Poe was by no means immune from defects and affectations. His pretence to profound and obscure scholarship, his blundering ventures in stilted and laboured pseudo-humour, and his often vitriolic bursts of critical prejudice must all be recognised and forgiven. Beyond and above them, and dwarfing them to insignificance, was a master's vision of the terror that stalks about and within us, and the worm that

writhes and slavers in the hideously close abyss. Penetrating to every festering
horror in the gaily painted mockery called existence, and in the solemn
masquerade called human thought and feeling, that vision had power to
project itself in blackly magical crystallisations and transmutations; till there
bloomed in the sterile America of the 'thirties and 'forties such a moon-
nourished garden of gorgeous poison fungi as not even the nether slope of
Saturn might boast. Verses and tales alike sustain the burthen of cosmic
panic. The raven whose noisome beak pierces the heart, the ghouls that
toll iron bells in pestilential steeples, the vault of Ulalume in the black
October night, the shocking spires and domes under the sea, the "wild,
weird clime that lieth, sublime, out of Space—out of Time"—all these
things and more leer at us amidst maniacal rattlings in the seething nightmare
of the poetry. And in the prose there yawn for us the very jaws of the pit—
inconceivable abnormalities slyly hinted into a horrible half-knowledge by
words whose innocence we scarcely doubt till the cracked tension of the
speaker's hollow voice bids us fear their nameless implications; daemoniac
patterns and presences slumbering noxiously till waked for one phobic second
into a shrieking revelation that cackles itself to sudden madness or explodes
in memorable and cataclysmic echoes. A Witches' Sabbath of horror flinging
off decorous robes is flashed before us—a sight the more monstrous because
of the scientific skill with which every particular is marshalled and brought
into an easy apparent relation to the known gruesomeness of material life.

H. P. Lovecraft, "Supernatural Horror in Literature" (1927), *Dagon and Other Macabre
Tales*, ed. S. T. Joshi (Sauk City, WI: Arkham House, 1986), pp. 395–97

EDWARD H. DAVIDSON   ⟨. . .⟩ we might define the Poesque
version of horror as that region or mysterious middle ground where the
normal, rational faculties of thinking and choice have, for reasons beyond
knowing, been suspended; ethical and religious beliefs are still the portion
of men, but are powerless to function. All power of choice and all sense of
direction have been lost; in fact, they have been so long lost that the
nightmare world of presumed reality obeys no laws of reason or stability. It
is a highly complex metaphysical condition wherein the constants of heaven
and hell are fixed at their opposite polarity, but between them is the vast
region wherein the human will is situated and is powerless to effect any
variation of its own existence. It is a realm where the will cannot exist,
not because it never had an existence but because it somehow lost its power
to function. It is a world like that in "The City in the Sea": moral man
once lived in that long-ago world, but now everything is shadowy and

atrophied. In such a horror world men are moral mutes or paralytics; they are like Roderick Usher, the "Last of the Visigoths," at the very end of a long line of ethically directed ancestors. Horror is, then, the urgent need for moral knowledge and direction—and its total lack. The characters in such a situation can only dream of a condition which once existed but which they would never be able to follow, even if they were able to recapture it. They are like the creatures in Poe's most complete allegorical presentations, those in the apocalyptic visions like "The Conversation of Eiros and Charmion" (1839) and "The Colloquy of Monos and Una" (1841): they are the victims of an Apocalypse which has had no perceptible reason for being.

Yet even the lack or the negation of a moral principle had to be based on some system of good and evil. A Christian view, such as Hawthorne propounded, conceived that sin entered the world with man and remains with man forever, while nature exists outside either in a dualism with man or in an implacable state of indifference to him. The naturalism of a Melville or Mark Twain, to draw a brief contrast, found the basis for evil not in man but in the primal order of nature and at the center of the universe itself: man is thereby lodged in a universe of evil, and his tragedy is that he alone of all forms of life can both know and strive to meliorate his condition. This naturalism, as it was with Twain, can be driven far enough to exonerate man of all blame or consequence for the rigidly deterministic order.

With Poe we are hardly concerned with "evil" at all, insofar as evil might be considered inherent in man or in the phenomenal order; in a sense, his one prescription for evil is its absence: never to know evil nor to have been engaged in any moral struggle is the condition of horror in which the Poe protagonist must exist. In such a nightmare world all the prescriptions for evil and good are matters of being from which man has moved or which has long passed from the earth. Only when these protagonists are, like Michaelangelo in "Al Aaraaf" or the strange creatures in "Silence" or "The Colloquy of Monos and Una," on, as it were, the "other side" can they at last realize what it was they never knew.

Edward H. Davidson, *Poe: A Critical Study* (Cambridge, MA: Harvard University Press, 1957), pp. 122–23.

RICHARD WILBUR   Like many romantic poets, Poe identified imagination with dream. Where Poe differed from other romantic poets was in the literalness and absoluteness of the identification, and in the clinical precision with which he observed the phenomena of dream, carefully distin-

guishing the various states through which the mind passes on its way to
sleep. A large number of Poe's stories derive their very structure from this
sequence of mental states: "MS. Found in a Bottle," to give but one example,
is an allegory of the mind's voyage from the waking world into the world
of dreams, with each main step of the narrative symbolizing the passage of
the mind from one state to another—from wakefulness to reverie, from
reverie to the hypnagogic state, from the hypnagogic state to the deep
dream. The departure of the narrator's ship from Batavia represents the
mind's withdrawal from the waking world; the drowning of the captain and
all but one of the crew represents the growing solitude of reverie; when the
narrator is transferred by collision from a real ship to a phantom ship, we
are to understand that he has passed from reverie, a state in which reality
and dream exist in a kind of equilibrium, into the free fantasy of the
hypnagogic state. And when the phantom ship makes its final plunge into
the whirlpool, we are to understand that the narrator's mind has gone over
the brink of sleep and descended into dreams.

What I am saying by means of this example is that the scenes and
situations of Poe's tales are always concrete representations of states of mind.
If we bear in mind Poe's fundamental plot—the effort of the poetic soul to
escape all consciousness of the world in dream—we soon recognize the
significance of certain scenic or situational motifs which turn up in story
after story. The most important of these recurrent motifs is that of *enclosure*
or *circumscription*; perhaps the latter term is preferable, because it is Poe's
own word, and because Poe's enclosures are so often more or less circular
in form. The heroes of Poe's tales and poems are violently circumscribed
by whirlpools, or peacefully circumscribed by cloud-capped Paradisal valleys;
they float upon circular pools ringed in by steep flowering hillsides; they
dwell on islands, or voyage to them; we find Poe's heroes also in coffins,
in the cabs of balloons, or hidden away in the holds of ships; and above
all we find them sitting alone in the claustral and richly furnished rooms
of remote and mouldering mansions. ⟨. . .⟩

What does it mean that Poe's heroes are invariably enclosed or circumscribed? The answer is simple: circumscription, in Poe's tales, means the
exclusion from consciousness of the so-called real world of time and reason
and physical fact; it means the isolation of the poetic soul in visionary
reverie or trance. When we find one of Poe's characters in a remote valley,
or a claustral room, we know that he is in the process of dreaming his way
out of the world.

        Richard Wilbur, "The House of Poe," *Anniversary Lectures 1959* by Robert Hillyer,
        Richard Wilbur, and Cleanth Brooks (Washington, DC: Reference Department,
        Library of Congress, 1959), pp. 24–25

DANIEL HOFFMAN   It is self-evident that Poe's most impressive works do in fact derive from four traditions of popular fiction: the Gothic horror story, the tale of exploration, the science-fiction story, and the detective tale. It is also true that Poe so rationalized the detective story and so boldly adapted the appearance of scientificism in fiction that modern practitioners of these popular arts regard him as their virtual inventor.

The Gothic conventions inherited from Mrs. Radcliffe, Walpole, Beckford, Hoffmann, Tieck, and the contributors to magazines like *Blackwood's* were used by Poe's contemporaries for purposes other than his. Wilkie Collins exploited them for their inherent sensational effects. Hawthorne moralized them. Dickens, and later James, interlaced such Gothic themes as the haunted house, the ancestral curse, the ghost, the double who represents the unlived life, with a realistic imitation of widely varied characters and situations in a believable society. Such novels as theirs were as far beyond Poe's capacities as they were foreign to his intentions.

Poe is perhaps the more purely Gothic writer than any of these, since for him the conventions which others used as a convenience became the substance as well as the method of his fictions. For Poe the attributes of Gothicism open the way into the murky interiors of encrimsoned light, they lead through the narrow and dank passageways of the self, making available to his imagination, and to the control which his method required of a work of art, those energies, those attachments to numinous objects, which in reality we try, with as great success as we can, to repress. Such total honesty, such uncompromising knowledge of the self, is so wounding to our own esteem that we do not usually seek it with any expectation of pleasure. Poe, baring his own heart, shows us his inescapable truths, in tales (and a few poems) whose design is so consistent with their ends that we, despite ourselves, take pleasure in what appalls us. Perhaps a part of that pleasure is the reflected knowledge of our own selves which, but for Poe, we might not have had the means or the courage to confront. I would do him just that honor which requites his terrible gift.

Daniel Hoffman, *Poe Poe Poe Poe Poe Poe Poe* (Garden City, NY: Doubleday, 1972), pp. 320–21.

G. R. THOMPSON   The whole of Poe's Gothic fiction can be read not only as an ambivalent parody of the world of Gothic horror tales, but also as an extended grotesquerie of the human condition. Nothing quite works out for his heroes, even though they sometimes make superhuman efforts, and even though they are occasionally rescued from their predicaments. They undergo extended series of ironic reverses in fictional structures so ironically twisted that the form itself, even the very plot, approaches an absurd hoax perpetrated on the characters. The universe created in Poe's fiction is one in which the human mind tries vainly to perceive order and meaning. The universe is deceptive; its basic mode seems almost to be a constant shifting of appearances; reality is a flux variously interpreted, or even created, by the individual human mind. In its deceptiveness, the universe of Poe's Gothic fiction seems not so much malevolent as mocking or "perverse." The universe is much like a gigantic hoax that God has played on man, an idea which is the major undercurrent of Poe's essay on the universe, *Eureka*.

Indeed, it is not too extravagant to claim that the basic structuring force of *Eureka* is an elaborate conceit on "nothing." In searching for the key to unlock the secrets that lie just beyond appearances, the "Poe" persona finds (just as do the characters in Poe's tales) that the great discovery is of nothingness, of illusion only. Thus, the hoaxlike irony of Poe's technique has its parallel in the dramatic world in which his characters move and in the overall philosophical vision that structures at every level all of Poe's fiction. ⟨. . .⟩

Poe's fiction developed from a basically satiric mode into an ironic mode in which a tragic response to the perversities of fortune and to the treacheries of one's own mind is contrasted by a near-comic perception of the absurdity of man's condition in the universe. Such a double perception, we have seen in Romantic theory, leads, through art, to a momentary transcendence of the dark chaos of the universe. If the artist (and through him the reader) can mock man's absurd condition at the same time that he feels it deeply, he transcends earthly or finite limits in an artistic paralleling of God's infinite perception. In Poe, however, such transcendence is always at the expense of the less perceptive mind. Poe plays a constant intellectual game with his readers; he tries to draw the reader into the "Gothic" world of the mind, but he is ready at any moment to mock the simplistic Gothic vision (under the trappings of which Poe saw man's real estrangement and isolation) that contemporary readers insisted on in the popular magazines.

G. R. Thompson, *Poe's Fiction: Romantic Irony in the Gothic Tales* (Madison: University of Wisconsin Press, 1973), pp. 165–66

TZVETAN TODOROV   ⟨One⟩ consequence of the extreme choice made by Poe (against imitation, in favor of construction) is the disappearance of narrative, or at least of its simple and basic form. One might find such an assertion surprising, given that Poe is often judged a narrator par excellence; but an attentive reading will convince us that one almost never finds in his writing a straightforward linking of consecutive events. Even in the adventure stories that come the closest, such as "MS. Found in a Bottle" or *Narrative of A. Gordon Pym*, the story, which begins as a simple series of adventures, turns into a mystery, and compels us to turn back on it, to reread its enigmas more attentively. The same is true of the tales of ratiocination which, in this respect, are very far from contemporary forms of the detective novel: the logic of the action is replaced by that of the search for knowledge, so that we never witness the linking of causes and effects, only their deduction after the fact.

Thus traditional narrative is absent, and so too is ordinary psychology as a means of construction of the story. The determinism of facts takes the place of psychological motivation, as has often been noted, and Poe's characters, victims of a causality that surpasses them, always lack depth. Poe is incapable of constructing a true alterity: the monologue is his preferred style, and even his dialogues ("The Colloquy of Monos and Una," "The Conversation of Eiros and Charmion") are disguised monologues. Psychology arouses his interest only as a problem among others, a mystery to unravel; as an object, not a method of construction. The proof is found in a tale like "The Purloined Letter," in which Dupin, a puppet-character lacking in all "psychology" in the novelistic sense, offers lucid formulations of the laws of human psychic life.

Narrative is by its nature imitative, repeating in the succession of events it evokes that of the pages turned by the reader; Poe will thus find ways of getting rid of it. And first of all the most obvious way: he will replace narrative with description, in which the immobility of the phenomena described opposes the movement of the words. This leads to strange descriptive tales such as "The Island of the Fay," or "The Domain of Arnheim," or "Landor's Cottage," in which Poe introduces a succession of events after the fact; however, this succession belongs to the process of observation, not to the phenomenon observed. Still more importantly, this same tendency transforms "narrative" tales into a discontinuous juxtaposition of immobile moments. What is "The Masque of the Red Death," if not a static arrangement of three tableaux: the ball, the troubling masque, the spectacle of death? Or "William Wilson," in which a whole life is reduced to a few moments described with the greatest precision? Or "Berenice," in which a long narrative in past tenses indicating repeated actions rather than unique ones is followed by the image of the dead woman and then—after a line of suspension points—by a description of the narrator's room? In the pause

—in the white space on the page—the essential is played out: the violation of the sepulcher, Berenice's awakening, the mad act that has brought her teeth to an ebony box lying on Egaeus's desk. The only presence is that of the immobility that makes it possible to guess at the whirlwind of actions.

Poe describes fragments of a whole; and, within these fragments, he chooses the detail; thus in rhetorical terms he practices a double synecdoche. Dostoevsky had pointed out this feature too: "There is in his imaginative faculty a peculiarity that exists nowhere else: the power of the details." The human body in particular is reduced to one of its components; thus, for example, Berenice's teeth: "They were here, and there, and everywhere, and visibly and palpably before me; long, narrow and excessively white, with the pale lips writhing about them, as in the very moment of their first terrible development." Or the eye of the old man in "The Tell-Tale Heart": "One of his eyes resembled that of a vulture—a pale dull blue, with a hideous veil over it that chilled the very marrow in my bones" (this old man consists of an eye and a beating heart, nothing more). We cannot forget, either, the missing eye of the black cat.

Tzvetan Todorov, "The Limits of Edgar Poe," Genres in Discourse [1978], tr. Catherine Porter (Cambridge: Cambridge University Press, 1990), pp. 100–101.

JOAN DAYAN   〈. . .〉 Poe uses his fiction to violate his critical conjunction between the death of a beautiful woman and the creation of a beautiful poem. He first empties the woman of actuality, turning her into an ideal, then he kills off that figure and resurrects dead beauty not as a spectral object, but as an earthly—and very unpoetical—subject. I suspect that Poe, having read well his Milton, recognized how the apparent idealization of woman was quite convertible with—and even necessary for—her brutalization. So he takes the angel of the house and turns her into a demon in order to dramatize the reversals, provocations, and delusions latent in male attempts at projection—and protection. By alternately sanctifying and demonizing woman, Poe jolts his reader out of the misrecognition necessary to maintaining society's mechanisms of hierarchy and control. The excesses of love and hate she inspires in his narrators coerce all kinds of categories and distinctions into confusion. And it is through this chaos of matter and spirit, purity and filth that Poe attacks the reductiveness of mere morality, and the vanity of self-complacency.

Joan Dayan, Fables of Mind: An Inquiry into Poe's Fiction (New York: Oxford University Press, 1987), pp. 226–27.

MARK KINKEAD-WEEKES   What is immediately impressive about 'The Fall of the House of Usher' is the care with which it sets out to establish the kind of reader it requires. As opposed, it turns out, to Coleridge's notion of an aeolian lute, which resounds to every capricious gust of feeling or idea, there is to be scruple and discrimination, a challenge to put imagination, and feeling, and critical intelligence to work, in controlled harmony. The mode then is not merely Gothick, but rather a 'Gothick' which at every turn signals a consciousness of its own operation, its own language and vision. From the outset we have before us, too, a narrator we must both respond to, and carefully watch responding:

> During the whole of a dull, dark, and soundless day in the autumn
> of the year, when the clouds hung oppressively low in the heavens,
> I had been passing alone, on horseback, through a singularly
> dreary tract of country, and at length found myself, as the
> shades of the evening drew on, within view of the melancholy
> House of Usher. I know not how it was—but with the first
> glimpse of the building, a sense of insufferable gloom pervaded
> my spirit.

This could be the opening script for a thousand 'horror' stories and films: the adjectival atmospherics, the *compositio loci* as the titles come up, the dreary landscape, the gathering darkness, the melancholy house, the lonely horseman, the preternatural feeling of gloom.

But just as the sense of something worked-up becomes conscious, becomes overdone with the word 'insufferable'—we are made aware of it as a word through a scruple, made to stand back and *look*, at both the Gothick and the motives of its audience. In other words, Poe keeps a controlling distance on what the opening paragraph terms 'that half-pleasurable, because poetic, sentiment with which the mind usually receives even the sternest natural images of the desolate or terrible'; this story will be no mere sensationalist exercise in 'horror'. Still less are we offered that darker romanticism which seeks in hallucination or drug some goading or torturing of the imagination into the sublime—but rather something more like the aftermath of that: the hideous awakening from illusion into sick depression and hangover, so that everyday reality seems poisoned and bitter. The narrator is both suspect and comes through. If there is a touch of 'romantick' or even decadent expertise, of one who has known the pull of the Gothick theatre and the opium den, nevertheless the outcome is a clearing away, from what we are to attend to, of those self-pleasing but necessarily falsifying and even sick-

ening kinds of veil. We can hope for good Poe when the temptations to
what can be bad in him are so clearly renounced.

Mark Kinkead-Weekes, "Reflections on, and in, 'The Fall of the House of Usher,' "
Edgar Allan Poe: The Design of Order, ed. A. Robert Lee (London: Vision Press;
Totowa, NJ: Barnes & Noble, 1987), pp. 17–18

KENNETH SILVERMAN   Poe's mood following his failed
courtship of ⟨Sarah⟩ Helen ⟨Whitman⟩ seems most fully recorded in "Hop-
Frog," a briskly narrated tale of revenge, written about a month after his
final trip to Providence. Here the also touchy and explosive protagonist is
a court jester, doubly plagued in being both a dwarf and a cripple. He and
his companion Trippetta, "a young girl very little less dwarfish than himself,"
have been kidnapped from their homes and sent as presents to the king.
This sadistic practical joker enjoys commanding Hop-Frog to drink, although
even a little wine befuddles him. Wishing to host a masquerade, the king
summons Hop-Frog and orders him to invent some novel sport for it. He
also forces the dwarf to drink, which Hop-Frog does, looking around with
a "half-insane stare." Trippetta tries to intervene, but the king pushes her
away and dashes wine in her face. Seething, Hop-Frog drinks some more,
and vengefully suggests that the king entertain his guests with a costumed
skit.

On the evening of the masquerade, the king and his seven ministers
gleefully consent to be coated with tar and flax, to look like escaped orang-
utans. They rush into the grand salon, hoping to frighten the company, as
they do. Apparently aiding their jest, Hop-Frog hoists them to the ceiling,
chained together. A grating sound is heard: "it came from the fang-like
teeth of the dwarf, who ground them and gnashed them as he foamed at
the mouth, and glared, with an expression of maniacal rage." Then Hop-
Frog torches the combustible costumes, cremating the men in a sheet of
flame that leaves a "fetid, blackened, hideous, and indistinguishable mass."
Having murdered the king, Hop-Frog runs off with Trippetta, neither of
them to be seen again.

The conflict between the mighty king and the crippled jester dramatizes
years of accumulated gripes and griefs. In the king's indifference to the
suffering of others, his callous affronts, his demands to be entertained, Poe
summoned up a small army of people by whom he had come to feel abused
and misled—the Elector of Moldavia, cronies who induced him to drink,
editors ("We want characters—*characters*, man," the jaded king tells Hop-
Frog, "something novel—out of the way"), friends of Helen. In the jester
Poe portrayed much of himself, kidnapped from home and presented to the

king, bearing a name not given in baptism but "conferred upon him," protective of the girlish Trippetta, and susceptible to wine, which "excited the poor cripple almost to madness"—a touch-and-go bullethead who when insulted and forced to drink becomes insane with rage. Over the conflict between these characters, too, hangs a sense of the future. X-ing himself, the murderous dwarf announces to the masqueraders, at the end of the tale, his own disappearance. "I am simply Hop-Frog the jester," he declares, prophetically for Poe, "and *this is my last jest.*"

> Kenneth Silverman, *Edgar A. Poe: Mournful and Never-Ending Remembrance* (New York: HarperCollins, 1991), pp. 406–7

Bibliography

Tamerlane and Other Poems. 1827.

Al Aaraaf, Tamerlane, and Minor Poems. 1829.

Poems. 1831.

The Narrative of Arthur Gordon Pym of Nantucket. 1838.

The Conchologist's First Book; or, A System of Testaceous Malacology. 1839.

Tales of the Grotesque and Arabesque. 1840. 2 vols.

Prospectus of The Penn Magazine. 1840.

Prose Romances: The Murders in the Rue Morgue; The Man That Was Used Up. 1843.

Tales. 1845.

The Raven and Other Poems. 1845.

Mesmerism "in Articulo Mortis" ("The Facts in the Case of M. Valdemar"). 1846.

Prospectus of The Stylus. 1848.

Eureka: A Prose Poem. 1848.

Works. Ed. Rufus W. Griswold. 1850–56. 4 vols.

Tales of Mystery and Imagination. 1855.

Works. Ed. John H. Ingram. 1874–75. 4 vols.

Works. Ed. Richard Henry Stoddard. 1884. 8 vols.

Works. Ed. Edmund Clarence Stedman and George Edward Woodberry. 1894–95. 10 vols.

Complete Works. Ed. James A. Harrison. 1902. 17 vols.

Last Letters to Sarah Helen Whitman. Ed. James A. Harrison. 1909.

Complete Poems. Ed. J. H. Whitty. 1911.

Poems. Ed. Killis Campbell. 1917.

Letters. Ed. Mary Newton Stanard. 1925.

Best Known Works. Ed. Hervey Allen. 1931.

Complete Poems and Stories. Ed. Arthur Hobson Quinn. 1946. 2 vols.

Letters. Ed. John Ward Ostrom. 1948. 2 vols.

Selected Prose, Poetry, and Eureka. Ed. W. H. Auden. 1950.

Literary Criticism. Ed. Robert L. Hough. 1965.

Poems. Ed. Floyd Stovall. 1965.

Collected Works. Ed. Thomas Ollive Mabbott et al. 1969–78. 3 vols. (incomplete).

The Science Fiction of Edgar Allan Poe. Ed. Harold Beaver. 1976.

Collected Writings. Ed. Burton R. Pollin et al. 1981– .

The Annotated Edgar Allan Poe. Ed. Stephen Peithman. 1981.

Poetry and Tales. Ed. Patrick Quinn. 1984.

Essays and Reviews. Ed. G. R. Thompson. 1984.

❖ ❖ ❖

Ann Radcliffe
1764–1823

ANN WARD RADCLIFFE was born in London on July 9, 1764, the daughter of William Ward, a London haberdasher. In 1772 her family moved to Bath, and in 1787 she married William Radcliffe, a journalist and owner and manager of the *English Chronicle*. Little else is known about Ann Radcliffe's private life, despite the fact that she was for some time the most popular novelist in England. Her first two books were *The Castles of Athlin and Dunbayne* and *A Sicilian Romance*, published anonymously in 1789 and 1790, respectively. It was her next novel, *The Romance of the Forest* (1791), that first made her name known to the public, but her greatest success came in 1794 with the publication of *The Mysteries of Udolpho*. The book was widely imitated, and among those who claimed to be influenced by it was Matthew Gregory Lewis, who introduced a new element into the Gothic genre when he mixed sexual titillation with terror in his Gothic novel *The Monk* (1796). Lewis's book reportedly infuriated Mrs. Radcliffe, who feared it would bring about the moral degradation of a genre so closely linked with her own name. Accordingly, she set herself to producing a novel that in many respects was a bowdlerized version of Lewis's, published in 1797 as *The Italian*.

After 1797 Radcliffe published no more Gothics, although she was then at the height of her popularity; perhaps she no longer wished to have her name linked with a genre that had become associated in the public mind with scandal and insanity. Her *Poems* (consisting mostly of the verses inserted in her novels) appeared in 1815, but in general she lived such a retired existence that rumors began to circulate that she was already dead or in an insane asylum. Radcliffe suffered in later life from asthma, and died of pneumonia on February 7, 1823. After her death T. Noon Talfourd published her final novel, *Gaston de Blondeville* (1826), to which he attached a lengthy memoir.

Radcliffe also published a travel account, *A Journey Made in the Summer of 1794, through Holland and the West Frontier of Germany* (1795), relating her only trip to the Continent; the descriptions in her novels of French and Italian landscapes are entirely based on books and pictures.

◙ *Critical Extracts*

MATTHEW GREGORY LEWIS   I have taken up my romance;
and perhaps by this time ten years, I may make shift to finish it fit for
throwing in the fire. I was induced to go on with it by reading the *Mysteries
of Udolpho*, which is, in my opinion, one of the most interesting books that
has ever been published. I would advise you to read it by all means; but I
must warn you, that it is not very entertaining till St. Aubyn's death. His
travels, to my mind, are uncommonly dull, and I wish heartily that they
had been left out, and something substituted in their room. I am sure you
will be particularly interested by the part, when Emily returns home after
her father's death: and when you read it, tell me whether you think there is
any resemblance between the character given of Montoni, in the seventeenth
chapter of the second volume, and my own. I confess that it struck me; and
as he is the villain of the tale, I did not feel much flattered by the likeness.

Matthew Gregory Lewis, Letter to His Mother (18 May 1794), *The Life and Correspondence of Matthew Gregory Lewis*, ed. Margaret Baron-Wilson (London: Henry Colburn, 1839), Vol. 1, pp. 124–25

SAMUEL TAYLOR COLERIDGE

> Thine too these golden keys, immortal boy!
> This can unlock the gates of joy,
> Of horror that, and thrilling fears,
> Or ope the sacred source of sympathetic tears.

Such were the presents of the muse to the infant Shakespeare, and though
perhaps to no other mortal has she been so lavish of her gifts, the keys
referring to the third line Mrs. Radcliffe must be allowed to be completely
in possession of. This, all who have read the *Romance of the Forest* will
willingly bear witness to. Nor does the present production ⟨*The Mysteries
of Udolpho*⟩ require the name of its author to ascertain that it comes from
the same hand. The same powers of description are displayed, the same
predilection is discovered for the wonderful and the gloomy—the same
mysterious terrors are continually exciting in the mind the idea of a supernatural appearance, keeping us, as it were, upon the very edge and confines of
the world of spirits, and yet are ingeniously explained by familiar causes;
curiosity is kept upon the stretch from page to page, and from volume to
volume, and the secret, which the reader thinks himself every instant on
the point of penetrating, flies like a phantom before him, and eludes his
eagerness until the very last moment of protracted expectation. This art of

escaping the guesses of the reader has been improved and brought to perfection along with the reader's sagacity; just as the various inventions of locks, bolts and private drawers in order to secure, fasten, and hide, have always kept pace with the ingenuity of the pickpocket and house-breaker, whose profession is to unlock, unfasten, and lay open what you have taken so much pains to conceal. In this contest of curiosity on one side, and invention on the other, Mrs. Radcliffe certainly has the advantage. She delights in concealing her plan with the most artifical contrivance, and seems to amuse herself with saying, at every turn and doubling of the story, 'Now you think you have me, but I shall take care to disappoint you.' This method is, however, liable to the following inconvenience, that in the search of what is new, an author is apt to forget what is natural; and, in rejecting the more obvious conclusions, to take those which are less satisfactory. The trite and the extravagant are the Scylla and Charybdis of writers who deal in fiction. With regard to the work before us, while we acknowledge the extraordinary powers of Mrs. Radcliffe, some readers will be inclined to doubt whether they have been exerted in the present work with equal effect as in the *Romance of the Forest*. Four volumes cannot depend entirely on terrific incidents and intricacy of story. They require character, unity of design, a delineation of the scenes of real life, and the variety of well supported contrast. *The Mysteries of Udolpho* are indeed relieved by much elegant description and picturesque scenery; but in the descriptions there is too much of the sameness: the pine and the larch tree wave, and the full moon pours its lustre through almost every chapter. Curiosity is raised oftener than it is gratified; or rather, it is raised so high that no adequate gratification can be given it; the interest is completely dissolved when once the adventure is finished, and the reader, when he is got to the end of the work, looks about in vain for the spell which had bound him so strongly to it.

Samuel Taylor Coleridge, "*The Mysteries of Udolpho, a Romance* by Ann Radcliffe" (1794), *Coleridge's Miscellaneous Criticism*, ed. Thomas Middleton Raysor (London: Constable, 1936), pp. 355–57

JOHN DUNLOP   Of this justly celebrated woman, the principal object seems to have been to raise the powerful emotions of surprise, awe, and especially terror, by means and agents apparently supernatural. To effect this, she places her characters, and transports her readers, amid scenes which are calculated to strongly excite the mind, and to predispose it for spectral illusion: Gothic castles, gloomy abbeys, subterraneous passages, the haunts of banditti, the sobbing of the wind, and the howling of the storm, are all employed for this purpose; and in order that these may have their full effect, the principal character in her romances is always a lovely and unprotected female, encompassed by snares, and surrounded by villains. But, that in which the works of Mrs. Radcliffe chiefly differ from those by which they were preceded is, that in the *Castle of Otranto* and *Old English Baron*, the machinery is in fact supernatural, whereas the means and agents employed by Mrs. Radcliffe are in reality human, and as such can be, or, at least, are professed to be, explained by natural events. By these means she certainly excites a very powerful interest, as the reader meanwhile experiences the full impression of the wonderful and terrific appearances; but there is one defect which attends this mode of composition, and which seems to be inseparable from it. As it is the intention of the author, that the mysteries should be afterward cleaned up, they are all mountains in labour, and even when she is successful in explaining the marvellous circumstances which have occurred, we feel disappointed that we should have been so agitated by trifles. But the truth is, they never are properly explained, and the author, in order to raise strong emotions of fear and horror in the body of the work, is tempted to go lengths, to account for which the subsequent explanations seem utterly inadequate. Thus, for example, after all the wonder and dismay, and terror and expectation, excited by the mysterious chamber in the castle of Udolpho, how much are we disappointed and disgusted to find that all this pother has been raised by an image of wax! In short, we may say not only of Mrs. Radcliffe's castles, but of her works in general, that they abound "in *passages* that lead to nothing."

> John Dunlop, *The History of Fiction* (1814; rev. ed. London: Carey & Hart, 1842), Vol. 2, pp. 411–12

ANN RADCLIFFE   Terror and horror are so far opposite, that the first expands the soul, and awakens the faculties to a high degree of life; the other contracts, freezes, and nearly annihilates them. I apprehend, that neither Shakespeare nor Milton by their fictions, nor Mr. Burke by his reasoning, anywhere looked to positive horror as a source of the sublime, though they all agree that terror is a very high one; and where lies the great difference between horror and terror, but in the uncertainty and obscurity that accompany the first, respecting the dreaded evil?

> Ann Radcliffe, "On the Supernatural in Poetry," *New Monthly Magazine and Literary Journal* 16 (1826): 150–51

SIR WALTER SCOTT   In working upon the sensation of natural and superstitious fear, Mrs. Radcliffe has made much use of obscurity and suspense, the most fertile source, perhaps, of sublime emotion; for there are few dangers that do not become familiar to the firm mind, if they are presented to consideration as certainties, and in all their open and declared character; whilst, on the other hand, the bravest have shrunk from the dark and the doubtful. To break off the narrative, when it seemed at the point of becoming most interesting—to extinguish a lamp, just when a parchment containing some hideous secret ought to have been read—to exhibit shadowy forms and half-heard sounds of woe, are resources which Mrs. Radcliffe has employed with more effect than any other writer of romance. It must be confessed, that in order to bring about these situations, some art or contrivance, on the part of the author, is rather too visible. Her heroines voluntarily expose themselves to situations, which in nature a lonely female would certainly have avoided. They are too apt to choose the midnight hour for investigating the mysteries of a deserted chamber or secret passage, and generally are only supplied with an expiring lamp, when about to read the most interesting documents. The simplicity of the tale is thus somewhat injured—it is as if we witnessed a dressing up of the very phantom by which we are to be startled; and the imperfection, though redeemed by many beauties, did not escape the censure of criticism.

Sir Walter Scott, "Ann Radcliffe" (1824), *Lives of the Novelists* (1825; rpt. London: J. M. Dent; New York: E. P. Dutton [Everyman's Library], 1910), pp. 230–31

LEIGH HUNT   Mrs. Radcliffe, a beautiful little woman of delicate constitution and sequestered habits, as fond, as her own heroines, of lonely sea-shores, picturesque mountains, and poetical meditations, perfected that discovery of the capabilites of *an old house* or *castle* for exciting a romantic interest, which lay ready to be made in the mind of every child and poet, but which (if Gray did not put it into his head) first suggested itself to the feudal dilettantism of Horace Walpole. Horace had more genius in him than his contemporaries gave him credit for; but the reputation which his wit obtained him, the material philosophy of the day, and the pursuit of fashionable amusements, did it no good. He lost sight of the line to be drawn between the imposing and the incredible; and though there is real merit in the *Castle of Otranto*, and grandeur of imagination, yet the conversion of dreams into gross daylight palpabilities, which nothing short of iron-founders could create—swords that take a hundred men to lift them, and supernatural yet substantial helmets, big as houses and actually serving for prisons—turn the sublime into the ridiculous, and has completely spoilt an otherwise interesting narrative. Mrs. Radcliffe, frightened perhaps by

Walpole's failure (for this great mistress of Fear was too often a servant of it), went to another extreme; and except in what she quoted from other story-tellers, resolved all her supernatural effects into common-place causes. Those effects, however, while they lasted, and everything else capable of frightening people out of their wits—old haunted houses and corridors, mysterious music, faces behind curtains, cowled and guilty monks, inquisitors, nuns, places to commit murder in, and the murders themselves—she understood to perfection. To dress these in appropriate circumstances, she possessed also the eye of a painter as well as the feeling of a poetess. She conceived to a nicety the effect of a storm on a landscape, the playing of a meteor on a point of a spear, and the sudden appearance of some old castle to which travellers have been long coming, and which they have reasons to fear living in. It has been objected to her that she is too much of a melodramatic writer, and that her characters are inferior to her circumstances; the background (as Hazlitt says) of more importance than the figures. This in a great measure is true; but she has painted characters also, chiefly weak ones, as in the querulous duped aunt in *Udolpho,* and the victim of error, St. Pierre, in the *Romance of the Forest.* It must be considered, however, that her effects, however produced, are successful, and greatly successful; and that Nature herself deals in precisely such effects, leaving men to be operated upon by them passively, and not to play the chief parts in the process by means of their characters. Mrs. Radcliffe brings on the scene Fear and Terror themselves, the grandeurs of the known world, and the awes of the unknown; and if human beings become puppets in her hands, it is as people in storm and earthquake are puppets in the hands of Nature.

> Leigh Hunt, "Ludovico in the Haunted Chamber," *A Book for a Corner* (London: Chapman & Hall, 1849), Vol. 1, pp. 103–4

MARGARET OLIPHANT   The chief distinction of her power to the more commonplace reader is the skill with which she manages her mysteries—leading us from step to step through dim corridors, by uncertain lights, which have a way of going out at the the most thrilling moment, across deserted chambers, where curtains rustle and sliding panels open, and the supernatural is feared yet always averted. She was a great deal too enlightened ever to have anything to say to a ghost. In those days the ancient love of superstition had faded, and the new groping after spiritual presences had not begun. There are a hundred apparitions in her pages, but they are all elaborately accounted for, and never turn out to be anything more alarming than flesh and blood. Sometimes the effect, so carefully worked up to, is a failure, as in the case of the mystery of the veiled recess in Udolpho, where our imagination refuses to accept as anything but a flagrant imposition and deception the waxen image of death which is supposed to shock every beholder out of his wits. But as a matter of fact, no mysterious terror which is not supernatural will stand investigation even by the most skilful hands. The reader is angry at being defrauded of his alarm, and knows that he has no right to be so frightened by anything that can be explained.

Margaret Oliphant, *The Literary History of England in the End of the Eighteenth and Beginning of the Nineteenth Century* (London: Macmillan, 1882), Vol. 2, pp. 279–80

CLARA FRANCES McINTYRE   In this matter of structure, one can hardly deny that Mrs. Radcliffe made a contribution ⟨to the novel⟩ which was distinctive and important. Her deliberate use of suspense as an artistic principle is something entirely different from the method of Richardson and Fielding in shaping the incidents of their stories to fit into a general plan. Just how far her method affected later writers is a question which it would be difficult to answer conclusively. Scott had a strong feeling for the individual scene, and we know that in many ways he was influenced by Radcliffe's work. The great novels of the nineteenth century show a combination of the picaresque and the dramatic methods, with the emphasis, probably, upon the latter. The short stories, from Poe down to the latest attempts in our magazines, are founded upon the principle of suspense; and the modern detective story, with its elaborate mystification, and its often disappointing solution, no doubt owes much to Mrs. Radcliffe's methods. She gave a new emphasis to action—not action in and for itself, as in the picaresque novel, but action as bringing about complications, and resolving them.

It seems hardly fair, then, to think of the 'Gothic' novel as a mere side-issue in the development of the type—a 'blind alley' leading nowhere. Walpole, with his clumsy beginnings, and Mrs. Radcliffe, with the perfected method, added something to the plot as Richardson and Fielding had conceived it, and so had their direct share in the development of the novel.

Clara Frances McIntyre, *Ann Radcliffe in Relation to Her Time* (New Haven: Yale University Press, 1920), pp. 88–89

J. M. S. TOMPKINS   Briefly, Mrs. Radcliffe approached the terrible with all the tremors of a highly-strung nervous system. Not for her the crude vigour of Otranto or the piecemeal manifestations of the good

Alfonso; these portents, as Scott suggested, are somewhat too definite in outline; like the crash of the falling helmet, they stun rather than stimulate the imagination. She is the poet of apprehension. Her theme is not the dreadful happening—very often nothing dreadful happens—but the interval during which the menace takes shape and the mind of the victim is reluctantly shaken by its impedance. Sources of and parallels to her devices can be found in the Elizabethan drama, but the drama has no room for the slow subjection of the mind to terror. For that we must wait for the psychological novel, towards the development of which Mrs. Radcliffe has made a contribution in her analysis of fear. Her procedures can be traced in those chapters of *The Romance of the Forest* that lead up to and include Adeline's discovery and perusal of the manuscript; or in even greater length in those describing Emily's sojourn at Udolpho. A sensitive but spirited girl is brought to a Gothic building and exposed to its influence. She is lonely, helpless, in unhappy circumstances and presently threatened by real peril, and her reasonable fears gradually sap her defences against the unaccountable terrors with which her surroundings and the confused stories of ignorant servants inspire her. Her nerves are subjected to a series of slight, harassing attacks, in which intimations of earthly and ghostly terror are blended. One notes the delicacy of means by which these effects are evoked, a sigh, a moving light, an unfamiliar tone of voice, the reflection in a mirror of a cloaked and striding figure. Thus her senses are excited and her reason is bewildered, and she is delivered over to the "mystic and turbulent promptings of the imagination." It was no small achievement, in an age of rough-and-ready assaults on the sensibilities, to trace Adeline to the point when she sits reading the prisoner's manuscript, at midnight, by her failing lamp, and, shaken by mysterious sympathies, dare hardly raise her eyes to the mirror, lest she should see another face beside her own. In thus tracing the growth of fear, Mrs. Radcliffe takes a few steps in the direction of that science that was to become the guiding light of fiction a hundred years hence. Her innovation was noticed by her contemporaries, and Mary Hays in the preface to *Emma Courtney* (1796) ranks her among those writers who, by tracing the progress and consequence of one strong, indulged passion, have afforded material for philosophers to calculate the powers and estimate the motives of the human mind. Her study of abnormal mental states, however, is strictly limited by the bias of her own tastes and opinions. Of all the passions she studies only fear, and fear, through the intervention of her sense of dignity, never reaches such a pitch as to deprave the fearful. Her heroines are timid but steadfast. They have no enemy within; they are sure that innocence will be divinely shielded, and they never doubt their innocence. Those pits

of agony into which Maturin cast a glance, where lie the souls of those who
feel an involuntary pollution darkening their minds and dread lest their
natures should conform to those of their persecutors, were beyond her scan.
Under the pressure of fear Adeline, Emily and the lovers of *The Italian*
remain devout, merciful and essentially courageous. Beyond this point terror
ceases to be "a pleasing luxury," and dream passes into nightmare.

J. M. S. Tompkins, "The Gothic Romance," *The Popular Novel in England 1770–1800*
(London: Constable, 1932), pp. 258–59

ALINE GRANT   ⟨By 1801⟩ Ann Radcliffe had decided to write
no more for publication. Since Matthew Lewis' phenomenal success with
The Monk, less than two years after the appearance of *The Mysteries of
Udolpho*, there had been numerous other sensational novels, some scurrilous,
some merely silly, that all quite obviously owed their primary inspiration
to Mrs. Radcliffe however much their tone and style differed from hers.
Also the titles as well as the plots of her own novels appeared in the blue-
covered chapbooks that sold for sixpence or a shilling according to their
length, under such slight disguises as *The Bloody Monk of Udolpho*, *Romance
of the Cavern*, *Mysteries of the Forest*, and *The Midnight Assassin; or, Confession
of the Monk Rinaldi*.

There were satires, too, upon the Gothic novel, such as *More Ghosts!* by
Mrs. Patrick, even while Mrs. Meeke and many another industrious lady
fed the Minerva Press and the circulating libraries with *The Abbey of Clugny*,
The Mysterious Wife, *The Mysterious Husband*, and many another mysterious
being.

Ann Radcliffe felt herself made ridiculous even more by her ardent
imitators than by those who satirized her work. She was too gentle to take
any pleasure in ridiculing others and too sensitive not to feel ridicule deeply
when it was directed towards herself. Even the knowledge that a scholar
like Joseph Warton, headmaster of Winchester, or such brilliant statesmen
as Sheridan and Fox had found her works enthralling, could not give her
courage to brave publication again. She did write one more romance but
it did not appear in print during her lifetime. This novel, which she called
Gaston de Blondeville, was directly inspired by the visit which she made to
Kenilworth Castle in the autumn of 1802.

Aline Grant, *Ann Radcliffe* (Denver: Alan Swallow, 1951), pp. 111–12

DEVENDRA P. VARMA   Her ingenuity fostered a new style
of romanticism distinct from the poetical marvels of conventional tales of

magic and chivalry or the realistic manner of Richardson and Fielding. Yet the wondrous and the credible are both woven into her fabric: the gossamer dreams of bygone times across the grim realities of her own days. She had not the art of stimulating the fancy by deft, light sketches of life and manners. Her most powerful effects are gained by the passion of fear, and this base emotion is raised to the dignity of romance. In the silence of nature we listen to echoes from beyond the grave, and with a tremulous eagerness we follow the sequence of events. She fascinates and appals us at the same time, and stirs up those secret springs of mortal apprehension which join our earthly existence and our spiritual self. This art is not melodramatic, but is very similar to the essence of tragic power, "which is felt not merely in the greatness of actions, or sorrows, which it exhibits, but in its nice application to the inmost sources of terror and pity" ⟨Anna Laetitia Barbauld⟩. ⟨. . .⟩

She excited the imagination by supernatural apprehensions, by phantom effects and half-hearted sounds. In her hands the gusts of wind, the creaking door, even the sound of a common footstep became sources of terror and mystery. The crude machinery of Walpole's story—secret trap doors, sliding panels, spiral staircases, and subterranean vaults—in her hands became artistic instruments to evoke an atmosphere of suspense and beauty.

She was skilful in producing terror by awakening a sense of mystery. The sequence of her narrative is so managed that it moves our minds to a feeling of impending danger, and we hold our breath in suspense. Her vast, antique chambers have about them a sense of unearthly presences; where an ominous silence prevails; where echoing footsteps die away in prolonged gloom, and where phantoms lurk in dark corridors, and whispers come from behind the tapestry, as it flutters in the gusts of wind. "She alarms with terror; agitates with suspense, prolonged and wrought up to the most intense feeling; by mysterious hints and obscure intimations of unseen danger", according to Mrs. Barbauld. ⟨. . .⟩

Mrs. Radcliffe, a mistress of hints, associations, silence and emptiness, only half-revealing her picture, leaves the rest to the imagination. She knows, as Burke has asserted, that obscurity is a strong ingredient in the sublime; but she knew the sharp distinction between Terror and Horror, which was unknown to Burke.

Devendra P. Varma, *The Gothic Flame* (London: Arthur Barker, 1957), pp. 101–3

JOEL PORTE   It is surprising, particularly in view of the evidence that lies readily to hand, how little systematic consideration has been given to Gothic fiction as the expression of a fundamentally Protestant theological or religious disquietude. Beginning in 1756, when Burke published his *Philosophical Inquiry into the Origin of Our Ideas of the Sublime and Beautiful*, it became commonplace among both writers and readers to consider the emotions of terror and awe as sources of "the Sublime"—a ready conduit to ideas of Divinity, Omnipotence, and all Final Things. Mrs. Radcliffe, for example, had conned her Burke and knew that the proper business of the orthodox novel of Terror was to expand the soul religiously. So, in the very first chapter of *The Mysteries of Udolpho*, and interminably thereafter, the impeccably well-instructed Emily St. Aubert is sent off, as to a sylvan Sunday school, not into "the soft and glowing landscape," but to "the wild wood-walks, that skirted the mountain; and still more the mountain's stupendous recesses, where the silence and grandeur of solitude impressed a sacred awe upon her heart, and lifted her thoughts to the GOD OF HEAVEN AND EARTH."

So far as serious religious ideas or emotions are concerned, *Udolpho* does not often get beyond such simple exercises in majuscular Sublimity. One possible exception, but an important one in this context, concerns the shadowy and pathetically mad Sister Agnes, who is finally revealed to be none other than Signora Laurentini di Udolpho, the passion-crazed destroyer of Emily's aunt (the Marchioness de Villeroi) whose story contains the central mystery of the book. In a frightening interview with the dying nun, the *aes triplex* of Emily's innocence is subjected to its most profound threat—intimations of universal sinfulness and the reality of damnation. Asserting that the guilty forfeit the protection of God, Agnes both unburdens herself and moralizes at large:

> "Yet who is he, that shall dare to call himself innocent!—
> all earthly innocence is but comparative. Yet still how wide
> asunder are the extremes of guilt, and to what an horrible depth
> may we fall! Oh!"—
> The nun, as she concluded, uttered a shuddering sigh, that
> startled Emily, who, looking up, perceived the eyes of Agnes
> fixed on hers, after which the sister rose, took her hand, gazed
> earnestly upon her countenance, for some moments, in
> silence, and then said,
> "You are young—you are innocent! I mean you are yet
> innocent of any great crime!—But you have passions in your
> heart,—scorpions; they sleep now—beware how you awaken
> them!—they will sting you, even unto death!"
> Emily, affected by these words and by the solemnity, with
> which they were delivered, could not suppress her tears.

"Ah! is it so?" exclaimed Agnes, her countenance softening
from its sternness—"so young, and so unfortunate! We are
sisters, then indeed. Yet, there is no bond of kindness among
the guilty," she added, while her eyes resumed their wild
expression, "no gentleness,—no peace, no hope! I knew them
all once—my eyes could weep—but now they burn, for now,
my soul is fixed, and fearless!—I lament no more!"

Here, in a scene that probably influenced Hawthorne's treatment of the
Miriam-Hilda relationship in *The Marble Faun*, Mrs. Radcliffe modulates,
though only briefly, to that somber key of psychological-cum-moral ambiguity and anxiety which is fundamental to the most affecting Gothic writing.
    Joel Porte, "In the Hands of an Angry God: Religious Terror in Gothic Fiction,"
    The Gothic Imagination: Essays in Dark Romanticism, ed. G. R. Thompson (Pullman:
    Washington State University Press, 1974), pp. 43–44

DAVID DURANT   Following the Gothic convention, Mrs. Radcliffe made her heroines discover a nightmare world beneath the pastoral,
after they had been expelled from secure family life. Her underground is a
world of chaos, where the forces of the supernatural and of the illicit
hold full sway. The ruined castles and abbeys are graphic symbols of the
disintegration of a stable civilization; their underground reaches are the
hiding places for all those forces which cannot stand the light of day. A
Sicilian Romance establishes the gothic geography. Once she flees from her
home, Julia finds that the world consists of an interconnected series of
underground sites, each one peopled with viler felons than the last. Her
villainous father lurks in the dark passageway through which she attempts
her first escape; bandits, rapists, and murderers fill the other caverns, subterranean crypts, tunnels, and secret passageways of the novel. What makes the
underground so terrible is that its inhabitants include the supernatural as
well as the wicked. The wicked forces of the Inquisition who people the
underground in *The Italian* are joined by supernatural figures who can apparently pass through walls and come back from the dead to work their revenge.
The intrusion of the supernatural into the world of depravity allows Mrs.
Radcliffe to explain its malevolence. In the fallen world, there are forces
which reason cannot explain: the true authority of reason which had
restrained vice has been lost. Once out of the family, the heroine finds that
chaos is loosed.

    The contrast between the true family and chaos is exemplified by Mrs.
Radcliffe's use of a false father as villain. The innovation came in *A Sicilian
Romance*, which involves a mutation of the usual sentimental struggle

between a heroine's love and a father's authority. Mazzini is the typical misguided, overbearing father, but he also has some aspects of the character of a Lovelace. He is seducer as well as father: he has imprisoned his real wife; pretended she has died; and taken a younger woman to please his lusts. Even his demand that his daughter marry Luovo comes from his illicit consort's depraved love for the hero and jealousy of the heroine. The other novels continue this father-villain combination. In *Udolpho*, the villain Montoni is parental only by virtue of his marriage to Emily's legal guardian. But in both *The Romance of the Forest* and *The Italian*, the parental status of the villain is explicit. Adeline's father plucks her from from her convent, exposes her to danger, has her exiled, tries to seduce her, and plots to kill her. In *The Italian*, Schedoni is the monkish henchman of the hero's family who kidnaps Ellena, breaks up her wedding after she escapes, imprisons her fiancé, and finally plots her murder. The climax of the novel comes when he discovers that this plaything is his daughter. There is more than a hint of incest in this formula, but the main focus lies on the definition of an adult world in which the normal, loving relationships of fathers and children are replaced by unnatural and unprovoked enmity by the father. To Mrs. Radcliffe, the world outside the family is utterly perverse in its villainy.

David Durant, "Ann Radcliffe and the Conservative Gothic," *Studies in English Literature 1500–1900* 22, No. 3 (Summer 1982): 523–25

MARGARET L. CARTER   Radcliffe has the characters in her early work, *A Sicilian Romance* (1790), debate the reality and theological import of hauntings. (By "Radcliffe," I mean of course, the implied author-within-the-text.) The heroine's governess, discussing the possible existence of ghosts, says, "Who shall say that anything is impossible to God? We know that he has made us, who are embodied spirits; he, therefore, can make unembodied spirits." Much like Imlac, the same speaker further asserts, "Such spirits, if indeed they have ever been seen, can have appeared only by the express permission of God, and for some very singular purposes." Here the existence of ghosts is made contingent on that of God. If the former cannot exist without the latter, then the true apparition of a ghost constitutes a strong argument for the reality of the Divine. Radcliffe is far from denying the reality of the spiritual realm, yet avoids lending support to credulous superstition unworthy of an enlightened age. Her novels maintain a balance between these two attitudes by keeping their apparitions suspended in the realm of the fantastic until the end of the story. This conversation from *A Sicilian Romance* is a good example of Radcliffe's calling up ghosts in order to subdue them. In her world we can entertain belief in the supernatural in general but disbelieve every particular supernatural event. Radcliffe's "suggestive obscurity" allows us to "feel the full impression of the world of shadows although she stops short of anything really supernatural" (Devendra P. Varma). In other words she gives us the awareness of a reality beyond the material world without demanding a positive act of belief from us; we have our Enlightenment cake and eat it with Gothic icing. In Joel Porte's words, she demonstrates that "the proper business of the orthodox novel of terror" is "to expand the soul religiously."

Margaret L. Carter, "The Fantastic Uncanny in Radcliffe," Specter or Delusion: The Supernatural in Gothic Fiction (Ann Arbor, MI: UMI Research Press, 1986), pp. 28–29

▣ *Bibliography*

The Castles of Athlin and Dunbayne: A Highland Story. 1789.

A Sicilian Romance. 1790. 2 vols.

The Romance of the Forest. 1791. 3 vols.

The Mysteries of Udolpho: A Romance. 1794. 4 vols.

A Journey Made in the Summer of 1794, through Holland and the West Frontier of Germany, with a Return down the Rhine. 1795.

The Italian; or, The Confessional of the Black Penitents: A Romance. 1797. 3 vols.

Poems. 1815.

Novels. 1824.

Gaston de Blondeville; or, The Court of Henry III. Keeping Festival in Ardienne: A Romance; St. Alban's Abbey: A Metrical Tale; with Some Poetical Pieces. 1826. 4 vols.

Poetical Works. 1834. 2 vols.

❖ ❖ ❖

Mary Shelley
1797–1851

MARY WOLLSTONECRAFT SHELLEY was born in London on August 30, 1797, the only daughter of the philosopher William Godwin and the writer Mary Wollstonecraft. Her mother died giving birth to her, and in 1801 Godwin took a second wife, whom Mary passionately disliked. In 1812 Godwin sent Mary to live in Dundee, where she remained, except for brief visits, until 1814. During one of these visits, at the end of 1812, Mary met Percy Bysshe Shelley and his wife Harriet. After meeting a second time in 1814, Percy and Mary fell in love and left England together, traveling through France, Switzerland, Germany, and Holland. In 1815, after they had returned to England, Mary gave birth to a daughter, who died less than two weeks later; of their four children only one, Percy (b. 1819), was to survive infancy. Shelley and Mary Godwin were married in 1816, shortly after Harriet Shelley's death by drowning.

In 1817 Mary Shelley published anonymously the *History of a Six Weeks' Tour*, cowritten with Percy. The following year her most famous work—and one of the most famous novels of the nineteenth century—was published: *Frankenstein; or, The Modern Prometheus*. It was the product of a contest among Mary Shelley, Percy Shelley, Lord Byron, and John William Polidori as to who could write the most frightening tale; Mary's was the only one brought to a conclusion, although Polidori produced the able short story "The Vampyre." *Frankenstein* was published anonymously, as were several of Mary's later books, and was thought to be the work of a man until the revised edition appeared in 1831.

Shortly after the publication of *Frankenstein*, Mary and Percy left for Italy, where on July 28, 1822, Shelley was drowned in the Bay of Spezia during a heavy squall. Because Mary did not wish to surrender her only remaining child, Percy, to Shelley's father, Sir Timothy, the latter refused to give any financial support, and it became necessary for Mary to support herself by writing. Between Shelley's death and her own in 1851 she produced five novels: *Valperga* (1823), *The Last Man* (1826), *The Fortunes of Perkin*

Warbeck (1830), *Lodore* (1835), *and Falkner* (1837). She also wrote five volumes of biographical sketches of "eminent literary and scientific men" for *Lardner's Cabinet Cyclopedia* (1835–38); a two-volume travel book, *Rambles in Germany and Italy in 1840, 1842, and 1843* (1844); and a number of poems, essays, and short stories, mostly published in the periodical *Keepsake.* Mary Shelley edited and published her husband's *Complete Poetical Works* (4 vols., 1839) and his *Essays, Letters from Abroad, Translations and Fragments* (2 vols., 1840). She died in London on February 1, 1851.

▣ *Critical Extracts*

JOHN WILSON CROKER   Our readers will guess from this summary, what a tissue of horrible and disgusting absurdity this work ⟨*Frankenstein*⟩ presents.—It is piously dedicated to Mr. Godwin, and it is written in the spirit of his school. The dreams of insanity are embodied in the strong and striking language of the insane, and the author, notwithstanding the rationality of his preface, often leaves us in doubt whether he is not as mad as his hero. Mr. Godwin is the patriarch of a literary family, whose chief skill is in delineating the wanderings of the intellect, and which strangely delights in the most afflicting and humiliating of human miseries. His disciples are a kind of *out-pensioners of Bedlam*, and like 'Mad Bess' or 'Mad Tom,' are occasionally visited with paroxysms of genius or fits of expression, which make sober-minded people wonder and shudder. ⟨. . .⟩

But when we have thus admitted that *Frankenstein* has passages which appal the mind and makes the flesh creep, we have given it all the praise (if praise it can be called) which we dare to bestow. Our taste and our judgment alike revolt at this kind of writing, and the greater the ability with which it may be executed the worse it is—it inculcates no lesson of conduct, manners, or morality; it cannot mend, and will not even amuse its readers, unless their taste have been deplorably vitiated—it fatigues the feelings without interesting the understanding; it gratuitously harasses the heart, and wantonly adds to the store, already too great, of painful sensations. The author has powers, both of conception and language, which employed in a happier direction might, perhaps (we speak dubiously,) give him a name among those whose writings amuse or amend their fellow-creatures; but we take the liberty of assuring him, and hope that he may be in a temper to listen to us, that the style which he has adopted in the present publication merely tends to defeat his own purpose, if he really had any other object in view than that of leaving the wearied reader, after a struggle between laughter and loathing, in doubt whether the head or the heart of the author be the most diseased.

John Wilson Croker, [Review of *Frankenstein*], *Quarterly Review* No. 36 (January 1818): 382, 386

SIR WALTER SCOTT   It is no slight merit in our eyes, that the tale ⟨*Frankenstein*⟩, though wild in incident, is written in plain and forcible English, without exhibiting that mixture of hyperbolical Germanisms with which tales of wonder are usually told, as if it were necessary that the language should be as extravagant as the fiction. The ideas of the author are always clearly as well as forcibly expressed; and his descriptions of landscape have in them the choice requisites of truth, freshness, precision, and beauty. The self-education of the monster, considering the slender opportunities of acquiring knowledge that he possessed, we have already noticed as improbable and overstrained. That he should not only have learned to speak, but to read, and, for aught we know, to write—that he should have become acquainted with *Werter*, with *Plutarch's Lives*, and with *Paradise Lost*, by listening through a hole in the wall, seems as unlikely as that he should have acquired, in the same way, the problems of *Euclid*, or the art of book-keeping by single and double entry. The author has however two apologies—the first, the necessity that his monster should acquire those endowments, and the other, that his neighbours were engaged in teaching the language of the country to a young foreigner. His progress in self-knowledge, and the acquisition of information is, after all, more wonderful than that of *Hai Eben Yokhdan*, or *Automathes*, or the hero of the little romance called *The Child of Nature*, one of which works might perhaps suggest the train of ideas followed by the author of *Frankenstein*. We should also be disposed, in support of the principles with which we set out, to question whether the monster, how tall, agile, and strong however, could have perpetrated so much mischief undiscovered; or passed through so many countries without being secured, either on account of his crimes, or for the benefit of some such speculator such as Mr Polito, who would have been happy to add to his museum so curious a specimen of natural history. But as we have consented to admit the leading incident of the work, perhaps some of our readers may be of the opinion, that to stickle upon lesser improbabilities, is to incur the censure bestowed by the Scottish proverb on those who "start at straws, after swallowing *windlings*."

Sir Walter Scott, "Remarks on *Frankenstein; or, The Modern Prometheus*," *Blackwood's Edinburgh Magazine* No. 12 (March 1818): 619

PERCY BYSSHE SHELLEY   This novel ⟨*Frankenstein*⟩ rests its claim on being a source of powerful and profound emotion. The elementary feelings of the human mind are exposed to view; and those who are accustomed to reason deeply on their origin and tendency will, perhaps, be the only persons who can sympathize, to the full extent, in the interest of the actions which are their result. But, founded on nature as they are, there is perhaps no reader who can endure anything beside a new love story, who will not feel a responsive string touched to his inmost soul. The sentiments are so affectionate and so innocent—the characters of the subordinate agents in this strange drama are clothed in the light of such a mild and gentle mind—the pictures of domestic manners are of the most simple and attaching character: the pathos is irresistible and deep. Nor are the crimes and malevolence of the single Being, though indeed withering and tremendous, the offspring of any unaccountable propensity to evil, but flow irresistibly from certain causes fully adequate to their production. They are the children, as it were, of Necessity and Human Nature. In this the direct moral of the book consists; and it is perhaps the most important, and of the most universal application, of any moral that can be enforced by example. Treat a person ill, and he will become wicked. Requite affection with scorn;—let one being be selected, for whatever cause, as the refuse of his kind—divide him, a social being, from society, and you impose upon him the irresistible obligations—malevolence and selfishness. It is thus that, too often in society, those who are best qualified to be its benefactors and its ornaments are branded by some accident with scorn, and changed, by neglect and solitude of heart, into a scourge.

The Being in *Frankenstein* is, no doubt, a tremendous creature. It was impossible that he should not have received among men that treatment which led to the consequences of his being a social nature. He was an abortion and an anomaly; and though his mind was such as its first impressions framed it, affectionate and full of moral sensibility, yet the circumstances of his existence are so monstrous and uncommon, that, when the consequences of them became developed in action, his original goodness was gradually turned into inextinguishable misanthropy and revenge.

Percy Bysshe Shelley, "On *Frankenstein*" (1818), cited in William Veeder, *Mary Shelley and* Frankenstein: The Fate of Androgyny (Chicago: University of Chicago Press, 1987), pp. 225–26

MARY SHELLEY   In the summer of 1816 we visited Switzerland and became the neighbours of Lord Byron. At first we spent our pleasant hours on the lake or wandering on its shores; and Lord Byron, who was writing the third canto of *Childe Harold,* was the only one among us who put his thoughts down upon paper. These, as he brought them successively to us, clothed in all the light and harmony of poetry, seemed to stamp as divine the glories of heaven and earth, whose influences we partook with him.

But it proved a wet, ungenial summer, and incessant rain often confined us for days to the house. Some volumes of ghost stories translated from the German into the French fell into our hands. ⟨. . .⟩

'We will each write a ghost story,' said Lord Byron, and his proposition was acceded to. ⟨. . .⟩ I busied myself *to think of a story*—a story to rival those which had exicted us to this task. One which would speak to the mysterious fears of our nature and awaken thrilling horror—one to make the reader dread to look round, to curdle the blood, and quicken the beatings of the heart. If I did not accomplish these things, my ghost story would be unworthy of its name. I thought and pondered—vainly. I felt that blank incapability of invention which is the greatest misery of authorship, when dull Nothing replies to our anxious invocations. 'Have you thought of a story?' I was asked each morning, and each morning I was forced to reply with a mortifying negative. ⟨. . .⟩

Many and long were the conversations between Lord Byron and Shelley, to which I was a devout but nearly silent listener. During one of these, various philosophical doctrines were discussed, and among others the nature of the principle of life, and whether there was any probability of its ever being discovered and communicated. They talked of the experiments of Dr Darwin (I speak not of what the doctor really did, or said that he did, but as more to my purpose, of what was then spoken of as having been done by him), who preserved a piece of vermicelli in a glass case till by some extraordinary means it began to move with voluntary motion. Not thus, after all, would life be given. Perhaps a corpse would be reanimated; galvanism had given token of such things: perhaps the component parts of a creature might be manufactured, brought together, and endued with vital warmth.

Night waned upon this talk, and even the witching hour had gone by before we retired to rest. When I placed my head on my pillow, I did not sleep, nor could I be said to think. My imagination, unbidden, possessed and guided me, gifting the successive images that arose in my mind with a vividness far beyond the usual bounds of reverie. I saw—with shut eyes, but acute mental vision—I saw the pale student of unhallowed arts kneeling beside the thing he had put together. I saw the hideous phantasm of a man stretched out, and then, on the working of some powerful engine, show signs of life, and stir with an uneasy, half-vital motion. Frightful must it be; for supremely frightful would be the effect of any human endeavour to mock the stupendous mechanism of the Creator of the world. His success would terrify the artist; he would rush away from his odious handiwork, horror-stricken. He would hope that, left to itself, the slight spark of life which he had communicated would fade; that this thing which had received such imperfect animation would subside into dead matter, and he might sleep in the belief that the silence of the grave would quench forever the transient existence of the hideous corpse which he had looked upon as the cradle of life. He sleeps; but he is awakened; he opens his eye; behold, the horrid thing stands at his bedside, opening his curtains and looking on him with yellow, watery, but speculative eyes.

I opened mine in terror. The idea so possessed my mind that a thrill of fear ran through me, and I wished to exchange the ghastly image of my fancy for the realities around. I see them still: the very room, the dark parquet, the closed shutters with the moonlight struggling through, and the sense I had the glassy lake and white high Alps were beyond. I could not so easily get rid of my hideous phantom; still it haunted me. I must try to think of something else. I recurred to my ghost story—my tiresome, unlucky ghost story! Oh! If I could only contrive one which would frighten my reader as I myself had been frightened that night!

Swift as light and as cheering was the idea that broke in upon me. 'I have found it! What terrified me will terrify others; and I need only describe the spectre which had haunted my midnight pillow.' On the morrow I announced that I had *thought of a story*. I began that day with the words, 'It was on a dreary night of November,' making only a transcript of the grim terrors of my waking dream.

> Mary Shelley, "Author's Introduction to the Standard Novels Edition" (1831), *Three Gothic Novels*, ed. Peter Fairclough (Harmondsworth: Penguin, 1968), pp. 260–64

RICHARD HENRY HORNE   The Monster in *Frankenstein*, sublime in his ugliness, his simplicity, his passions, his wrongs and his strength, physical and mental, embodies in the wild narrative more than one distinct and important moral theory or proposition. In himself he is the type of a class deeply and cruelly aggrieved by nature—the Deformed or hideous figure in countenance, whose sympathies and passions are as strong as their bodily deformity renders them repulsive. An amount of human woe, great beyond reckoning, have such experienced. When the monster pleads his cause against cruel man, and when he finally disappears on his raft on the icy sea to build his own funeral pile, he pleads the cause of all that class who have so strong a claim on the help and sympathy of the world, yet find little else but disgust or, at best, neglect.

The Monster created by Frankenstein is also an illustration of the embodied consequences of our actions. As he, when formed and endowed with life, became to his imaginary creator an everlasting ever-present curse, so may one single action, nay a word, or it may be thought, thrown upon the tide of time become to its originator a curse, never to be recovered, never to be shaken off.

Frankenstein suggests yet another analogy. It teaches the tragic results of attainment when an impetuous irresistible passion hurries on the soul to its doom. Such tragic results are the sacrificial fires out of which humanity arises purified. They constitute one form of the great ministry of Pain. The conception of *Frankenstein* is the converse of that of the delightful German fiction of Peter Schlemil, in which the *loss* of his shadow (reputation or honour) leads on the hero through several griefs and troubles to the great simplicity of nature and truth; while in *Frankenstein* the *attainment* of a gigantic reality leads through crime and desolation to the same goal, but it is only reached in the moment of death.

Richard Henry Horne, "Mrs. Shelley," *A New Spirit of the Age*, ed. Richard Henry Horne (New York: Harper & Brothers, 1844), pp. 318–19

HELEN MOORE   Regarded as a mere tale, it is difficult to account for the hold this story has always had upon the minds of the reading world. As a story it does not justify its own success. To say that it is remarkable as a work of imagination does not meet the difficulty. By a work of the imagination, as used in the current criticism of *Frankenstein*, is simply meant that it is a fantastic romance, such as we find in the *Arabian Nights*, or in the prose tales of Poe. But a position utterly different from these is accorded to *Frankenstein*.

We have intimated that there was a dual quality in it, to which it owed its singular power and place in literature. One element is doubtless the horror of the tale and the weird fancy of the author's imagination in the ordinary acceptation of that word. But it is to an entirely different department of mental conception that we must look for the secret of its peculiar influence. The faculty of imagination is something more than the recalling and rearrangements of past impressions. Profoundly considered, it is that function of the mind which formulates, as though real, a state of things which if present would so appear. It is the power of projecting the mind into unhappened realities. It is the faculty of picturing unseen verities. There is thus in it a prophetic element, not at all miraculous, but dependent upon subtle laws of association and suggestion. It is to this element that *Frankenstein* owes its power over thoughtful minds. It is by virtue of the allegorical element that it holds its high position as a work of imagination. Yet so unobtrusively is the allegory woven through the thread of the romance, that, while always felt, it can scarcely be said to have been detected. Certain it is that no one has directed attention to this phase, or carefully attempted an analysis of the work, with the view of deducing the meaning thus legible between the lines.

That Mrs. Shelley herself was conscious of this element is certain, by the double title she gave it,—*Frankenstein, or the Modern Prometheus*. Furthermore, that she would thus embody, under the apparent guise of a weird story, suggestions of moral truths, development of mental traits,—normal and abnormal,—and hints at, and solutions of, social questions, was in strict accord both with her own intellectual state and with the circumstances under which *Frankenstein* was produced. And yet nothing is more improbable than that it was written with such design, or that the youthful author was fully aware or even conscious of the extent to which the allegorical overlies largely the narrative in her work. This very unconsciousness of result, this obliviousness to hidden truths, is a distinguishing mark of genius. To take daily account of stock proclaims the small trader, not the merchant prince. Placed in a congenial atmosphere, genius in breathing the breath of life will exhale truths. The very gist of genius is embodied in this hidden relation to truth. That mind has genius which, detecting germs of truth under forms where the common eye sees them not, affords itself the place and pabulum for their growth.

Helen Moore, "Frankenstein, and Other Writings," *Mary Wollstonecraft Shelley* (Philadelphia: J. B. Lippincott Co., 1886), pp. 248–50

EDITH BIRKHEAD   Like *Alastor*, *Frankenstein* was a plea for human sympathy, and was, according to Shelley's preface, intended to "exhibit the amiableness of domestic affection and the excellence of universal virtue." The monster has the perception and desire of goodness, but, by the circumstances of his abnormal existence, is delivered over to evil. It is this dual nature that prevents him from being a mere automaton. The monster indeed is far more real than the shadowy beings whom he pursues. Frankenstein is less an individual than a type, and only interests us through the emotions which his conflict with the monster arouses. Clerval, Elizabeth and Frankenstein's relatives are passive sufferers whose psychology does not concern us. Mrs. Shelley rightly lavishes her skill on the central figure of the book, and succeeds, as effectually as Frankenstein himself, in infusing into him the spark of life. Mrs. Shelley's aim is to "awaken thrilling horror," and, incidentally, to "exhibit the excellence of domestic virtue," and for her purpose the demon is of paramount importance. The involved, complex plot of a novel seemed to pass beyond Mrs. Shelley's control. A short tale she could handle successfully, and Shelley was unwise in inciting her to expand *Frankenstein* into a long narrative. So long as she is completely carried away by her subject Mrs. Shelley writes clearly, but when she pauses to regard the progress of her story dispassionately, she seems to be over-whelmed by the wealth of her resources and to have no power of selecting the relevant details. The laborious introductory letters, the meticulous record of Frankenstein's education, the story of Felix and Sofie, the description of the tour through England before the creation of the second monster is attempted, are all connected with the main theme by very frail links and serve to distract our attention in an irritating fashion from what really interests us. In the novel of mystery a tantalising delay may be singularly effective. In a novel which depends chiefly for its effect on sheer horror, delays are merely dangerous. By resting her terrors on a pseudo-scientific basis and by placing her story in a definite locality, Mrs. Shelley waives her right to an entire suspension of disbelief. If it be reduced to its lowest terms, the plot of *Frankenstein*, with its bewildering confusion of the prosaic and the fantastic, sounds as crude, disjointed and inconsequent as that of a nightmare. Mrs. Shelley's timid hesitation between imagination and reality, her attempt to reconcile incompatible things and to place a creature who belongs to no earthly land in familiar surroundings, prevents *Frankenstein* from being a wholly satisfactory and alarming novel of terror. She loves the fantastic, but she also fears it. She is weighted down by commonsense, and so flutters instead of soaring, unwilling to trust herself far from the material world. But the fact that she was able to vivify her grotesque skeleton of a plot with some degree of success is no mean tribute to her gifts. The energy and vigour of her style, her complete and serious absorption in her subject, carry us safely over many an absurdity.

Edith Birkhead, *The Tale of Terror: A Study of the Gothic Romance* (New York: Dutton, 1921), pp. 163–65.

MURIEL SPARK   If *The Last Man* were to be called a Gothic novel, the qualification must be added that it exists as such only in so far as an improbable theme of horror maintains an illusion of probability. As in *Frankenstein*, this story offers nothing supernatural, and very little except plain horror that is proper to the Gothic convention. But this horror is enough to reveal its Gothic affinities. It is true that the plague does not descend from the clouds as from the wrath of a fiend; but it does descend from the earth, evolving from microbe to monster and sinuously progressing across the whole terrestrial scene. And the Greek Princess Evadne, her exotic temperament, her high-flown actions and her final passionate prophecy, are in the Gothic style. As in *Frankenstein*, however, the effects are horrific but the methods are not those of the horror novel proper; as in *Frankenstein*, the Gothic element is chastened by the rational.

It is further chastened by realism, and still further by a domestic note. It is not, therefore, a Gothic novel entirely; nor is it realist fiction, for the whole work is a fantasy; and neither is it a domestic tale for the work deals with society at large as well as family life; moreover, it is not a sociological novel, since the disintegration of the social scene leaves a large portion of the book to the study of individual man. *The Last Man*, in fact, defies classification in any accepted fictional genre; but that is not to question its value as such. I would describe it as a triptych of fiction—a group of three pictures, associated with, yet distinct from each other.

Muriel Spark, *Child of Light: A Reassessment of Mary Wollstonecraft Shelley* (Hadleigh, UK: Tower Bridge, 1951), p. 157

HAROLD BLOOM   I am suggesting that what makes *Frankenstein* an important book, though it is only a strong, flawed, frequently clumsy novel, is that it vividly projects a version of the Romantic mythology of the self, found among other places, in Blake's *Book of Urizen*, Shelley's *Prometheus Unbound* and Byron's *Manfred*. It lacks the sophistication and imaginative complexity of such works but precisely because of that *Frankenstein* affords a unique introduction to the archetypal world of the Romantics. ⟨...⟩

If we stand back from Mary Shelley's novel, in order to better view its archetypal shape, we see it as the quest of a solitary and ravaged consciousness first for consolation, then for revenge, and finally for a self-destruction that will be apocalyptic, that will bring down the creator with his creature. Though Mary Shelley may not have intended it, her novel's prime theme is a necessary counterpoise to Prometheanism, for Prometheanism exalts the increase in consciousness despite all cost. Frankenstein breaks through the barrier that separates man from God, and apparently becomes the giver of life, but all he actually can give is death-in-life. The profound dejection endemic to Mary Shelley's novel is fundamental to the Romantic mythology of the self, for all Romantic horrors are diseases of excessive consciousness, of the self unable to bear the self. Kierkegaard remarks that Satan's despair is absolute, because Satan as pure spirit is pure consciousness, and for Satan (and all men in his predicament) every increase in consciousness is an increase in despair. Frankenstein's desperate creature attains the state of pure spirit through his extraordinary situation, and is racked by a consciousness in which every thought is a fresh disease.

A Romantic poet fought against self-consciousness through the strength of what he called imagination, a more than rational energy, by which thought could seek to heal itself. But Frankenstein's daemon, though he is in the archetypal situation of the Romantic Wanderer or Solitary, who sometimes was a poet, can win no release from his own story by telling it. His desperate desire for a mate is clearly an attempt to find a Shelleyan Epipsyche or Blakean Emanation for himself, a self within the self. But as he is the nightmare actualization of Frankenstein's desire, he is himself an emanation of Promethean yearnings, and his only double is his creator and denier.

Harold Bloom, "Frankenstein, or the New Prometheus," *Partisan Review* 32, No. 4 (Fall 1965): 613, 617

ELLEN MOERS   Mary Shelley was a unique case, in literature as in life. She brought birth to fiction not as realism but as Gothic fantasy, and thus contributed to Romanticism a myth of genuine originality: the mad scientist who locks himself in his laboratory and secretly, guiltily, works at creating human life, only to find that he has made a monster.

> It was on a dreary night of November, that I beheld the
> accomplishment of my toils. With an anxiety that almost
> amounted to agony, I collected the instruments of life around
> me, that I might infuse a spark of being into the lifeless
> thing that lay at my feet. . . . The rain pattered dismally against
> the panes, and my candle was nearly burnt out, when, by
> the glimmer of the half-extinguished light, I saw the dull yellow
> eye of the creature open; it breathed hard, and a convulsive
> motion agitated the limbs. . . . His yellow skin scarcely covered
> the work of muscles and arteries beneath; his hair was of a
> lustrous black, and flowing . . . but these luxuriances only formed
> a more horrid contrast with his watery eyes, that seemed
> almost of the same color as the dun white sockets in which they
> were set, his shrivelled complexion and straight black lips.

That is very good horror, but what follows is more horrid still: Franken-stein, the scientist, runs away and abandons the newborn Monster, who is and remains nameless. Here, I think, is where Mary Shelley's book is most interesting, most powerful, and most feminine: in the motif of revulsion against newborn life, and the drama of guilt, dread, and flight surrounding birth and its consequences. Most of the novel, roughly two of its three volumes, can be said to deal with the retribution visited upon Monster and creator for deficient infant care. *Frankenstein* seems to be distinctly a *woman's* mythmaking on the subject of birth precisely because its emphasis is not upon what precedes birth, not upon birth itself, but upon what follows birth: the trauma of the afterbirth.

Ellen Moers, "Female Gothic" (1974), *The Endurance of* Frankenstein, ed. George Levine and U. C. Knoepflmacher (Berkeley: University of California Press, 1979), pp. 80–81

PAUL A. CANTOR   In dramatizing the position of an alien being in an uncomprehending community, *Frankenstein* embodies what gradually emerged as the Romantic conception of the artist's relation to society. Victor is the epitome of the isolated Romantic genius: a man with a special power of insight, a rebel against convention, living on the fringes of society, losing touch with his fellow men even as he works to transform their existence. Both Frankenstein and the monster stand out from the ranks of ordinary men. What distinguishes the creator from the creature is that he glories in his sense of being different: "I could not rank myself with the herd of common projectors." The monster, by contrast, does not like to dwell upon the ways in which he excels ordinary men, but only craves their acceptance in normal life. Frankenstein, who evidently could enjoy a successful family life with Elizabeth, gives it up for the sake of his creativity, while the monster, who is free of all ties and could, for example, achieve success as an Arctic explorer beyond Robert Walton's wildest dreams, longs for nothing more than lingering by the sort of family hearth both Frankenstein and Walton despise. Deep down, the creator and the creature in *Frankenstein* yearn to exchange roles: the monster craves the home life Frankenstein rejects, and Frankenstein covets the freedom from personal bonds which the monster views as his curse.

Perhaps then we can view the monster's attitude toward Frankenstein as the creature in man rebelling against the creator in man. The monster expresses the resentment of man's creaturely instincts against his creative impulses, which cause him to suffer and be lonely in his life. Reduced to its essentials, the monster's charge against Frankenstein is: "You've made me miserable for the sake of your creativity." One can think of this reproach as the human half of a poet saying to the artistic half: "For the sake of your art, you've ruined my life." If we take seriously the idea of Frankenstein and the monster as a composite being, we see that in portraying the conflict of creator and creature, Mary Shelley's novel begins to explore the tension between art and life that became such a central theme in nineteenth-century literature.

Paul A. Cantor, *Creature and Creator: Myth-Making and English Romanticism* (Cambridge: Cambridge University Press, 1984), pp. 129–30

JOYCE CAROL OATES   ⟨. . .⟩ it is a mistake to read *Frankenstein* as a modern novel of psychological realism, or as a "novel" at all. It contains no characters, only points of view; its concerns are pointedly moral and didactic; it makes no claims for verisimilitude of even a poetic Wordsworthian nature. (The Alpine landscapes are all self-consciously sublime and theatrical; Mont Blanc, for instance, suggests "another earth, the habitations of another race of beings.") If one were to choose a literary antecedent for *Frankenstein* it might be, surprisingly, Samuel Johnson's *Rasselas*, rather than a popular Gothic like Mrs. Radcliffe's *Mysteries of Udolpho*, which allegedly had the power to frighten its readers. (A character in Jane Austen's *Northanger Abbey* says of this once famous novel: "I remember finishing it in two days—my hair standing on end the whole time.") Though *Frankenstein* and *Dracula* are commonly linked, Bram Stoker's tour-de-force of 1897 is vastly different in tone, theme, and intention from Shelley's novel: its "monster" is not at all monstrous in appearance, only in behavior; and he is thoroughly and irremediably evil by nature. But no one in *Frankenstein* is evil—the universe is emptied of God and theistic assumptions of "good" and "evil." Hence its modernity.

Tragedy does not arise spontaneous and unwilled in so "modern" a setting, it must be made—in fact, manufactured. The Fates are not to blame; there *are* no Fates; only the brash young scientist who boasts of never having feared the supernatural. ("In my education my father had taken the greatest precautions that my mind should be impressed with no supernatural horrors. I do not ever remember to have trembled at a tale of superstition, or to have feared the apparition of a spirit. . . . A churchyard was to me merely the receptacle of bodies deprived of life, which, from being the seat of beauty and strength, had become food for the worm.") Where *Dracula* and other conventional Gothic works are fantasies, with clear links to fairy tales and

legends, and even popular ballads, *Frankenstein* has the theoretical and cautionary tone of science fiction. It is meant to prophecize, not to entertain.
    Joyce Carol Oates, "Afterword: Frankenstein's Fallen Angel," *Frankenstein; or, The Modern Prometheus* (West Hatfield, CT: Pennyroyal Press, 1984), pp. 248–49

CHRIS BALDICK   That Victor Frankenstein assembles his monster from parts of corpses collected from charnel houses and dissecting rooms is one of the most memorable and enduring features of the story, even to those who have never read Mary Shelley's novel. The monstrosity of the creature is clearly enough the consequence of its assembly from different parts, but it still sets us a puzzle which James Whale's 1931 film version evades by introducing a faulty component, the Abnormal Brain: why should a creature constructed from parts which Victor selects as perfect and indeed beautiful specimens turn out to be hideously repulsive? The novel provides no explanation for the creature's ugliness, and if we are tempted to account for it psychologically as a mere projection of Frankenstein's guilty revulsion from his deed, we run up against the evidence of the other characters' reactions. The monster appears frighteningly ugly not just to his creator but to all who see him, even to himself as he studies his reflection in water. By stressing clearly the beauty of the component parts and the ugliness of the finished combination, Mary Shelley is isolating and dramatizing a problem which was in her time central to philosophical, and by extension to aesthetic and political discussion; namely the question of the relation of parts to wholes.

Just as for Kant the mind had to be more than the sum of its sense impressions, so for Coleridge, the British avatar of German Idealism, any living 'whole'—whether a plant, a poem, or a nation—was always more than a mere aggregation of its constituent parts. It was upon this principle that Romantic Idealism founded its critique of the empiricist thought of the preceding century and set the terms of that central opposition between the mechanical and the organic which was to define so many of the conflicts within nineteenth century culture.

⟨. . .⟩ The fragmented society, the patchwork or clockwork individual— these become the themes of Romantic social analysis from Schiller through Carlyle and beyond. Mary Shelley's *Frankenstein* takes its place within this pattern of Romantic contrasts between lifeless parts and living wholes, partly as a dramatization of that principle of inorganic aggregation which Schiller saw as the modern disease. Viewed in this light, Victor Frankenstein's error is to have confused the beauty of the dead limbs he has collected with the beauty of the whole organism. According to the Idealist philosophy of the Romantics, the beauty of the whole can arise only from a pure vital principle within, to which all subordinate parts and limbs will then conform. The parts, in a living being, can only be as beautiful as the animating principle which organizes them, and if this 'spark of life' proceeds, as it does in Victor's creation, from tormented isolation and guilty secrecy, the resulting assembly will only animate and body forth that condition and display its moral ugliness.

> Chris Baldick, "The Monster Speaks: Mary Shelley's Novel," In *Frankenstein's Shadow: Myth, Monstrosity, and Nineteenth-Century Writing* (Oxford: Clarendon Press, 1987), pp. 33–35

DAVID SOYKA   Since Mary Shelley's "Frankenstein's Monster" has become such a commonplace expression, with a legion of authors indebted to her for inspiring their own imaginative works, it is easy to lose sight of the originality of Mary Shelley's invention. As ⟨Anne K.⟩ Mellor points out, "All other creation myths . . . depend on female participation or some form of divine interpretation. . . . The idea of an entirely man-made monster is Mary Shelley's own." The significance of this is best illustrated by Northrop Frye's observation that the "creation myth suggests planning and intelligence, and planning and intelligence suggest a creator who could have originally produced only a perfect or model world. . . . To account for the contrast between the model world that such a God must have made and the actual world that we find ourselves in now, a myth of human 'fall' must be added, an alienation myth which expresses the present human condition *but does not attach it directly to the work of creation*" (emphasis added).

Mary Shelley's unique literary achievement is that she creates a myth in which evil is not separate from creation, but is intertwinably fated with the act. Man creates evil because he lacks foresight to anticipate the outcomes of creation. Therefore, if God exists, and if evil has entered into God's Creation, then it must be through some similar shortcoming of God. This raises the question of whether a fallible God, if there is one at all, deserves to be worshiped. And, if not, wherein lies salvation?

The novel's conclusion suggests that if there is any hope of salvation, it is through humanity's, not God's, doing. Frankenstein and his Monster have self-destructed, the latter, ironically, by fire, Prometheus's gift to humanity. Robert Walton, though not without regret, is persuaded to abandon his own Promethean quest in recognition of the potential harm he might inflict upon his fellow beings. Despite the shortcomings of God's Creation, Mary

Shelley puts faith in humanity's ability to learn from its mistakes, that individual will and foresight allow for at least the chance that evil need not be inevitable. That as we enter the twenty-first century we continue to live with the Frankenstein Complex hints that this viewpoint may be overly optimistic.

> David Soyka, "*Frankenstein* and the Miltonic Creation of Evil," *Extrapolation* 33, No. 2 (Summer 1992): 175–76

❖ *Bibliography*

History of a Six Weeks' Tour through a Part of France, Switzerland, Germany and Holland (with Percy Bysshe Shelley). 1817.

Frankenstein; or, The Modern Prometheus. 1818. 3 vols.

Valperga; or, The Life and Adventures of Castruccio, Prince of Lucca. 1823. 3 vols.

Posthumous Poems by Percy Bysshe Shelley (editor). 1824.

The Last Man. 1826. 3 vols.

The Fortunes of Perkin Warbeck: A Romance. 1830. 3 vols.

Lodore. 1835. 3 vols.

Falkner. 1837. 3 vols.

Poetical Works by Percy Bysshe Shelley (editor). 1839. 4 vols.

Essays, Letters from Abroad, Translations and Fragments by Percy Bysshe Shelley (editor). 1840. 2 vols.

Rambles in Germany and Italy in 1840, 1842 and 1843. 1844. 2 vols.

The Choice: A Poem on Shelley's Death. Ed. H. Buxton Forman. 1876.

Tales and Stories. Ed. Richard Garnett. 1891.

Letters, Mostly Unpublished. Ed. Henry H. Harper. 1918.

Proserpine and Midas: Mythological Dramas. Ed. André Henri Koszul. 1922.

Harriet and Mary: Being the Relations between P. B., Harriet and Mary Shelley and T. J. Hogg as Shown in Letters between Them (with others). Ed. Walter Sidney Scott. 1944.

Letters. Ed. Frederick L. Jones. 1944. 2 vols.

Journal. Ed. Frederick L. Jones. 1947.

My Best Mary: Selected Letters. Ed. Muriel Spark and Derek Stanford. 1953.

Matilda. Ed. Elizabeth Nitchie. 1959.

Shelley's Posthumous Poems: Mary Shelley's Fair Copy Book (editor). Ed. Irving Massey. 1969.

Collected Tales and Stories. Ed. Charles E. Robinson. 1976.

Letters. Ed. Betty T. Bennett. 1980–88. 3 vols.

Journals. Ed. Paula R. Feldman and Diana Scott-Kilvert. 1987. 2 vols.

The Mary Shelley Reader. Ed. Betty T. Bennett and Charles E. Robinson.
    1990.

⊠ ⊠ ⊠

Robert Louis Stevenson
1850–1894

ROBERT LOUIS BALFOUR STEVENSON was born in Edinburgh on November 13, 1850, the only son of a lighthouse engineer. In 1867 he entered Edinburgh University to study engineering, but in 1871 decided to study law instead. In 1875 he was admitted to the Scottish bar, but by then had already decided to become a writer.

In 1878, after he had published a number of articles in various periodicals and several minor works of juvenilia, Stevenson brought out *An Inland Voyage*, describing a tour by canoe of Belgium and France in 1876. This was followed by *Deacon Brodie* (1880), the first of several undistinguished plays written in collaboration with his friend William Ernest Henley; the others were *Admiral Guinea* (1884), *Beau Austin* (1884), and *Macaire* (1885). *Travels with a Donkey in the Cévennes* appeared in 1879, the same year Stevenson went to America in pursuit of Fanny Osbourne, whom he married in 1880. He returned to England the following year, and traveled frequently over the next two years on the Continent and in the Scottish Highlands in search of better health.

In 1881 Stevenson published *Virginibus Puerisque*, a collection of short stories, essays, and travel pieces. This was followed by *Familiar Studies of Men and Books* (1882) and the episodic novels *New Arabian Nights* (1882) and *More New Arabian Nights: The Dynamiter* (1885; with Fanny Van de Grift Stevenson). In 1883 Stevenson published *The Silverado Squatters*, an account of his adventures on his honeymoon near an abandoned silver mine, and also brought out his first full-length novel, *Treasure Island*, which made him famous. It was followed by such works as *A Child's Garden of Verses* (1885), the novels *Kidnapped* (1886) and *The Black Arrow* (1888), and *Underwoods* (1887), a volume of poetry.

Stevenson's weird work is restricted to the short novel *The Strange Case of Dr. Jekyll and Mr. Hyde* (1886) and some short stories, notably "Thrawn Janet," "Markheim," "Olalla," and "The Body-Snatcher," most of which were first collected in *The Merry Men and Other Tales and Fables* (1887).

Dr. Jekyll and Mr. Hyde is the prototypical tale of a *Doppelgänger* or "double"; its portrayal of a split personality, although perhaps inspired by Poe's "William Wilson" and other earlier examples, has made it one of the most influential works in the history of horror fiction. *New Arabian Nights* and *More New Arabian Nights* also have their weird touches, especially the section in the first book entitled "The Suicide Club"; in form these novels appear to have inspired Arthur Machen's *The Three Impostors* (1895).

Stevenson and his family spent 1887 in America, then in 1888 sailed to the South Seas, still in search of a beautiful environment. In 1889 he purchased an estate in Vailima, Samoa, where he settled permanently. During the few remaining years of his life Stevenson published his novels *The Wrong Box* (1889), written with his stepson Lloyd Osbourne, and *The Master of Ballantrae* (1889), as well as a short-story collection, *Island Nights' Entertainments* (1893), which contains his famous story "The Beach of Falesá."

In 1893 Fanny Stevenson suffered a nervous breakdown. Despite this Stevenson brought out one more novel, *The Ebb-Tide*, written with Lloyd Osbourne, before dying of a brain hemorrhage on December 3, 1894. At the time of his death Stevenson was at work on yet another novel, *Weir of Hermiston*, published as a fragment in 1896. A *Life* by Graham Balfour appeared in 1901, and there have been several editions of his collected letters.

◈ *Critical Extracts*

GERARD MANLEY HOPKINS   A friend recommended me if I met with them to read L. Stevenson's stories, the *New Arabian Nights* and others since. I read a story by him in *Longman's*, I think, and a paper by him on Romance. His doctrine, if I apprehend him, is something like this. The essence of Romance is incident and that only, the type of pure Romance the *Arabian Nights*: those stories have no moral, no character-drawing, they turn altogether on interesting incident. The incidents must of course have a connection, but it need be nothing more than that they happen to the same person, are aggravations and so on. As history consists essentially of events likely or unlikely, consequences of causes chronicled before or what may be called chance, just retributions or nothing of the sort, so Romance, which is fictitious history, consists of event, of incident. His own stories

are written on this principle: they are very good and he has all the gifts
a writer of fiction should have, including those he holds unessential, as
characterisation, and at first you notice no more than an ordinary well told
story, but on looking back in the light of this doctrine you see that the
persons illustrate the incident or strain of incidents, the plot, *the story*, not
the story and incidents the persons.

Gerard Manley Hopkins, Letter to R. W. Dixon (15 August 1883), *The Correspondence of Gerard Manley Hopkins and Richard Watson Dixon,* ed. Claude Colleer Abbott (London: Oxford University Press, 1935), p. 114

JOHN ADDINGTON SYMONDS   I doubt whether anyone
has the right so to scrutinise "the abysmal depths of personality." You see
I have been reading *Dr. Jekyll.* At least I think he ought to bring more of
distinct belief in the resources of human nature, more faith, more sympathy
with our frailty, into the matter than you have done. The art is burning
and intense. The *Peau de Chagrin* disappears, and Poe's work is water. Also
one discerns at once that this is an allegory of all twy-natured souls who
yield consciously to evil. Most of us are on the brink of educating a Mr.
Hyde at some epoch of our being. But the scientific cast of the allegory will
only act as an incentive to moral self-murder with those who perceive the
allegory's profundity. Louis, how had you the "ilia dura, ferro et aere triplici
duriora," to write Dr. Jekyll? I know now what was meant when you were
called a sprite.

You see I am trembling under the magician's wand of your fancy, and
rebelling against it with the scorn of a soul that hates to be contaminated
with the mere picture of victorious evil. Our only chance seems to me to
be to maintain, against all appearances, that evil can never and in no way
be victorious. ⟨. . .⟩

The suicide end of Dr. Jekyll is too commonplace. Dr. Jekyll ought to
have given Mr. Hyde up to justice. This would have vindicated the sense
of human dignity which is so horribly outraged in your book.

John Addington Symonds, Letter to Robert Louis Stevenson (1 March 1886), cited in Horatio N. Brown, *John Addington Symonds: A Biography* (1893; rev. ed. London: Smith, Elder & Co., 1903), pp. 407–8

HENRY JAMES   Is *Dr. Jekyll and Mr. Hyde* a work of high philo-
sophic intention, or simply the most ingenious and irresponsible of fictions?
It has the stamp of a really imaginative production, that we may take it in
different ways, but I suppose it would be called the most serious of the

author's tales. It deals with the relation of the baser parts of man to his nobler—of the capacity for evil that exists in the most generous natures, and it expresses these things in a fable which is a wonderfully happy invention. The subject is endlessly interesting, and rich in all sorts of provocation, and Mr. Stevenson is to be congratulated on having touched the core of it. I may do him injustice, but it is, however, here, not the profundity of the idea which strikes me so much as the art of the presentation—the extremely successful form. There is a genuine feeling for the perpetual moral question, a fresh sense of the difficulty of being good and the brutishness of being bad, but what there is above all is a singular ability in holding the interest. I confess that that, to my sense, is the most edifying thing in the short, rapid, concentrated story, which is really a masterpiece of concision. There is something almost impertinent in the way, as I have noticed, in which Mr. Stevenson achieves his best effects without the aid of the ladies, and *Dr. Jekyll* is a capital example of his heartless independence. It is usually supposed that a truly poignant impression cannot be made without them, but in the drama of Mr. Hyde's fatal ascendency they remain altogether in the wing. It is very obvious—I do not say it cynically—that they must have played an important part in his development. The gruesome tone of the tale is, no doubt, deepened by their absence; it is like the late afternoon light of a foggy winter Sunday, when even inanimate objects have a kind of wicked look. I remember few situations in the pages of mystifying fiction more to the purpose than the episode of Mr. Utterson's going to Dr. Jekyll's to confer with the butler, when the doctor is locked up in his laboratory and the old servant, whose sagacity has hitherto encountered successfully the problems of the sideboard and the pantry, confesses that this time he is utterly baffled. The way the two men, at the door of the laboratory, discuss the identity of the mysterious personage inside, who has revealed himself in two or three inhuman glimpses to Poole, has those touches of which irresistible shudders are made. The butler's theory is that his master has been murdered, and that the murderer is in the room, personating him with a sort of clumsy diabolism. "Well, when that masked thing like a monkey jumped from among the chemicals and whipped into the cabinet, it went down my spine like ice." That is the effect upon the reader of most of the story. I say of most rather than all, because the ice rather melts in the sequel, and I have some difficulty in accepting the business of the powders, which seems to me too explicit and explanatory. The powders constitute the machinery of the transformation, and it will probably have struck many readers that this uncanny process would be more conceivable (so far as one may speak of the conceivable in such a case), if the author had not made it so definite.

Henry James, "Robert Louis Stevenson," *Century Magazine* 35, No. 6 (April 1888): 877–78

ARTHUR MACHEN   Don't you see how thoroughly *physical* the actual plot ⟨of *Dr. Jekyll and Mr. Hyde*⟩ is? and if one escapes for a moment from the atmosphere of the laboratory it is only to be confronted by the most obvious vein of moral allegory; and from this latter light *Jekyll and Hyde* seems almost the vivid metaphor of a clever preacher. You mustn't imagine, you know, that I condemn the powder business as bad in itself, for (let us revert for a moment to philosophy) man is a sacrament, soul manifested under the form of body, and art has to deal with each and both and to show their interaction and interdependence. ⟨. . .⟩ But (in our age, at all events) a prose romance ⟨. . .⟩ must have incident, corporeity, relation to material things, and all these will occupy a considerable part of the whole. To a certain extent, then, the idea must be materialised, but still it must always shine through the fleshly vestment; the body must never be mere body but always the body of the spirit, existing to conceal and yet to manifest the spirit; and here it seems to me that Stevenson's story breaks down. The transformation of Jekyll into Hyde is solely material as you read it, without artistic significance; it is simply an astounding incident, and not an outward sign of an inward mystery. As for the possible allegory I have too much respect for Stevenson as an artificer to think that he would regard this element as anything but a grave defect. Allegory, as Poe so well observed, is always a literary vice, and we are only able to enjoy *The Pilgrim's Progress* by forgetting that the allegory exists. Yes, that seems to me the *vitium* of *Jekyll and Hyde*: the conception has been badly realised, and by badly I do not mean clumsily, because from the logical, literal standpoint the plot and the construction are marvels of cleverness; but I mean inartistically: ecstasy, which as we have settled is the synonym of art, gave birth to the idea, but immediately abandoned it to artifice, and to artifice only, instead of presiding over and inspiring every further step in plot, in construction and in style.

Arthur Machen, *Hieroglyphics: A Note upon Ecstasy in Literature* (1902; rpt. New York: Knopf, 1923), pp. 73–74

EINO RAILO   ⟨In *Dr. Jekyll and Mr. Hyde*⟩ the element of evil is actually wrenched apart from a human being and transmuted into a new being, not only in a spiritual sense but bodily. The division, or more rightly, transformation is effected by the invention, in itself a little mysterious, of an unknown drug. So Stevenson rejects the Devil's elixir and turns for help to science, whereby he eliminates the mystical element from his story and substitutes for it that instinctive impression aroused in the mind by the mention of strange and terrible unknown drugs discovered by the "adepts" of science. The effect of the drug on Dr. Jekyll is to cause everything good in him to disappear. His noble appearance becomes the prototype of wickedness, his soul a nest of baseness and iniquity; for this new being sinning is fraught with devilish joy. His pleasure is increased by the knowledge that he need never fear being brought to book for his excesses, as he can at any time regain his former respect-awakening exterior simply by a new dose of the same drug. The position could not have been better for a personation of human wickedness. ⟨. . .⟩

The merit of this tale of horror, put together with cool-headed Scotch calculation, lies in its power of affecting the reader, even though it lacks the suggestive power of the story of Medardus ⟨in E. T. A. Hoffmann's "The Elixir of the Devil"⟩, with its realistic, human and yet demoniac representative of the principle of evil and with the allegorical force with which the growing power of evil over its proselytes is depicted. The detachment and quasi-scientific stamp of the novel tempt one to deny to it the atmosphere of romanticism, but its masterly manner of depicting evil in the guise of a human being, capable of being evolved from the noblest soul, awakens a series of compelling moods.

Eino Railo, *The Haunted Castle: A Study of the Elements of English Romanticism* (London: George Routledge & Sons; New York: E. P. Dutton, 1927), pp. 187–88

MASAO MIYOSHI   Then there is "Markheim" (1884), which somewhat resembles *Crime and Punishment*. The hero, intent on robbery, enters a pawnshop on Christmas eve on the pretext of looking for a present. There, like Dorian Gray prematurely encountering his portrait, the sight of himself in an antique hand-mirror unhinges him: "Why, look here—look in it—look at yourself!" he cries to the pawnbroker, "Do you like to see it? No! nor I—nor any man." There is too awful a self-recognition in the mirror, a "damned reminder of years, and sins and follies [in] this hand conscience." At the height of the self-aversion Markheim murders the man, only to be confronted at every turn in the stifling little room by some presence, some "shadow of himself." In one glass after another "he saw his face repeated and repeated, as it were an army of spies; his own eyes met and detected him."

Out of his anguish, there appears another man Markheim at once recognizes as a "likeness to himself." The double is that other self, his conscience. Markheim at first tries to justify himself to this double. What he seems to be, he argues, is not his true nature but merely a disguise, a mask: "I have lived to belie my nature. All men do; all men are better than this disguise that grows about and stifles them." Arguing in the Godwinian vein, he is, he insists, merely what the "giants of circumstance" have made of him, his true self having no responsibility for anything the "lie" happens to do. Underneath his false face anyone can see the "clear writing of conscience." The double admonishes him for all this self-defensiveness, and when the shopkeeper's servant girl suddenly returns he advises killing her and running. However, Markheim, realizing that he is still free and, like the hero in *Sartor Resartus,* can still prefer good to evil, confronts her and tells his crime. During this confession, the features of his double brighten and soften, and he gradually disappears. Markheim has reconciled the double agents of action: his true free self and circumstance. The "other self" has no reason any longer to live.

Masao Miyoshi, *The Divided Self: A Perspective on the Literature of the Victorians* (New York: New York University Press, 1969), pp. 294–95

VLADIMIR NABOKOV   Please completely forget, disremember, obliterate, unlearn, consign to oblivion any notion you may have had that *Jekyll and Hyde* is some kind of a mystery story, a detective story, or movie. It is of course quite true that Stevenson's short novel, written in 1885, is one of the ancestors of the modern mystery story. But today's mystery story is the very negation of style, being, at the best, conventional literature. Frankly, I am not one of those college professors who coyly boasts of enjoying detective stories—they are too badly written for my taste and bore me to death. Whereas Stevenson's story is—God bless his pure soul—lame as a detective story. Neither is it a parable nor an allegory, for it would be tasteless as either. It has, however, its own special enchantment if we regard it as a phenomenon of style. It is not only a good "bogey story," as Stevenson exclaimed when awakening from a dream in which he had visualized it much in the same way I suppose as magic cerebration had granted Coleridge the vision of the most famous of unfinished poems. It is also, and more importantly, "a fable that lies nearer to poetry than to ordinary prose fiction" (Stephen Gwynn) and therefore belongs to the same order of art as, for instance, *Madame Bovary* or *Dead Souls.*

Vladimir Nabokov, "*The Strange Case of Dr. Jekyll and Mr. Hyde* (1885)," *Lectures on Literature*, ed. Fredson Bowers (New York: Harcourt Brace Jovanovich, 1980), pp. 179–80

ED BLOCK, JR.   In "Olalla," which a recent editor ⟨Michael Hayes⟩—opposing most previous critical opinion—says "must surely be counted in the handful of truly great horror stories in the English language," most of the characters including the soldier-narrator show similar tendencies to recapitulate primitive modes of consciousness. In different ways all three members of a once-great Spanish family exhibit the decline of their race to the soldier who comes to recuperate at their residencia. Felipe, the son, is a half-wit whose preconceptual language appears focused on sensation. He "seemed to live . . . by the senses, taken and possessed by the visual object of the moment and unable to discharge his mind of that impression." His speech is a "disjointed babble . . . and yet somehow with an effect that was natural and pleasing, like that of the song of birds." The Señora, mother of Felipe and Olalla, has just as little use for speech, also living in the moment. A more frightening manifestation of her primitiveness, however, is her violent bloodlust. Aroused by the sight of blood from the soldier's cut hand, the Señora suddenly attacks the soldier and bites the hand. As in the case of Hyde's attack on Sir Danvers Carew, the unexpected impulsive act reveals prehuman instincts. The Señora's attraction to blood is significant as it represents another modification of a traditional Gothic convention. In the context of the story's concern with Galtonian notions of heredity, bloodlust represents a manifestation of "degeneracy" such as Walter Bagehot, for instance, had forecast in *Physics and Politics*. In this way the age-old trope is legitimized in the evolutionist context and as a result invested with a fresh load of sinister connotations. The Señora's bloodlust also anticipates the interest in vampirism evidenced most clearly a decade later in Bram Stoker's *Dracula*.

> Ed Block, Jr., "James Sully, Evolutionist Psychology, and Late Victorian Gothic Fiction," *Victorian Studies* 25, No. 4 (Summer 1982): 459–60

STEPHEN HEATH   This *Strange Case of Dr Jekyll and Mr Hyde* can stand as one of those works in which the unconscious is glimpsed but not heard, an example of the challenge to 'the very fortress of identity' in the latter part of the nineteenth century, contemporary with von Hartmann, Nietzsche and so on whose ideas could be made to provide parallels with Stevenson's version of the human duality. Jekyll's I is overwhelmed by what lies beneath it, by its inner fissures and depths, but this underconsciousness is then only representable as darkness and animality, 'the beast Hyde' with all his 'ape-like' tricks. The reader, 'every thinking creature', can then recognise himself in this telling of 'man's double being', find his own Hyde (we need to keep to the text's conventional male generalisations here); thus ⟨Gerard Manley⟩ Hopkins: 'You are certainly wrong about Hyde being overdrawn: my Hyde is worse'. As for what this recognition might involve, Stevenson ⟨. . .⟩ plays down sexuality, the problem is hypocrisy: 'The harm was in Jekyll, because he was a hypocrite . . . The hypocrite let out the beast Hyde'. But not just in Jekyll, rather in Jekyll in society: it is the desire 'to carry [his] head high' and to stand with grave countenance 'before the public' that leads him to 'a profound duplicity of life'. Or as Freud will put it some twenty years later: 'Experience teaches us that for most people there is a limit beyond which their constitution cannot comply with the demands of civilization. All who wish to be more noble-minded than their constitution allows fall victims to neurosis; they would have been more healthy if it could have been possible for them to be less good'. Indeed, Stevenson's world in the *Strange Case of Dr Jekyll and Mr Hyde* is very much that of Freud's ' "Civilized" Sexual Morality and Modern Nervous Illness' (1908), the essay from which that previous quotation was drawn, and of all the other discussions of sexual-social standards that are rife in the last decades of the nineteenth century. The argument for Stevenson too is about harm, the harm done by a false morality and *its* ideas of harm: there is 'none— no harm whatever—in what prurient fools call "immorality" ', nothing 'diabolic' in 'this poor wish to have a woman, that they make such a cry about'. Later, in his dying years, Stevenson returned to the question: 'If I had to begin again . . . I believe I should try to honour Sex more religiously. The worst of our education is that Christianity does not recognize and hallow Sex. It looks askance at it, over its shoulder, oppressed as it is by reminiscences of hermits and Asiatic self-tortures.' The sexual, in other words, is not a problem, the problem is everything else—social attitudes, morality, hypocrisy.

Stephen Heath, "Psychopathia Sexualis: Stevenson's *Strange Case*," *Critical Quarterly* 28, Nos. 1 & 2 (Spring–Summer 1986): 97–98

JOYCE CAROL OATES   The visionary starkness of *The Strange Case of Dr. Jekyll and Mr. Hyde* anticipates that of Freud in such late melancholy meditations as *Civilization and Its Discontents* (1929–30): there is a split in man's psyche between ego and instinct, between civilization and "nature," and the split can never be healed. Freud saw ethics as a reluctant concession of the individual to the group, veneer of a sort overlaid upon an unregenerate primordial self. The various stratagems of culture— including, not incidentally, the "sublimation" of raw aggression by way of art and science—are ultimately powerless to contain the discontent, which must erupt at certain periodic times, on a collective scale, as war. Stevenson's quintessentially Victorian parable is unique in that the protagonist initiates his tragedy of doubleness out of a fully lucid sensibility—one might say a scientific sensibility. Dr. Jekyll knows what he is doing, and why he is doing it, though he cannot, of course, know how it will turn out. What is unquestioned throughout the narrative, by either Jekyll or his circle of friends, is mankind's fallen nature: sin is *original*, and *irremediable*. For Hyde, though hidden, will not remain so. And when Jekyll finally destroys him he must destroy Jekyll too.

Joyce Carol Oates, "Jekyll/Hyde," *Hudson Review* 40, No. 4 (Winter 1988): 607–8

PATRICK BRANTLINGER and RICHARD BOYLE

Stevenson was indeed a "fictitious article"—the storyteller-hero whose stories formed key episodes in a picaresque career. His "heroic industry" in the face of disease and death, his fabled bohemianism, his South Seas adventures—these also were chapters of the Stevenson romance, the general story that can be read between the lines of such clearly "fictitious" or perhaps even factitious stories as *Jekyll and Hyde*. By the late nineteenth century, the writer as "personality" or "celebrity" had also become an important commodity that publishers and critics sought to market. From the outset of his career, Stevenson was taken up by such fellow writers as Leslie Stephen, Sidney Colvin, and Andrew Lang, for whom, as Jenni Calder says, "literature . . . had grown demoralised, and needed to be rescued." Stevenson appeared to them as a potential rescuer, though his mass cultural ventures threatened to demoralize them further. But for his critics and admirers, even those stories and essays most removed from autobiography arranged themselves as episodes in a version of that quite typical modern genre—the Carlylean saga of "The Hero as Man of Letters." *Jekyll and Hyde* can thus be read as a palimpsest between or beneath whose lines the knowing reader will discern the well-advertised originary dream, the incineration of the first draft, and the subsequent allegorization of the story at Fanny's behest.

Stevenson's "Gothic gnome," in other words, mirrors the story of an exemplary struggling artist, torn between the desire to produce "masterpieces" and the knowledge that popular success lay in the contrary directions of "shilling shocker" and "moral allegory." For the supposedly undiscriminating mass readership, there was the "crawler" plain and simple, though this was also a palimpsest in which the form of the gothic thriller, as Hirsch and Lawler have shown, was overwritten by the patterns of the detective story and science fiction. For a supposedly more sophisticated sort of reader, there was the moral allegory about good and evil; *Jekyll and Hyde* served as the subject, we are told, for numerous late-Victorian sermons. But for the discriminating elite such as Henry James and Edmund Gosse, there would also be the heroic and self-pitying story of its writer's struggle against adversity, which included the adversity of having to cater to the cultural mass market of the late-Victorian age.

Patrick Brantlinger and Richard Boyle, "The Education of Edward Hyde: Stevenson's 'Gothic Gnome' and the Mass Readership of Late-Victorian England," *Dr Jekyll and Mr Hyde After One Hundred Years*, ed. William Veeder and Gordon Hirsch (Chicago: University of Chicago Press, 1988), pp. 271–72

◫ Bibliography

The Pentland Rising: A Page of History, 1666. 1866.

The Charity Bazaar: An Allegorical Dialogue. 1868.

On the Thermal Influence of Forests. 1873.

An Appeal to the Clergy of the Church of Scotland, with a Note for the Laity. 1875.

An Inland Voyage. 1878.

Edinburgh: Picturesque Notes. 1879.

Travels with a Donkey in the Cévennes. 1879.

Deacon Brodie; or, The Double Life (with W. E. Henley). 1880.

The Surprise. 1880. 1 no.

To F. J. S. 1881.

Virginibus Puerisque and Other Papers. 1881.

The Story of a Lie. 1882.

Familiar Studies of Men and Books. 1882.

New Arabian Nights. 1882. 2 vols.

Black Canyon; or, Wild Adventures in the Far West: A Tale of Instruction and Amusement. 1882.

Not I and Other Poems. 1882.

Moral Emblems: A Collection of Cuts and Verses. 1882.

Moral Emblems: A Second Collection of Cuts and Verses. 1882.

A Martial Elegy for Some Lead Soldiers. 1882.

The Graver & the Pen; or, Scenes from Nature, with Appropriate Verses. 1882.

Robin and Ben; or, The Pirate and the Apothecary. 1882.

The Silverado Squatters: Sketches from a Californian Mountain. 1883.

Treasure Island. 1883.

We found him first as in the dells of day. 1883.

To the Thompson Class Club, "from Their Stammering Laureate." 1883.

Admiral Guinea (with W. E. Henley). 1884.

Beau Austin (with W. E. Henley). 1884.

Prince Otto: A Romance. 1885.

A Child's Garden of Verses. 1885.

More New Arabian Nights: The Dynamiter (with Fanny Van de Grift Stevenson). 1885.

Macaire (with W. E. Henley). 1885.

The Laureat Ste'enson to the Thamson Class. 1885.

The Strange Case of Dr. Jekyll and Mr. Hyde. 1886.

Kidnapped: Being Memoirs of the Adventures of David Balfour in the Year 1751. 1886.

Some College Memories. 1886.

The Merry Men and Other Tales and Fables. 1887.

Thomas Stevenson, Civil Engineer. 1887.

Memories and Portraits. 1887.

Underwoods. 1887.

Ticonderoga. 1887.

The Hanging Judge (with Fanny Van de Grift Stevenson). 1887.

Memoir of Fleeming Jenkin. 1887.

The Black Arrow: A Tale of the Two Roses. 1888.

The Misadventure of John Nicholson: A Christmas Story. 1888.

The Master of Ballantrae: A Winter's Tale. 1889.

The Wrong Box (with Lloyd Osborne). 1889.

On Board the Old "Equator." 1889.

The South Seas: A Record of Three Cruises ⟨In the South Seas⟩. 1890.

Father Damien: An Open Letter to the Reverend Dr. Hyde of Honolulu. 1890.

Ballads. 1890.

Across the Plains, with Other Memories and Essays. 1892.

The Wrecker (with Lloyd Osborne). 1892.

A Footnote to History: Eight Years of Trouble in Samoa. 1892.

Three Plays (with W. E. Henley). 1892.

The Beach of Falesá. 1892.

Island Nights' Entertainments. 1893.

Catriona: A Sequel to Kidnapped, *Being Memoirs of the Further Adventures of David Balfour at Home and Abroad*. 1893.

The Ebb-Tide: A Trio and Quartette (with Lloyd Osborne). 1894.

Works. Ed. Sidney Colvin. 1894–98. 28 vols.

The Amateur Emigrant from the Clyde to Sandy Hook. 1895.

Vailima Letters: Being Correspondence Addressed to Sidney Colvin, November 1890–October 1894. 1895.

The Body-Snatcher. 1895.

Fables. 1896.

Weir of Hermiston: An Unfinished Romance. 1896.

Songs of Travel and Other Verses. 1896.

Familiar Epistles in Prose and Verse. 1896.

A Mountain Town in France: A Fragment. 1896.

Plays (with W. E. Henley). 1896.

St Ives: Being the Adventures of a French Prisoner in England (with A. T. Quiller-Couch). 1897.

Three Short Poems. 1898.

A Lowden Sabbath Morn. 1898.

Letters to His Family and Friends. Ed. Sidney Colvin. 1899. 2 vols.

R.L.S. Teuila. 1899.

The Morality of the Profession of Letters. 1899.

A Stevenson Medley. Ed. Sidney Colvin. 1899.

A Christmas Sermon. 1900.

Three Letters. 1902.

Some Letters. Ed. Horace Townsend. 1902.

Essays and Criticisms. 1903.

Prayers Written at Vailima. 1905.

Tales and Fantasies. 1905.

Essays of Travel. 1905.

Essays in the Art of Writing. 1905.

Essays. Ed. William Lyon Phelps. 1906.

Works. Ed. Edmund Gosse. 1906–07. 20 vols.

Collected Works. Ed. Charles Scribner and Sons. 1908–12. 31 vols.

Pan's Pipes. 1910.

Letters. Ed. Sidney Colvin. 1911. 4 vols.

Lay Morals and Other Papers. 1911.

Works. 1911–12. 25 vols.

Records of a Family of Engineers. 1912.

Memoirs of Himself. 1912.

The Flight of the Princess and Other Pieces. 1912.

Verses by R.L.S. Ed. L. S. Livingston. 1912.

Poems and Ballads. 1913.

Desiderata: 1895. 1914.

Letters to Charles Baxter. 1914.

Letters to an Editor. Ed. Clement K. Shorter. 1914.

Poetical Fragments. 1915.

An Ode of Horace: Book II, Ode III: Experiments in Three Metres (translator). 1916.

On the Choice of a Profession. 1916.

The Waif Woman. 1916.

Poems Hitherto Unpublished. Ed. George S. Hellman. 1916 (2 vols.), 1921 (ed. George S. Hellman and William P. Trent).

New Poems and Variant Readings. 1918.

Hitherto Unpublished Prose Writings. Ed. Henry H. Harper. 1921.

Confessions of a Unionist. Ed. Flora V. Livingston. 1921.

Works. Ed. Lloyd Osborne and Fanny Van de Grift Stevenson. 1922–23. 26 vols.

The Manuscripts of Stevenson's Records of a Family of Engineers: The Unfinished Chapters. Ed. J. Christian Bay. 1929.

Henry James and Robert Louis Stevenson: A Record of Friendship and Criticism. Ed. Janet Adam Smith. 1948.

Collected Poems. Ed. Janet Adam Smith. 1950, 1971.

Silverado Journal. Ed. John E. Jordan. 1954.

RLS: Stevenson's Letters to Charles Baxter. Ed. De Lancey Ferguson and Marshall Waingrow. 1956.

From Scotland to Silverado. Ed. James D. Hart. 1966.

Complete Short Stories, with a Selection of the Best Short Novels. Ed. Charles Neider. 1969. 3 vols.

Travels to Hawaii. Ed. A. Grove Day. 1973.

Selected Short Stories. Ed. Ian Campbell. 1980.

An Old Song and Edifying Letters of the Rutherford Family. Ed. Roger C. Swearingen. 1982.

From the Clyde to California: Robert Louis Stevenson's Emigrant Journey. Ed. Andrew Noble. 1985.

Island Landfalls: Reflections from the South Seas. Ed. Jenni Calder. 1987.

The Lantern-Bearers and Other Essays. Ed. Jenny Treglawn. 1988.

The Scottish Stories and Essays. Ed. Kenneth Gelder. 1989.

Complete Shorter Fiction. Ed. Peter Stoneley. 1991.

⊠ ⊠ ⊠

Bram Stoker
1847–1912

BRAM STOKER was born Abraham Stoker in Dublin on November 8, 1847, the second son of Abraham and Charlotte Stoker. He was ill throughout his early childhood and was unable to stand upright until the age of seven. By the time he was twenty, however, he had outgrown this invalidism to become an outstanding athlete at Trinity College, Dublin, and for the remainder of his life he exhibited great physical strength. At the university he also excelled in academics, receiving awards in history, composition, oratory, and mathematics, and was head of both the Historical Society and the Philosophical Society.

Following his graduation Stoker worked unhappily for ten years as an Irish civil servant, a period of service that produced the nonfiction *Duties of Clerks of Petty Sessions* (1879). In 1871 he began a five-year stint as the unpaid drama critic of the Dublin *Mail*. During this time he also worked as a freelance journalist and became a barrister of the Inner Temple. In the late 1870s Stoker attended a performance given by the noted actor Henry Irving. The mutual attraction was so strong that Irving named Stoker his personal manager and manager of the actor's Lyceum Theatre in December 1878. Stoker retained the post until Irving's death in 1905. In this capacity Stoker worked long and hard, later estimating that he had written half a million letters on Irving's behalf. He accompanied Irving on his American tours, and then, back in England, gave a series of lectures on American life for the benefit of Britons, who he believed knew little about it. One lecture was subsequently published as the pamphlet *A Glimpse of America* (1886); it came to the attention of the explorer H. M. Stanley, who encouraged Stoker to become a writer.

Stoker had already published a collection of macabre children's stories in 1882, *Under the Sunset*. His first novel, *The Snake's Pass*, appeared in 1890, the same year he began research on the novel that was to bring him enduring fame, *Dracula* (1897). Though not the first novel concerning vampires, *Dracula* was a great popular success that would eventually be adapted for stage, screen, radio, and television, and would become the prototype for most vampire fiction that followed it. Stoker went on to write other books, including four non-supernatural novels, *Miss Betty* (1898), *The Mystery of the Sea* (1902), *The Man* (1905), and *Lady Athlyne* (1908); the horror novels *The Jewel of Seven Stars* (1903), *The Lady of the Shroud* (1909), and *The Lair of the White Worm* (1911); and a memoir of Henry Irving that appeared in 1906. None, however, were to match the success of *Dracula*.

In his later years Stoker was on the literary staff of the London *Telegraph* and worked briefly as an opera manager. He died in London on April 20, 1912. In 1914 his widow assembled the collection *Dracula's Guest and Other Weird Stories*, which gathered together Stoker's best short fiction, some of which had been published in separate pirated American editions in the 1890s. The volume includes such celebrated tales as "The Squaw," "The Judge's House," and the title piece, a chapter originally excised from *Dracula*.

Critical Extracts

UNSIGNED   Mr. Stoker is the purveyor of so many strange wares that *Dracula* reads like a determined effort to go, as it were, "one better" than others in the same field. How far the author is himself a believer in the phenomena described is not for the reviewer to say. He can but attempt to gauge how far the general faith in witches, warlocks, and vampires—supposing it to exist in any general and appreciable measure—is likely to be stimulated by this story. The vampire idea is very ancient indeed, and there are in nature, no doubt, mysterious powers to account for the vague belief in such beings. Mr. Stoker's way of presenting his matter, and still more the matter itself, are of too direct and uncompromising a kind. They lack the essential note of awful remoteness and at the same time subtle affinity that separates while it links our humanity with unknown beings and possibilities hovering on the confines of the known world. *Dracula* is highly sensational, but it is wanting in the constructive art as well as in the higher literary sense. It reads at times like a mere series of grotesquely incredible events; but there are better moments that show more power, though even these are never productive of the tremor such subjects evoke under the hand of a master. An immense amount of energy, a certain degree of imaginative faculty, and many ingenious and gruesome details are there. At times Mr. Stoker almost succeeds in creating the sense of possibility in impossibility; at others he merely commands an array of crude statements of incredible actions. The early part goes best, for it promises to unfold the roots of mystery and fear lying deep in human nature; but the want of skill and fancy grows more and more conspicuous. The people who band themselves together to run the vampire to earth have no real individuality of being. The German man of science is particularly poor, and indulges, like a German, in much weak sentiment. Still Mr. Stoker has got together a number of "horrid details," and his object, assuming it to be ghastliness, is fairly well fulfilled. Isolated scenes and touches are probably quite uncanny enough to please those for whom they are designed.

Unsigned, [Review of *Dracula*], *Athenaeum*, 26 June 1897, p. 835

BRAM STOKER   The self-restraint and reticence which many writers have through centuries exercised in behalf of an art which they loved and honoured has not of late been exercised by the few who seek to make money and achieve notoriety through base means. There is no denying the fact nor the cause; both are only too painfully apparent. Within a couple of years past quite a number of novels have been published in England that would be a disgrace to any country even less civilised than our own. The class of works to which I allude are meant by both authors and publishers to bring to the winning of commercial success the forces of inherent evil in man. The word man here stands for woman as well as man; indeed, women are the worst offenders in this form of breach of moral law. As to the alleged men who follow this loathsome calling, what term of opprobrium is sufficient, what punishment could be too great? This judgment of work which claims to be artistic may seem harsh, and punishment may seem vindictive; the writer has no wish to be either harsh or vindictive—except in so far as all just judgment may seem harsh and all punishment vindictive. For look what those people have done. They found an art wholesome, they made it morbid; they found it pure, they left it sullied. Up to this time it was free—the freest thing in the land; they so treated it, they so abused the powers allowed them and their own opportunities, that continued freedom becomes dangerous, even impossible. They in their selfish greed tried to deprave where others had striven to elevate. In the language of the pulpit, they have 'crucified Christ afresh.' The merest glance at some of their work will justify any harshness of judgment; the roughest synopsis will horrify. It is not well to name either these books or their authors, for such would make known what is better suppressed, and give the writers the advertisement which they crave. It may be taken that such works as are here spoken of deal not merely with natural misdoing based on human weakness, frailty, or passions of the sense, but with vices so flagitious, so opposed to even the decencies of nature in its crudest and lowest forms, that the poignancy of moral disgust is lost in horror. This article is no mere protest against academic faults or breaches of good taste. It is a deliberate indictment of a class of literature so vile that it is actually corrupting the nation.

> Bram Stoker, "The Censorship of Fiction," *Nineteenth Century* 64, No. 3 (September 1908): 484–85

DOROTHY SCARBOROUGH   It is in Bram Stoker's *Dracula* that one finds the tensest, most dreadful modern story of vampirism. This novel seems to omit no detail of terror, for every aspect of vampire horror is touched upon with brutal and ghastly effect. The combination of ghouls, vampires, ghosts, werewolves, and other awful elements is almost unendurable, yet the book loses in effect toward the last, for the mind cannot endure four hundred pages of vampiric outrage and respond to fresh impressions of horror. The initial vampire here is a Hungarian count, who, after terrorizing his own country for years, transports himself to England to start his ravages there. Each victim in turn becomes a vampire. The combination of modern science with medieval superstition to fight the scourge, using garlic and sprigs of the wild rose together with blood transfusion, is interesting. All the resources of modern science are pitted against the infection and the complications are dramatically thrilling. The book is not advised as suitable reading for one sitting alone at night.

> Dorothy Scarborough, *The Supernatural in Modern English Fiction* (New York: Putnam's, 1917), pp. 163–64

H. P. LOVECRAFT   Speaking of ⟨W. Paul⟩ Cook, he hath just lent me two books, one of which is Bram Stoker's last production, *The Lair of the White Worm*. The plot idea is colossal, but the development is so childish that I cannot imagine how the thing ever got into print—unless on the reputation of *Dracula*. The rambling and unmotivated narration, the puerile and stagey characterisation, the irrational propensity of everyone to do the most stupid possible thing at precisely the wrong moment and for no cause at all, and the involved development of a personality afterward relegated to utter insignificance—all this proves to me either that *Dracula* (Mrs. ⟨Edith⟩ Miniter saw *Dracula* in manuscript about thirty years ago. It was incredibly slovenly. She considered the job of revision but charged too much for Stoker) and *The Jewel of Seven Stars* were touched up Bushwork-fashion by a superior hand which arranged *all* the details, or that by the end of his life (he died in 1912, the year after the *Lair* was issued) he trickled out in a pitiful and inept senility.

H. P. Lovecraft, Letter to Frank Belknap Long (7 October 1923), *Selected Letters 1911–1924* (Sauk City, WI: Arkham House, 1965), p. 255

MAURICE RICHARDSON   *Dracula,* I think, provides really striking confirmation of the Freudian interpretation. The source book here is Dr Ernest Jones's fascinating monograph *On the Nightmare,* which has a special chapter on the vampire superstition. ⟨. . .⟩ The vampire superstition, as Jones points out, embodies a particularly complex form of the interest, both natural and unnatural, which the living take in the dead. In ghoulism the necrophiliac traffic is one way, as it were, but in vampirism 'the dead first visits the living and then drags him into death being himself reanimated in the process'.

These are surface considerations. The starting point from which to investigate the hidden content of the superstition is once again Freud's dictum that morbid dread always signifies suppressed sexual wishes. In vampirism they become plainly visible. Here we enter a twilight borderland, a sort of homicidal lunatic's brothel in a crypt, where religious and psychopathological motives intermingle. Ambivalence is the keynote. Death wishes all round exist side by side with the desire for immortality. Frightful cruelty, aggression and greed is accompanied by a madly possessive kind of love. Guilt is everywhere and deep. Behaviour smacks of the unconscious world of infantile sexuality with what Freud called its polymorph perverse tendencies. There is an obvious fixation at the oral level, with all that sucking and biting, also a generous allowance of anality. We are left in no doubt about the origin of the frightful smell, compost of charnel house and cloaca, that attaches to the vampire.

It is very remarkable how in *Dracula,* Stoker makes use of all the traditional mythical properties and blends them with a family type of situation of his own contriving that turns out to be a quite blatant demonstration of the Oedipus complex. From a Freudian standpoint—and from no other does the story really make any sense—it is seen as a kind of incestuous, necrophilous, oral-anal-sadistic all-in wrestling match. And this is what gives the story its force.

Maurice Richardson, "The Psychoanalysis of Ghost Stories," *Twentieth Century* No. 994 (December 1959): 426–27

C. F. BENTLEY   Nothing in Stoker's other writings or in what is
known of his life suggests that he would consciously write quasi-pornography,
and it must be assumed that he was largely unaware of the sexual content
of his book ⟨*Dracula*⟩. In common with almost all respectable Victorian
novelists, Stoker avoids any overt treatment of the sexuality of his characters.
The obscenity laws, the tyranny of the circulating libraries, and the force of
public opinion were, throughout the greater part of the nineteenth century,
powerful constraints on any author who wrote for the general public, but
it is probable that for many writers, including Stoker himself, an even
stronger reason for avoiding sexual matters was a personal reticence
amounting to repression. Stoker's 'living' characters (that is, those other
than vampires) are, both the women and the men, models of chastity. One
male-female relationship, that of Jonathan Harker and Miss Mina Murray,
is of primary importance to the story, and they marry at an early stage of
the plot, but the sexual elements that presumably exist in their relationships
are never revealed, much less discussed. However what is rejected or repressed
on a conscious level appears in a covert and perverted form through the
novel, the apparatus of the vampire superstition, described in almost obses-
sional detail in *Dracula*, providing the means for a symbolic presentation
of human sexual relationships.

   A close examination of certain episodes in the work shows that Stoker's
vampires are permitted to assert their sexuality in a much more explicit
manner than his 'living' characters. ⟨. . .⟩ With the exception of Dracula's
brief and abortive assault on Harker when momentarily aroused by the sight
of blood from a shaving cut trickling down the latter's chin, the prominent
vampire attacks in the novel are always on members of the other sex: the
female vampires attempt to make Harker their prey, and Dracula attacks
Mina Harker and Lucy Westenra, suggesting that vampirism is a perversion
of normal heterosexual activity.

   C. F. Bentley, "The Monster in the Bedroom: Sexual Symbolism in Bram Stoker's
Dracula," *Literature and Psychology* 22, No. 1 (1972): 27–29

CARROL L. FRY   Stoker had apparently done some research on
the folklore of vampirism, and most of the detail he gives is verified by the
work of Montague Summers. The vampire's inability to cast a reflection,
his fear of daylight, and the stake in the heart as a means of killing him
are all part of the folklore of Eastern Europe. But one element of this folklore
is particularly appropriate for melodramatic fiction: the contagious nature
of vampirism. Both the rake of the popular novel and the vampire of folklore

pass on their conditions (moral depravity in the former and vampirism in the latter) to their victims. In fiction, it is conventional for the fallen woman to become an outcast, alienated from the rest of mankind, or to die a painful death. If she lives, she often becomes a prostitute or the chattel of her seducer. ⟨. . .⟩

The change in Lucy Westenra's appearance after she receives Dracula's attention is marked. Physically, her features are altogether different. Dr. Seward describes her in her tomb when the group goes there to destroy her: "The sweetness was turned to adamantine, heartless cruelty, and the purity to wantonness." Instead of the "pure gentle orbs we knew," her eyes are "unclean and full of hell fire." She approaches Arthur with a "languorous, voluptuous grace," saying "My arms are hungry for you." In all, "The whole carnal and unspiritual appearance" seems "like a devilish mockery of Lucy's sweet purity." Throughout, the description of female vampires underscores their sexuality, and the words "voluptuous" and "wanton" appear repeatedly in these contexts, words that never could be used in describing a pure woman. Clearly, Lucy has fallen, but in the end she is saved from herself in rather conventional fashion. Her death and the smile of bliss on her face as she passes satisfy the reader's desire for a happy ending to her story and fulfill his expectation regarding the fate proper to a fallen woman.

Carrol L. Fry, "Fictional Conventions and Sexuality in *Dracula*," *Victorian Newsletter* No. 42 (Fall 1972): 21–22

LES DANIELS   The story is so well known that it has become the authoritative source on the care and feeding of vampires; Stoker's decisions regarding the legendary attributes of these lecherous leeches have been accepted as gospel truth. Unlike most of the vampires described in the purportedly factual manuscripts of olden days, Dracula can transform himself into a mist, a wolf, or a bat. He has a marked aversion for symbols of Christianity and a chauvinistic fondness for female victims. Other debatable points include Stoker's declaration that this cursed condition is contagious and that a proper cure is a wooden stake through the monster's heart (vampires were commonly burned by those who believed in them). At any rate, Stoker's deviations from tradition were dramatically sound, and they helped insure his book's success.

Dracula is a particularly fascinating monster because unlike the equally famous creations of Dr. Frankenstein and Dr. Jekyll, he is almost completely remorseless. Rich, immortal, irresistible, and nearly omnipotent, he is the embodiment of an unleashed id, sleeping all day and spending his nights creeping into bedrooms. The sexual side of his ungentlemanly behavior undoubtedly titillated Victorian readers; this is particularly evident in the incident of his first English victim, Lucy Westenra, who keeps three suitors at arm's length while Dracula is turning her into a lustful fiend like himself. The highly charged scene in which her admirers converge on her coffin to hammer a stake into her has overtones of a symbolic rape.

Les Daniels, *Living in Fear: A History of Horror in the Mass Media* (New York: Scribner's, 1975), p. 63

DANIEL FARSON   It has been stated unequivocally that Stoker was a member of the Hermetic Order of the Golden Dawn, a group of occultists headed by Liddell Matthews and W. B. Yeats which was eventually shattered by the intervention of 'The Great Beast', Aleister Crowley. The Order comprised both men and women and was devoted to ritual magic and astrology, with lodges in Edinburgh, Paris, London, and Weston-Super-Mare. At one point an actress called Florence Farr was put in charge and performed their 'Egyptian Rites' in Paris, charging admission. Conceivably, Bram might have known her professionally and been introduced to the order by her. His membership has always been assumed by the 'cognoscenti' according to Francis King, the historian of ritual magic, who adds the surprising information that Constance Wilde was another member. But George M. Harper, another authority, tells me that to the best of his knowledge, which is extensive, Stoker did not belong to the Golden Dawn; a secret list of members which goes up to 1905 confirms this.

However, there were many splinter groups after Crowley's disruption of the original order, and it seems likely that Stoker was involved in an off-shoot called 'Alpha et Omega' which was run by the author J. W. Brodie-Innes. In 1915 Brodie-Innes published an occult novel, *The Devil's Mistress*, which he dedicated 'To the memory of Bram Stoker to whom I am indebted'.

It would be misleading to read too much into this, but if Bram was a secret member of one of the splinter groups it shows that he was involved with the supernatural more deeply than hitherto suspected: not merely an observer but a participant. Equally, there could be the explanation that this was an excellent way to gather research material.

Daniel Farson, *The Man Who Wrote* Dracula (London: Michael Joseph, 1975), p. 207

JUDITH WEISSMAN   The difference between the sexuality of Dracula and the women vampires is, I think, the key to the psychological meaning of the book. For him, sex is power; for them, it is desire. He is the man whom all other men fear, the man who can, without any loss of power or freedom himself, seduce other men's women and make them sexually insatiable with a sexual performance that the others cannot match. He is related to Lovelace and to the tradition of noble rakes who ruin middle and lower class women and go scot-free, but the women who are the victims of Lovelace and the young squires of *The Vicar of Wakefield* and *Tom Jones* (the one who preceded Tom in Molly's bed) are not said to be ruined for other men because they are now insatiable. They are, supposedly, simply no longer respectable. And yet I think that *Dracula* reveals one of the reasons *why* they are no longer respectable, why there has been an obsession in western culture with marrying virgins. Our culture is founded on the belief that men are more powerful than women, and perhaps women who are not virgins have not been considered eligible for marriage because they may make invidious sexual comparisons between their husbands and their previous lovers. Fielding, that great man, recognizes this possibility without horror when Shamela Andrews complains that all men are "little" compared with Parson Williams and says that she might have been well enough satisfied, too, on her wedding night, if she had never been acquainted with Parson Williams.

For Fielding, differences in sexual capacity are not a cause for terror; for Stoker, they are. His band of trusty men, loyal and chaste, are not simply trying to destroy Dracula, who has come to England to "create a new and ever-widening circle of semi-demons to batten on the helpless" (Jonathan Harker's Journal, 30 June morning). Their fight to destroy Dracula and restore Mina to her purity is really a fight for control over women. It is a fight to keep women from knowing what the men and women of the Middle Ages, the Renaissance, the seventeenth and eighteenth centuries knew, and what people of the nineteenth century must also have known, even if they did not want to—that women's sexual appetites are greater than men's.

Judith Weissman, "Women and Vampires: *Dracula* as a Victorian Novel," *Midwest Quarterly* 18, No. 4 (July 1977): 404–5

CAROL A. SENF   Although Stoker did model Dracula on the historical Vlad V of Wallachia and the East European superstition of the vampire, he adds a number of humanizing touches to make Dracula appear noble and vulnerable as well as demonic and threatening; and it becomes difficult to determine whether he is a hideous bloodsucker whose touch breeds death or a lonely and silent figure who is hunted and persecuted.

The difficulty in interpreting Dracula's character is compounded by the narrative technique, for the reader quickly recognizes that Dracula is *never* seen objectively and never permitted to speak for himself while his actions are recorded by people who have determined to destroy him and who, moreover, repeatedly question the sanity of their quest.

The question of sanity, which is so important in *Dracula,* provides another clue to the narrators' unreliability. More than half the novel takes place in or near Dr. Seward's London mental institution; and several of the characters are shown to be emotionally unstable: Renfield, one of Dr. Seward's patients, is an incarcerated madman who believes that he can achieve immortality by drinking the blood of insects and other small creatures; Jonathan Harker suffers a nervous breakdown after he escapes from Dracula's castle; and Lucy Westenra exhibits signs of schizophrenia, being a model of sweetness and conformity while she is awake but becoming sexually aggressive and demanding during her sleepwalking periods. More introspective than most of the other narrators, Dr. Seward occasionally refers to the questionable sanity of their mission, his diary entries mentioning his fears that they will all wake up in straitjackets. Furthermore, his entries on Renfield's condition indicate that he recognizes the narrow margin which separates sanity from insanity: "It is wonderful, however, what intellectual recuperatve power lunatics have, for within a few minutes he stood up quite calmly and looked about him."

However, even if the reader chooses to ignore the question of the narrators' sanity, it is important to understand their reasons for wishing to destroy Dracula. They accuse him of murdering the crew of the *Demeter,* of killing Lucy Westenra and transforming her into a vampire, and of trying to do the same thing to Mina Harker. However, the log found on the dead body of the *Demeter*'s captain, which makes only a few ambiguous allusions to a fiend or monster, is hysterical and inconclusive. Recording this "evidence," Mina's journal asserts that the verdict of the inquest was open-ended: "There is no evidence to adduce; and whether or not the man [the ship's captain] committed the murders there is now none to say." Lucy's death might just as easily be attributed to the blood transfusions (still a dangerous procedure at the time Stoker wrote *Dracula*) to which Dr. Van Helsing subjects her; and Mina acknowledges her complicity in the affair with Dracula by admitting that she did not want to prevent his advances. Finally, even if Dracula is responsible for all the Evil of which he is accused, he is tried, convicted, and sentenced by men (including two lawyers) who give him no opportunity to explain his actions and who repeatedly violate the laws which they profess to be defending: they avoid an inquest of Lucy's death, break into her tomb and desecrate her body, break into Dracula's houses, frequently resort to bribery and coercion to avoid legal involvement, and openly admit that they are responsible for the deaths of all five alleged vampires. While it can be argued that *Dracula* is a fantasy and therefore not subject to the laws of verisimilitude, Stoker uses the flimsiness of such "evidence" to focus on the contrast between the narrators' rigorous moral arguments and their all-too-pragmatic methods.

Carol A. Senf, "*Dracula*: The Unseen Face in the Mirror," *Journal of Narrative Technique* 9, No. 3 (Fall 1979): 162–63

A. N. WILSON   The *myth* to which all this second-rate subculture, this Dracula-cult, refers, is the invention of Bram Stoker. He invented it in the sense that the Empress Helena invented the True Cross. That is to say, he found it, reworked it, and left behind a cult which would have amazed his predecessors. His classic distinction is not artistic, but mythopoeic. He has created, or fixed in creation, a version of the old horrors concerning the living dead which has acquired mythological status. Count Dracula is as familiar to us as Robin Hood or King Arthur were to an earlier generation. When we think of King Arthur, we are probably thinking of stories which were first written down in English by Malory. But much more than a great artist (which he happened to be) Malory was a vehicle for a story. He had the luck, or the boldness, or the humility, to be arranging and passing on a set of stories unequalled in popular appeal since the classical myths of ancient Greece and Rome. The sheer *story*—of Excalibur, of Merlin's prophecies, of Launcelot and Guinevere, of Mordred's treachery—transcend any method in the telling. Likewise, in the old stories of classical times, we do not ask who was the *author* who wrote about Jason and the Argonauts or Orpheus and Eurydice; we simply know the story.

In a sinister way, Bram Stoker is largely responsible for perpetuating a popular mythology almost to this order. For every ten people who have actually read *Dracula*, you could find a thousand who could tell you what it is about. The ten would have had an experience which is much stronger than the thousand; such is the power of the book. Stoker did his work well, and I, for one, can never read his pages without a shudder of terror and disgust, compulsive in its guilty awfulness. It is a sinister story to have fed into the collective subconscious. But a case could be made for saying the reverse is true: that Stoker's most classic stroke was in his timing, that he wrote a tale for which his generation, and subsequent generations, were hungry. Much could doubtless be made of the fact that this widespread horror of the living dead, whipped up for purely sensationalist purposes, began at a phase when, for the first time in Christian history, there was widespread doubt about the real likelihood of a Resurrection of the Body. The generation who first avidly purchased *Dracula* were also the first who chose, in any considerable numbers, to dispose of corpses in a crematorium.

> A. N. Wilson, "Introduction," *Dracula* (Oxford: Oxford University Press, 1983), pp. xvi–xvii

---

ANNE McWHIR   In a sense, *Dracula* records the victory of the modern world against the irrational powers it cannot accommodate. The heroes rise up to destroy Dracula so that they can return to trains that run on time, to afternoon tea served by Mina in a pleasant English house. Purity and innocence seem to depend on this world of civilized order. But the novel undercuts its own vision of a world made safe for routine. Seward, Quincey Morris and Arthur are old friends who have hunted together, playing a deliberate game requiring heroism and courage. The young men whom Van Helsing describes as 'hunters of wild beasts' are meant to appear fit opponents to Dracula, who tells Harker, 'you dwellers in the city cannot enter into the feelings of the hunter.' The predatory animal is the type of the evil hunter, exemplifying nature red in tooth and claw, not the heroic enterprise of human strength. But the hunter who goes out against predators is one model for true heroism in *Dracula*. Harker is at first the most vulnerable of the young men simply because he is most completely the modern city-dweller, removed by profession, temperament and habit from the life of flesh and blood that Seward and Van Helsing know professionally and that Quincey and Arthur know as adventurers. Even fox-hunting, the ritual of gentlemen, seems to provide better preparation for dealing with Dracula than the desk-bound work of the solicitor. In the end the vampire-hunters go out against Dracula armed with Winchesters, but they never fire a shot. Shedding their rational assumptions and their technological defences as they go, they do the real work with knives—no longer Seward's or Van Helsing's sophisticated surgical tools, but real fighting weapons. Jonathan Harker, at last possessed by the power of the old centuries, is inseparable from his Ghoorka knife.

Thus, the distinction between civilization and savagery, between modernity and superstition, so dominant on the surface of the novel, breaks down not far beneath that surface. When Van Helsing tells Quincey Morris, 'A brave man's blood is the best thing on this earth when a woman is in trouble,' he is thinking of blood transfusion, a medical procedure, but his words also foreshadow Quincey's eventual sacrifice of his life. Science and ritual are brought together in the dominant image of the novel, the shedding or draining of blood. Similarly, the 'blood' that has made Dracula great allies him to the heroes of the novel at their most heroic moments. Emerging from the 'whirlpool of European races,' Dracula traces his ancestry back not only to Attila but also to Thor and Wodin; Arthur, civilized Christian child of the nineteenth century, sweating and gasping in his passion, drives a stake through Lucy's heart 'like a figure of Thor.' Throughout the novel categories and boundaries turn out to be less firm than they seem at first. The modern, categorical habit of mind organizes time and processes information, but it seems unable completely to separate myth from factual record, metaphor from scientific language: 'The blood is the life,' but in what sense?

> Anne McWhir, "Pollution and Redemption in *Dracula*," *Modern Language Studies* 27, No. 3 (Summer 1987): 32–33

ROSEMARY JANN   The real ideological thrust of the novel ⟨*Dracula*⟩ can be found in its correlation of sanity, adulthood, masculinity, deductive reasoning, and a moralized maturity. Stoker may suggest that the reality of the supernatural exposes the limitations of materialist science, but he ultimately lines up on the side of this science's truth-finding methods. Van Helsing may claim to put his trust in a faith that need not see in order to believe, but in its form the narrative insists that the medium is the message: subjective experience is ordered into reality and made factual by its inscription and interpretation. He may stress the mysterious nature of human psychology, but his success rests on the same assumption of a positivistic uniformity in human behavior that so often enables Sherlock Holmes to triumph. He reduces the protean Dracula to an example of the rigidly deterministic Lombrosoan model that equates crime with insanity and labels those "predestinate" to such deviance as lacking in "man-stature as to brain" and therefore condemned to the obsessive repetition of the same criminal act. This impulse to reduce the supernatural and the mysterious to a codified system also operates in Stoker's handling of vampire superstition as a whole. As Leonard Wolf has noted, he tries to turn "lore into law" by treating the inconsistent and undogmatic body of vampire legend as if it were fixed and systematic. At one point Stoker also tempers Dracula's supernatural powers by attributing them in part to the electrical and magnetic forces of his native Transylvania, forces that can still be demonstrated in the present.

Stoker's characters may profess faith in a higher religious truth, but their actions reaffirm the truths of a normative rationality. Seward's repeated tendency to assume madness in Lucy, Van Helsing, or even in himself when first confronted by evidence of vampirism is intended to underline the limitations his empiricist skepticism places upon him, and yet the second half of the novel does in fact affirm Seward's implicit equation of sanity with sequential logic and obedience to normative behavior. Although there is much typically Victorian lip-service paid in the novel to Mina's angelic womanhood and the conventional piety that abets it, many critics have argued persuasively for reading the novel as a projection of male fear of woman: Dracula must be defeated in order to free Mina from his control, but also to free the men from the threat of the insatiable female sexuality that his influence releases. It is appropriate that this defeat is effected by a group of men working together to exert their male rationality to protect— or to enforce conformity upon—a traditional female virtue. Mina—unlike Lucy—can finally be saved because she proves herself one of them: it is not her "woman's heart" but her "man's brain" that enables her to play a crucial part in Dracula's capture. She is rendered safe by putting "her great brain which is trained like a man's brain" into collaboration with a group of men who, as (Burton) Hatlen notes, represent key roles in the Victorian establishment: the aristocracy, the legal and medical professions, the paramilitary fighter. Stoker's *Dracula* titillates readers with fears of the repressed and the occult, but it implicitly seeks to reassure them that even the most protean supernatural evil can be dissolved into predictable categories and defeated by the pious cooperation of "good, brave men" and women who are willing to surrender desire to the discipline of order, logic, and reason. The continued emotional power of the novel rests on the failure rather than on the success of this effort, however; it rests on the fact that those dark anxieties displaced onto the foreign other resist the touch of reason and morality that reduces his body to dust at the end.

Rosemary Jann, "The Mixed Messages of Stoker's *Dracula*," *Texas Studies in Literature and Language* 31, No. 2 (Summer 1989): 283–84

BETTE B. ROBERTS   In some ways, Stoker's relationship to his predecessors parallels Samuel Richardson's experience with his own experiments in fiction. Learning from the limitations of his epistolary method in *Pamela*, specifically the totally subjective recording of experience, he found a way to moderate the unreliable subjectivity and provide a truer, more complex reality by having different voices write their experiences simultaneously. Similarly, Stoker apparently saw the aesthetic contradiction inherent in the majority of late-eighteenth-century Gothic novels, even

Radcliffe's, where the prevailing omniscient voice representing virtue, order, and rationality becomes merely a pretense for the irrational action conveyed through first-person narratives. Mary Shelley's *Frankenstein* is a transition of sorts to Stoker's *Dracula* in that she does take more pains to establish a thematic and moral link between the unlawful ambitions of her explorer Robert Walton writing letters home to his sister and the overreaching of Victor Frankenstein, who achieves self-knowledge before he perishes in the ice and warns Walton to "Seek happiness in tranquility and avoid ambition" (ch. 24).

Stoker removes the contradiction when he discards the omniscient authorial voice and the intermediary frame altogether in favor of the more Richardsonian, simultaneous realities. In so doing, he manages first of all to create a convincing, late-Victorian, middle-class milieu which is consistent throughout. Unlike many earlier Gothics, where the inset stories recount terrifying adventures of characters and ancestors in the past as explanations for conflicts in the present, in *Dracula* the threat is pervasive in the present action of the book from beginning to end, and since the reader realizes the extent of the vampire's presence long before the characters do, rather than after, we are thus drawn into the menace of the supernatural. Stoker maintains this suspense by using ironic effects created in the dramatic simultaneity of letters and journals written by characters who, without the whole picture, are unaware of the magnitude of evil. Further, Stoker builds distinct personalities for the characters and weaves their complicated relationships with one another. That he succeeds with this method of characterization is evident in the critical studies focusing on the ambivalent desires of those who, like Jonathan and Lucy, reveal more of their needs and selves than they intend in their letters. It is a psychological ambivalence emerging from the characterization, rather than a contradiction resulting from the didactic, authorial intent in earlier Gothics to reward virtue and advocate rational control while indulging in sensational narration. Perhaps most important is this coherence of form and content achieved in the complex epistolary style of *Dracula*, as the writing itself becomes associated with the very Victorian sources of moral victory: energy, fortitude, social community, and above all, work.

Bette B. Roberts, "Victorian Values in the Narration of *Dracula*," *Studies in Weird Fiction* No. 6 (Fall 1989): 13–14

⊠ *Bibliography*

The Duties of Clerks of Petty Sessions in Ireland. 1879.

Under the Sunset. 1882.

A Glimpse of America: A Lecture Given at the London Institution, 28th December,
    1885. 1886.

The Snake's Pass. 1890.

The Watter's Mou'. 1894.

Crooken Sands. 1894.

The Man from Shorrox's. 1894.

The Shoulder of Shasta. 1895.

Dracula. 1897.

Miss Betty. 1898.

Sir Henry Irving and Miss Ellen Terry in Robespierre, Merchant of Venice,
    The Bells, Nance Oldfield, The Amber Heart, Waterloo, *etc., Drawn*
    by Pamela Smith. 1899.

The Mystery of the Sea. 1902.

The Jewel of Seven Stars. 1903.

The Man ⟨The Gates of Life⟩. 1905.

Personal Reminiscences of Henry Irving. 1906. 2 vols.

Snowbound: The Record of a Theatrical Touring Party. 1908.

Lady Athlyne. 1908.

The Lady of the Shroud. 1909.

Famous Impostors. 1910.

The Lair of the White Worm. 1911.

Dracula's Guest and Other Weird Stories. 1914.

The Bram Stoker Bedside Companion. Ed. Charles Osborne. 1973.

Midnight Tales. Ed. Peter Haining. 1990.

Horace Walpole
1717–1797

HORACE WALPOLE, politician, connoisseur, collector, and man of letters, was born in London on September 24, 1717. The son of Sir Robert Walpole, he was educated at Eton (1727–34), where he formed the so-called "Quadruple Alliance" with his friends Thomas Gray, Richard West, and Thomas Ashton. In 1735 he entered King's College, Cambridge, which he attended irregularly for almost four years. Upon reaching his majority in 1738 Walpole was appointed to several lucrative sinecures, which supported him for the rest of his life.

In 1739 Walpole set off on a "Grand Tour" of the Continent with Thomas Gray, and while traveling began writing the letters that would ultimately bring him his greatest renown, including the "Epistle to Mr. Ashton from Florence." Gray and Walpole quarreled in 1741 and returned home separately; they were, however, reconciled by 1745. Walpole entered Parliament in 1741 as M.P. for the borough of Callington, Cornwall, and later represented Castle Rising and King's Lynn.

In 1747 Walpole moved to a house at Strawberry Hill, near Twickenham, an eccentric neo-Gothic castle in which he amassed a valuable library and art collection. In that year he published a catalogue of his father's art collection under the title *Aedes Walpolianae*. In 1757 Walpole founded a printing press at Strawberry Hill, and as his first publication prepared an edition of Gray's Pindaric odes (1757). This was followed in 1758 by the publication of his own *Catalogue of the Royal and Noble Authors of England* (much augmented by Thomas Park in 1806) and *Fugitive Pieces in Verse and Prose*. In 1762 Walpole published the first of four volumes of *Anecdotes of Painting in England* (1762–71), a survey of English art from medieval times to Walpole's own.

Walpole's novel *The Castle of Otranto* is dated 1765 but was published at Strawberry Hill on Christmas Eve 1764. It first appeared anonymously, as a translation from the Italian of "Onuphrio Muralto," but its great success impelled Walpole to admit authorship in the second edition. This novel inaugurated the Gothic tradition of the later eighteenth and early nineteenth centuries, and its influence was enormous. Walpole's play *The Mysterious Mother* (1768), although having little of the supernatural, could be thought to have initiated the school of Gothic drama, and as such is scarcely less influential than *The Castle of Otranto*. On the borderline of the weird is *Hieroglyphic Tales* (1785), a slim collection of short stories.

Walpole made the first of five visits to France in 1765 and there met Mme. du Deffand, with whom he formed a lasting friendship. After returning to England he retired from Parliament in 1768, then published *Historic Doubts on the Life and Reign of King Richard III* (1768), in which he attempted to prove that Richard had not committed the murders attributed to him by Thomas More.

In 1791, upon the death of his nephew, Walpole became the fourth Earl of Orford and inherited an estate burdened with debt. He died in London on March 2, 1797. Walpole's memoirs, begun in 1751, were removed from a sealed chest in 1818.   His *Memoirs of the Last Ten Years of the Reign of George II*, edited by Lord Holland, appeared in two volumes in 1822, while Sir Denis Le Marchant compiled the *Memoirs of the Reign of King George the Third* (1845). Walpole's correspondence, on which his literary reputation now largely rests, has been published in many editions, including a set of forty-eight volumes prepared by W. S. Lewis et al. (1937–81).

Critical Extracts

HORACE WALPOLE   I had time to write but a short note with *The Castle of Otranto*, as your messenger called on me at four o'clock as I was going to dine abroad. Your partiality to me and Strawberry have I hope inclined you to excuse the wildness of the story. You will even have found some traits to put you in mind of this place. When you read of the picture quitting its panel, did not you recollect the portrait of Lord Falkland all in white in my gallery? Shall I even confess to you what was the origin of this romance? I waked one morning in the beginning of last June from a dream, of which all I could recover was, that I had thought myself in an ancient castle (a very natural dream for a head filled like mine with Gothic story) and that on the uppermost bannister of a great staircase I saw a gigantic hand in armour. In the evening I sat down and began to write, without knowing in the least what I intended to say or relate. The work grew on my hands, and I grew fond of it—add that I was very glad to think of anything rather than politics— In short I was so engrossed with my tale, which I completed in less than two months, that one evening I wrote from the time I had drunk my tea, about six o'clock, till half an hour after one in the morning, when my hand and fingers were so weary, that I could not hold the pen to finish the sentence, but left Matilda and Isabella talking, in the middle of a paragraph. You will laugh at my earnestness, but if I have amused you by retracing with any fidelity the manners of ancient days, I am content, and give you leave to think me as idle as you please.

Horace Walpole, Letter to William Cole (9 March 1765), *Correspondence*, ed. W. S. Lewis (New Haven: Yale University Press, 1937), Vol. 1, p. 88

SIR WALTER SCOTT   It is doing injustice to Mr Walpole's memory to allege, that all which he aimed at in *The Castle of Otranto*, was "the art of exciting surprise and horror;" or, in other words, the appeal to that secret and reserved feeling of love for the marvellous and supernatural, which occupies a hidden corner in almost every one's bosom. Were this all which he had attempted, the means by which he sought to attain his purpose might, with justice, be termed both clumsy and puerile. But Mr Walpole's purpose was both more difficult of attainment, and more important when attained. It was his object to draw such a picture of domestic life and manners, during the feudal times, as might actually have existed, and to paint it checked and agitated by the action of supernatural machinery, such as the superstition of the period received as matter of devout credulity. The natural parts of the narrative are so contrived, that they associate themselves with the marvellous occurrences; and, by the force of that association, render those *speciosa miracula* striking and impressive, though our cooler reason admits their impossibility. Indeed, to produce, in a well-cultivated mind, any portion of that surprise and fear which are founded in supernatural events, the frame and tenor of the whole story must be adjusted in perfect harmony with this main-spring of the interest. He who, in early youth, has happened to pass a solitary night in one of the few ancient mansions which the fashion of more modern times has left undespoiled of their original furniture, has probably experienced, that the gigantic and preposterous fig-ures dimly visible in the defaced tapestry,—the remote clang of the distant doors which divide him from living society,—the deep darkness which involves the high and fretted roof of the apartment,—the dimly-seen pictures of ancient knights, renowned for their valour, and perhaps for their crimes, — the varied and indistinct sounds which disturb the silent desolation of a half-deserted mansion,—and, to crown all, the feeling that carries us back to ages of feudal power and papal superstition, join together to excite a corresponding sensation of supernatural awe, if not of terror. It is in such situations, when superstition becomes contagious, that we listen with respect, and even with dread, to the legends which are our sport in the garish light of sunshine, and amid the dissipating sights and sounds of everyday life. Now, it seems to have been Walpole's object to attain, by the minute accuracy of a fable, sketched with singular attention to the costume of the period in which the scene was laid, that same association, which might prepare his reader's mind for the reception of prodigies congenial to the creed and feelings of the actors. His feudal tyrant, his distressed damsel, his resigned yet dignified churchman,—the Castle itself, with its feudal arrangements of dungeons, trap-doors, oratories, and galleries,—the incidents of the trial, the chivalrous procession, and the combat;—in short, the scene, the performers, and action, so far as it is natural, form the accompaniments of his spectres and his miracles, and have the same effect on the mind of the reader, that the appearance and drapery of such a chamber as we have described may produce upon that of a temporary inmate. This was a task which required no little learning, no ordinary degree of fancy, no common portion of genius, to execute. The association of which we have spoken is of a nature peculiarly delicate, and subject to be broken and disarranged. It is, for instance, almost impossible to build such a modern Gothic structure as shall impress us with the feelings we have endeavoured to describe. It may be grand, or it may be gloomy; it may excite magnificent or melancholy ideas; but it must fail in bringing forth the sensation of supernatural awe, connected with halls that have echoed to the sounds of remote generations, and have been pressed by the footsteps of those who have long since passed away. Yet Horace Walpole has attained in composition, what, as an architect, he must have felt beyond the power of his art. The remote and superstitious period in which his scene is laid,—the art with which he has furnished forth its Gothic decorations,—the sustained, and, in general, the dignified tone of feudal manners,—prepare us gradually for the favourable reception of prodigies, which, though they could not really have happened at any period, were consistent with the belief of all mankind at that in which the action is placed. It was, therefore, the author's object, not merely to excite surprise and terror, by the introduction of supernatural agency, but to wind up the feelings of his reader till they became for a moment identified with those of a ruder age, which

Held each strange tale devoutly true.

Sir Walter Scott, "Introduction," *The Castle of Otranto* (Edinburgh: James Ballantyne & Co., 1811)

WILLIAM HAZLITT   *The Castle of Otranto* ⟨. . .⟩ is, to my notion, dry, meagre, and without effect. It is done upon false principles of taste. The great hand and arm, which are thrust into the court-yard, and remain there all day long, are the pasteboard machinery of a pantomime; they shock the senses, and have no purchase upon the imagination. They are a matter-of-fact impossibility; a fixture, and no longer a phantom. *Quod sic mihi ostendis, incredulus odi.* By realising the chimeras of ignorance and fear, begot upon shadows and dim likenesses, we take away the very grounds of credulity and superstition; and, as in other cases, by facing out the imposture, betray the secret to the contempt and laughter of the spectators.

William Hazlitt, *Lectures on the English Comic Writers* (1819), *The Complete Works of William Hazlitt*, ed. P. P. Howe (London: J. M. Dent, 1924), Vol. 6, p. 127

THOMAS BABINGTON MACAULAY   There is little skill in the delineation of characters ⟨in *The Castle of Otranto*⟩. Manfred is as commonplace a tyrant, Jerome as commonplace a confessor, Theodore as commonplace a young gentleman, Isabella and Matilda as commonplace a pair of young ladies, as are to be found in any of the thousand Italian castles in which *condottieri* have revelled or in which imprisoned duchesses have pined. We cannot say that we much admire the big man whose sword is dug up in one quarter of the globe, whose helmet drops from the clouds in another, and who, after clattering and rustling for some days, ends by kicking the house down. But the story, whatever its value may be, never flags for a single moment. There are no digressions, or unseasonable descriptions, or long speeches. Every sentence carries the action forward. The excitement is constantly renewed. Absurd as is the machinery, insipid as are the human characters, no reader probably ever thought the book dull.

Thomas Babington Macaulay, "Horace Walpole" (1833), *Critical, Historical, and Miscellaneous Essays* (Boston: Houghton Mifflin, 1860), Vol. 3, pp. 163–64

LESLIE STEPHEN   The *Castle of Otranto* and the *Mysterious Mother* were the progenitors of Mrs. Radcliffe's romances, and probably had a strong influence upon the author of *Ivanhoe*. Frowning castles and gloomy monasteries, knights in armour, and ladies in distress, and monks and nuns and hermits, all the scenery and the characters that have peopled the imagination of the romantic school, may be said to have had their origin on the night when Walpole lay down to sleep, his head crammed full of Wardour Street curiosities, and dreamt that he saw a gigantic hand in armour resting on the banister of his staircase. In three months from that time he had elaborated a story, the object of which, as defined by himself, was to combine the charms of the old romance and the modern novel, and which, to say the least, strikes us now like an exaggerated caricature of the later school. ⟨. . .⟩ Absurd as the burlesque seems, our ancestors found it amusing, and, what is stranger, awe-inspiring. Excitable readers shuddered when a helmet of more than gigantic size fell from the clouds, in the first chapter, and crushed the young baron to atoms on the eve of his wedding, as a trap smashes a mouse. ⟨. . .⟩

Yet, babyish as this mass of nursery tales may appear to us, it is curious that the theory which Walpole advocated has been exactly carried out. He wished to relieve the prosaic realism of the school of Fielding and Smollett by making use of romantic associations, without altogether taking leave of the language of common life. He sought to make real men and women out of mediaeval knights and ladies, or, in other words, he made a first experimental trip into the province afterwards occupied by Scott. The *Mysterious Mother* is in the same taste; and his interest in Ossian, in Chatterton, and in Percy's Relics, is another proof of his anticipation of the coming change of sentiment.

Leslie Stephen, "Horace Walpole" (1872), *Hours in a Library* (1874–79; rev. ed. London: Smith, Elder & Co., 1892), Vol. 1, pp. 372–74

EDITH BIRKHEAD   ⟨. . .⟩ apart from his characters, who are so colourless that they hardly hold our attention, Walpole bequeathed to his successors a remarkable collection of useful "properties." The background of the story is a Gothic castle, singularly unenchanted it is true, but capable of being invested by Mrs. Radcliffe with mysterious grandeur. Otranto contains underground vaults, ill-fitting doors with rusty hinges, easily extinguished lamps and a trap-door—objects trivial and insignificant in Walpole's hands, but fraught with terrible possibilities. Otranto would have fulfilled admirably the requirements of Barrett's Cherubina, who, when looking for lodgings demanded—to the indignation of a maidservant, who came to the door— old pictures, tapestry, a spectre and creaking hinges. ⟨. . .⟩ But Cherubina, whose palate was jaded by a surfeit of the pungent horrors of Walpole's successors, would probably have found *The Castle of Otranto* an insipid romance and would have lamented that he did not make more effective use of his supernatural machinery. His story offered hints and suggestions to those whose greater gifts turned the materials he had marshalled to better account, and he is to be honoured rather for what he instigated others to perform than for what he actually accomplished himself. *The Castle of*

Otranto was not intended as a serious contribution to literature, but will always survive in literary history as the ancestor of a thriving race of romances.

Edith Birkhead, *The Tale of Terror: A Study of the Gothic Romance* (New York: Dutton, 1921), pp. 22–23

BERTRAND EVANS   Walpole's tragedy ⟨*The Mysterious Mother*⟩ was not quite to Gothic drama as his novel was to Gothic fiction. *The Castle of Otranto* was at once the first Gothic novel and the fount of both Gothic fiction and drama. *The Mysterious Mother* was merely the first Gothic play. Without the novel there might have been no Gothic school. Without the play it is probable that later Gothic plays would have been written essentially as they were and in the number they were.

The dictates of dramatic form which lay heavily upon Walpole, a classicist, tended to curb the excess of horrific elements which characterizes *Otranto*. Though as novelist rules had restrained him not at all, as dramatist he respected and observed the unities, aimed at tragic dignity, and suppressed any lurking impulses to represent such monstrosities as he had assembled in the novel.

> Our Bard, whose head is fill'd with Gothic fancies,
> And teems with ghosts and giants and romances . . .

exploited, certainly, the attitude of his time toward the barbarous age, played exclusively with mystery, gloom, and terror, and indulged his Gothic propensity from beginning to end, but accomplished all in good "form." *The Mysterious Mother* is sound evidence that Walpole was not a rebel. It is a picture of the barbarous time as seen through the eyes of a classicist and painted in tones of horror for an age which viewed it similarly.

Bertrand Evans, *Gothic Drama from Walpole to Shelley* (Berkeley: University of California Press, 1947), p. 31

DEVENDRA P. VARMA   Besides the atmosphere and background of chivalry and enchantment typical of "old romances", there are three other literary forms shedding influences on *The Castle of Otranto*: the heroic romance, the fairy-story, and the tale of Oriental Magic; and these blend and fuse with three other elements from contemporary prose fiction: excessive sensibility, exemplary piety, and an explicit moral. Walpole's historical and antiquarian knowledge is well illustrated in his collection of books at Strawberry Hill. Over two hundred of the volumes were works on ancient chivalry and historical themes. These were sufficient to bestow a consistent atmosphere of chivalry on his romance, by means of stories of knights in armour and crusades, through descriptions of feudal tyrants and dungeons, and by recorded incidents of challenge and chivalric procession. Details, such as a lady arming her knight, his vow of eternal fealty to her, and knightly oaths as "by my halidane" (cf. Longsword), though this is oddly put into the mouth of a chattering domestic, does create an old-world chivalric atmosphere. We note the influence of heroic romance and drama in the struggle of generosity between the "sentimental, self-sacrificing heroines" and in the melting forgiveness of the pious hero for the barbarous treatment of the tyrant—the supernatural magnanimity of the heroic prince type (cf. for example Dryden's *Aurengzebe*). The temporary emergence of the "tender-hearted villain" in the scene where Manfred is 'touched' and weeps, seems to be influenced by ⟨John Leland's⟩ *Longsword*.

The supernatural element in the book is probably its greatest innovation, and is a curious blend of fairy-tale and magic, with one genuine spectre episode, the appearance of the skeleton hermit in the oratory, of which Scott said that it "was long accounted a masterpiece of the horrible". The appearance of this spectre as an instrument of fate, with its sepulchral warning, influenced the later Romanticism of Horror. But no one apparently ever attempted to imitate the much more elaborate but fantastic creation of the dismembered giant distributing himself piecemeal about the castle and at last shaking it to its foundations. This is quite different from the conventional ghosts, spirits, and spectres that stalk rampant through the pages of the later Gothic novels. In *The Castle of Otranto*, curiously, the word 'ghost' does not occur, but instead we find occasional references to 'sorcerer', 'talisman', and 'enchantment'. Certain episodes, too, such as the apparition of the giant seen by Bianca, when she was rubbing her ring, definitely suggest the fairy-tales of the East that Walpole was so fond of reading. The episode reminds us of the appearance of the genii in "Aladdin and the Wonderful Lamp", one of the stories in *Arabian Nights Entertainments*.

Devendra P. Varma, *The Gothic Flame* (London: Arthur Barker, 1957), pp. 50–51

CHARLES BEECHER HOGAN   The Gothic absurdities of *The Castle of Otranto* are appendages. They are not really inside the story, but are affixed, true gargoyles, on the outside of it. The skeleton, the statue that has a nosebleed, the big helmet and the big sword, the apotheosis of Alfonso, even the Poe-esque annihilation of the castle itself—all these exist only for their own immediate effect. They startle everybody, even the reader, for the moment, but they are never a determining element in the real progress of the story. Nor is their reception by any of the characters in any way permanent or destructive.

They are a bit like what the machinists and scene designers of the great Christmas pantomimes so endlessly popular in the eighteenth century and later were able to devise. These effects thrilled and terrified young and old alike who, two minutes later, were shouting with laughter at the sham battle between Harlequin and the Clown. Indeed, a further likeness to a pantomime or other showy spectacle is clearly to be seen in the description of Frederic's entourage in Act III. An entire page is devoted to a synopsis of his grand entry into Otranto: harbingers, then heralds, then footguards, then squires, then knights, etc., etc. Time after time lists such as this are to be encountered on the playbills of all the theatres of eighteenth-century London.

Charles Beecher Hogan, "The 'Theatre of Geo. 3,' " *Horace Walpole: Writer, Politician, and Connoisseur*, ed. Warren Hunting Smith (New Haven: Yale University Press, 1967), p. 239

FREDERICK R. KARL   If we view *The Castle of Otranto* as a vision of certain elements rather than as a novel in any traditional sense, we can gauge Walpole's achievement more effectively. As a novel, it is nonsense; as a vision (dream, nightmare, prophecy), it gains significance. Primarily, it is an observation of a life teeming with emotional crises denied in the contemporary literature of the period. It is a vision of omens, curses, extravagant stage sets (the helmet which crushes, the sword of monstrous size); a lustful, domineering father (Walpole's own was Fielding's model for Jonathan Wild) who goes well beyond the Harlowes; a devout, compliant, priest-ridden wife; a vision of doom, blood, terrified servants, apparitions, vengeance, and sadism. The novel suggests an imaginary, dreamlike state, one of ecstasy, in which the author stands "outside" normality and surveys the terrain of his own fantasies.

There is, in this vision, something of the Sadean view of man. Manfred is the resident tyrant who uses his strong will to dominate men and his sexual power to overwhelm his weakling son, Conrad. (Cf. Heathcliff and *his* weakling son, whom he drives into an arranged, unconsummated marriage.) As a tyrant, Manfred is a man of violent extremes, a man who assumes that whatever he is, nature is also, a man whose libido is so strong it must manifest itself in every situation. The cruelty of such a man is obvious if anyone attempts to interfere with his plans, needs, or lusts.

It is more than coincidence that Walpole's father figure, Manfred, should so closely resemble Fielding's interpretation of Sir Robert Walpole in *his* portrait of Jonathan Wild as a man of uncontrollable hands. Or that the son, Conrad, should be portrayed as a weakling, crushed under a helmet, while another, Theodore, eventually usurps the young man's role and marries his intended, Isabella. The vision is a fantasy of family life carried to extravagant extremes, a medievalism that has little relationship to eighteenth-century reality but considerable connection to a view of family life by one who sits outside normality and can turn his personal vision into opera.

Frederick R. Karl, *The Adversary Literature: The English Novel in the Eighteenth Century: A Study in Genre* (New York: Farrar, Straus & Giroux, 1974), pp. 245–46

WILLIAM PATRICK DAY   Manfred is ⟨. . .⟩ typical—is quite literally the prototype—of the Gothic patriarch struggling to establish his masculine identity. The two roles are, for Manfred, the same, for his struggle to preserve his individual identity is also a struggle to hold onto his patriarchal power, both as father and as prince of Otranto. In this struggle, Manfred confronts a crisis of inheritance. On the one hand, his inheritance of Otranto is illegitimate, for his grandfather Riccardo obtained the throne by murdering Alfonso the Good. On the other hand, his own line of succession has been broken by his son's mysterious death. Manfred's inability to pass his throne along threatens, not only his status as prince and patriarch, but, metaphorically, his personal identity. The illegitimacy of his rule is shadowed by Alfonso's curse; the failure of his line will mean the restoration of the legitimate line and the revelation that he is a fraud and a usurper. In order to hold together his own identity and Otranto, Manfred must become his own son, passing his corrupt inheritance on to himself as he fulfills both his own role and Conrad's.

Manfred's image of himself as an individual and as a ruler is tied to the masculine archetype's will to power. The sadism of the male protagonist is revealed, not simply as an accident of the Gothic spectacle, but rather as intrinsic to the masculine conception of identity, which defines the self by its ability to impose its will upon those around it. For Manfred, his family is both the instrument of his power and the symbol of his identity; his wife and children are tools and emblems. Because Matilda cannot extend the male line and is thus, unlike Conrad, an ineffective symbol of Manfred's identity, she is unimportant and her father ignores her. Because Hippolita cannot produce another male heir, she is useless, and Manfred will divorce her to marry Isabella, Conrad's intended. Manfred regards Isabella neither as a person nor even as a sexual object; she is just another human mechanism for the replication and maintenance of his identity and power.

William Patrick Day, *In the Circles of Fear and Desire: A Study of Gothic Fantasy* (Chicago: University of Chicago Press, 1985), pp. 92–93

IAN P. WATT   Walpole was at some pains to excuse the element of superstition in his story on the grounds that it was typical of the times depicted, and that he had in any case much restricted its operation, as compared to earlier writers of romance, where "the actors seem to lose their senses the moment the laws of nature lose their tone." So in general his motive for seeking the greater imaginative freedom of the supernatural must be seen as yet another aspect of how Gothic was a reaction of the intellectual temper of the century. Walpole liked *The Castle of Otranto* most among his works, he wrote to Madame du Deffand, because there alone he had given "reign to . . . imagination. . . . I am even persuaded that in the Future, when taste will be restored to the place now occupied by philosophy, my poor *Castle* will find admirers." His own time, alas, wanted "only cold reason," which had established a rigid distinction between the natural and the supernatural after Newton had cast light on nature's laws, and definitively depersonalized and demythologized the physical world.

The systematizing of this division between the natural and the supernatural orders inevitably affected general attitudes to the past and to the unseen world. By the time of Pope the supernatural had become to the enlightened a dubious and rather fanciful rival order, like the sylphs in *The Rape of the Lock*; and by the middle of the century such beliefs were becoming a sign of religious archaism, as in John Wesley and Parson Adams. To give the occult power of the past a real existence in fiction it was now necessary to set the narrative back in time into the Gothic past, to the times before the Reformation when Roman Catholic superstition held sway, and to the countries—most notably Italy—where it was still rampant.

To an Enlightenment sceptic like Walpole, of course, religious superstition was equally repulsive to political liberty and scientific reason; but it remained congenial to the aesthetic imagination. Hence Walpole compromised with his times both by setting the events back in times and places where credulity was universal, and by presenting his supernatural inventions in a selective way.

Walpole's supernature is entirely populated with beings who, for all their monstrous size and power, are essentially historical beings with rational human aims. This is typical of the Gothic novel in general; supernature is both secularized and individualized. Alfonso the Good, or whichever of his unseen adjutants is currently on duty to ruffle the helmet's plumes at the appropriate time, seems to be wholly concerned with bringing about a more satisfactory state of affairs in the secular world of his genealogical descendants; and when this rectifying mission has been accomplished, he can be trusted to hand Otranto back to the custody of Newtonian physics.

Ian P. Watt, "Time and Family in the Gothic Novel: *The Castle of Otranto*," *Eighteenth Century Life* 10, No. 3 (October 1986): 163–64

◙ *Bibliography*

The Lessons for the Day. 1742.

The Beauties: An Epistle to Mr. Eckhardt, the Painter. 1746.

Epilogue to Tamerlane, *on the Suppression of the Rebellion*. 1746.

Aedes Walpolianae; or, A Description of the Collection of Pictures at Houghton-Hall in Norfolk, the Seat of the Right Honourable Sir Robert Walpole, Earl of Orford. 1747.

A Letter to the Whigs: Occasion'd by The Letter to the Tories. 1747.

A Second and Third Letter to the Whigs. 1748.

Three Letters to the Whigs. 1748.

The Original Speech of Sir W⟨illia⟩m St⟨anho⟩pe. 1748.

The Speech of Richard White-Liver Esq; in Behalf of Himself and His Brethren. 1748.

A Letter from Xo Ho, a Chinese Philosopher at London, to His Friend Lien Chi at Peking. 1757.

A Catalogue of the Royal and Noble Authors of England. 1758. 2 vols.

Fugitive Pieces in Verse and Prose. 1758.

A Dialogue between Two Great Ladies. 1760.

Catalogue of Pictures and Drawings in the Holbein-Chamber, at Strawberry-Hill. 1760.

Catalogues of the Pictures of the Duke of Devonshire, General Guise, and the Late Sir Paul Methuen. 1760.

Anecdotes of Painting in England. 1762–71. 4 vols.

The Opposition to the Late Minister Vindicated. 1763.

A Counter-Address to the Public, on the Late Dismission of a General Officer. 1764.

The Magpie and Her Brood. 1764.

The Castle of Otranto: A Story. 1765.

An Account of the Giants Lately Discovered. 1766.

Historic Doubts on the Life and Reign of King Richard the Third. 1768.

The Mysterious Mother. 1768.

Works. 1770. 2 vols.

Reply to Dean Milles. 1770.

Memoires du Comte de Grammont by Anthony Hamilton (editor). 1772.

A Description of the Villa of Horace Walpole at Strawberry-Hill, Near Twicken-ham. 1774, 1784.

A Letter to the Editor of the Miscellanies of Thomas Chatterton. 1779.

Essay on Modern Gardening (with French tr. by Duc de Nivernois). 1785.

Hieroglyphic Tales. 1785.

Postscript to the Royal and Noble Authors. 1786.

PR830.T3 C57 1993   CU-Main

Bloom, Harold./Classic horror writers / edited and

3 9371 00013 0336

ENGLISH

Works. Ed. Mary Berry. 1798. 5 vols.

Notes on the Portraits at Woburn Abbey. 1800.

A Catalogue of the Royal and Noble Authors of England, Scotland and Ireland. Ed. Thomas Park. 1806. 5 vols.

Letters to George Montagu. Ed. John Martin. 1818.

Letters to the Rev. William Cole, and Others. Ed. John Martin. 1818.

Private Correspondence. 1820. 4 vols.

Memoires of the Last Ten Years of the Reign of George the Second. Ed. Lord Holland. 1822. 2 vols.

Letters to the Earl of Hertford. Ed. John Wilson Croker. 1825.

Letters to Sir Horace Mann. Ed. Lord Dover. 1833. 3 vols.

Letters. Ed. John Wright. 1840. 6 vols.

Memoirs of the Reign of King George the Third. Ed. Sir Denis Le Marchant. 1845.

Letters Addressed to the Countess of Ossory. Ed. R. Vernon Smith. 1848. 2 vols.

Correspondence of Horace Walpole and William Mason. Ed. John Mitford. 1851. 2 vols.

Letters. Ed. Peter Cunningham. 1857-59. 9 vols.

Journal of the Reign of King George the Third from the Year 1771 to 1783. Ed. John Doran. 1859. 2 vols.

Some Unpublished Letters. Ed. Sir Spencer Walpole. 1902.

Letters. Ed. Mrs. Paget Toynbee. 1903–05. 16 vols.

Supplement to the Letters. Ed. Paget Toynbee. 1918–25. 3 vols.

The Castle of Otranto and The Mysterious Mother. Ed. Montague Summers. 1925.

A Selection of the Letters. Ed. W. S. Lewis. 1926. 2 vols.

Miscellaneous Antiquities. Ed. W. S. Lewis. 1927. 16 vols.

Correspondence (Yale Edition). Ed. W. S. Lewis et al. 1937–81. 48 vols.

Memoirs and Portraits. Ed. Matthew Hodgart. 1963.

Selected Letters. Ed. W. S. Lewis. 1973.

Horace Walpole's Miscellany 1786–1795. Ed. Lars E. Troide. 1978.